W9-BXN-035

Security
Awareness

by Ira Winkler, CISSP®

for dummies®
A Wiley Brand

Security Awareness For Dummies®

Published by: **John Wiley & Sons, Inc.**, 111 River Street, Hoboken, NJ 07030-5774, www.wiley.com

Copyright © 2022 by John Wiley & Sons, Inc., Hoboken, New Jersey

Published simultaneously in Canada

Includes text used with permission from *You CAN Stop Stupid: Stopping Losses from Accidental and Malicious Actions* © 2021, John Wiley & Sons, Inc., Indianapolis, IN, authored by Ira Winkler and Tracy Celaya Brown.

For general information on our other products and services, please contact our Customer Care Department within the U.S. at 877-762-2974, outside the U.S. at 317-572-3993, or fax 317-572-4002. For technical support, please visit https://hub.wiley.com/community/support/dummies.

Wiley publishes in a variety of print and electronic formats and by print-on-demand. Some material included with standard print versions of this book may not be included in e-books or in print-on-demand. If this book refers to media such as a CD or DVD that is not included in the version you purchased, you may download this material at http://booksupport.wiley.com. For more information about Wiley products, visit www.wiley.com.

Library of Congress Control Number: 2022934265

ISBN 978-1-119-72092-8 (pbk); ISBN 978-1-119-72093-5 (ePDF); ISBN 978-1-119-72094-2 (epub)

SKY10033737_032222

Contents at a Glance

Table of Contents

Introduction

Creating security awareness among users is much more difficult and complicated than just telling them, "Bad people will try to trick you. Don't fall for their tricks." Not only is that advice usually insufficient, but you also have to account for much more than just bad people tricking your users. People lose equipment. They frequently know what to do, but have competing priorities. They may just not care. Relying on the user knowing what to do is not a silver bullet that creates a true firewall. However, with the right plan and strategy, you can make a measurable difference in improving user behavior. This book puts you on the right path to creating effective security awareness programs that meaningfully reduce risk to your organization.

About This Book

I started my career in cybersecurity performing social engineering and penetration tests. I put together teams of former special forces officers and intelligence operatives, and we targeted companies as nation-states would. I focused on black bag operations, which often consist of clandestine activities such as lock picking or safecracking, and otherwise infiltrating protected facilities. I went undercover to infiltrate organizations and persuade users to give me sensitive information. These operations led to the theft of reportedly billions of dollars of information and intellectual property. (I gave it all back.)

My "victims" then had me go back to their organizations and tell the stories about what I did, as a form of security awareness. The users were mesmerized by my stories. I heard about some successes in improved awareness, but when I went back for further assessments, the reality was that no real improvement had occurred. Just telling stories and telling people what not to do has limited impact.

Over two decades, I created and supported dozens, if not hundreds, of awareness programs for organizations of all types and sizes. I was able to see what worked best and what didn't. I found that many of the common beliefs and strategies just didn't work. They sounded great, but they were specious.

I also learned how to tell when awareness efforts were doomed to failure. More important though, I learned what works and how best to implement awareness programs.

This book shows how to implement the strategy that I found (through decades of experience) actually works. It helps you cut through hype and platitudes and begin doing what actually works. Platitudes and hype sound noble, but they are frequently misleading. Some of what I describe might go against what is considered common practice; however, you must consider that common practice has led to few improvements over decades. With that in mind, consider my perspective and determine what works best for your purposes. No guarantee exists of what will or won't work in any given situation.

Take this insight into account as you read this book and choose your own path.

To help you choose that path and make the content more accessible, I've divided this book into four parts:

>> **Part 1, "Getting to Know Security Awareness":** An overview of the fundamental concepts and philosophies of security awareness

>> **Part 2, "Building a Security Awareness Program":** The building blocks of an awareness program

>> **Part 3, "Putting Your Security Awareness Program into Action":** Creating and implementing your program

>> **Part 4, "The Part of Tens":** Quick guidance for optimizing your program

The appendix provides a sample assessment questionnaire.

Foolish Assumptions

My fundamental assumption is that I have no assumptions except that you are interested in addressing human vulnerabilities. You may be a CISO who wants to get a handle on how to better address the most common attacks against your organization. You may run awareness programs and want to enhance your current efforts. You may have been randomly assigned to run an awareness program and have little idea where to start. Or you may simply be interested in becoming a more well-rounded cybersecurity professional. This book definitely provides a valuable addition to your knowledge base.

Regardless of your role or position in your organization, if you're interested in addressing human vulnerabilities, you should find value in this book. I hope that you get to apply the information in a practical setting. As I finalize this manuscript, the 2021 Verizon Data Breach Investigations Report (DBIR) has been released, and it again reports that the targeting of users remains the top attack vector. It is my belief that this book can help to address this problem.

Icons Used in This Book

Throughout this book, icons in the margins highlight certain types of valuable information that call out for your attention. Here are the icons you encounter and a brief description of each:

The Tip icon marks tips and shortcuts you can use to make creating and running awareness programs easier.

Remember icons mark the information that's especially important to know. Frequently, paragraphs marked with this icon reiterate information that is presented previously in the book but bears repeating in the current context.

The Technical Stuff icon marks information that is specifically practical in implementing awareness programs. It involves information specific to the execution of programs.

When you see the Warning icon, you know to *watch out!* This icon marks important information that may save you headaches, or at least let you know when those headaches might pop up (and why).

Beyond the Book

In addition to the abundance of information and guidance related to creating a security awareness program that we provide in this book, you gain access to even more help and information online at Dummies.com. Check out this book's online Cheat Sheet. Just go to www.dummies.com and search for *security awareness for dummies cheat sheet.*

Where to Go from Here

This book follows a certain flow, but — as I identify in the description of the parts of this book, and as I write in the "Foolish Assumptions" section — you may be *anywhere* in the process of implementing an awareness program. For that reason, I intend for the chapters to stand alone as much as possible. Part 1 of this book covers my philosophies, biases, and experience, which may help you understand the perspective of the advice I provide, but you should be able to start with any chapter that seems most relevant to you.

If you have a functional program running and want to enhance it, I recommend turning to the chapters on gamification (see Chapter 11), running phishing simulations (see Chapter 12), or metrics (see Chapter 8). Otherwise, you can skim the chapters to see which one is the most relevant to your immediate needs. You may prefer, of course, to follow the flow of the book and read from front to back.

1

Getting to Know Security Awareness

IN THIS PART . . .

See what makes security awareness work.

Avoid the pitfalls that cause security awareness programs to fail.

Get the most from what science shows about human behavior.

Chapter 1

Knowing How Security Awareness Programs Work

A successful security awareness program motivates people to behave according to defined practices that decrease risk. Creating a program that successfully changes behavior throughout an organization involves more than simply communicating a bunch of facts about security awareness. Just because people are aware of a problem doesn't mean they will act on their awareness. In other words, awareness doesn't guarantee action. (Everyone knows that fast food isn't the healthiest choice, but most people still eat it.) This chapter sets the foundation for understanding the issues and the solutions.

Understanding the Benefits of Security Awareness

The thinking behind *security awareness* is that if people are aware of a problem, they're less likely to contribute to the problem — and more likely to respond appropriately when they encounter it.

Users who are *aware* don't pick up USB drives on the street and insert them into their work computers. They're aware of their surroundings and ensure that nobody is looking over their shoulders while they're working. They don't connect to insecure Wi-Fi networks. They're less likely to fall victim to phishing attacks. Essentially, users who are aware don't initiate losses for their organizations.

Organizations typically create security awareness programs to ensure that their employees, or *users,* are aware of cybersecurity problems that are already known to the organization. Phishing messages, which I cover in the next section, represent the most prolific attack against users.

Reducing losses from phishing attacks

Phishing attacks are common enough these days that many people are already familiar with the term. A working definition is "an email message that intends to trick a user into taking an action that is against the user's interests." A phishing awareness program would ideally train people to properly determine how to handle incoming emails in a way that reduces the likelihood of loss. For example, if a message asks for the disclosure of information, the ideal situation is that a user knows what information they can disclose and to whom while also determining whether the sender is valid. Chapter 6 discusses this topic in more detail.

To appreciate the losses that a phishing attack can cause, consider these prominent attacks:

>> **Sony:** The infamous 2014 Sony hack, which was reportedly perpetrated by North Korea, began with a phishing attack. The hack resulted in the leak of information about movies, the movies themselves, and embarrassing emails. Sony reported costs of the hack to be $35 million.

>> **Target:** The 2013 Target hack, which compromised more than 110 million credit card numbers and consumer records, began with a phishing attack of a Target vendor. Target reported the resulting costs to be $162 million.

>> **OPM:** The attack on the Office of Personnel Management (OPM), discovered in 2014, which compromised the security clearance files of 20 million US government employees and contractors, began with a phishing attack against a government contractor. The costs and losses are immeasurable because this attack is considered a major intelligence success for China, the perpetrator of the attack named by the US government.

>> **Colonial Pipeline:** The Colonial Pipeline ransomware attack in 2021 began with a phishing message that captured user credentials and allowed the criminals to establish a sustained presence on the network. This allowed the criminals to find the most critical systems and eventually install the ransomware, which caused Colonial Pipeline to shut down the pipeline, halting a primary oil delivery to the US east coast. Colonial Pipeline paid the criminals approximately $4.4 million, but the actual costs resulting from the shutdown were tens of millions of dollars to Colonial Pipeline and an incalculable cost to the economy.

TECHNICAL STUFF

The Verizon Enterprises Solutions' Data Breach Investigations Report, commonly referred to as the DBIR, is one of the most often cited studies in the cybersecurity field. The report, which is produced annually, is drawn from data collected directly by Verizon's managed security service. The DBIR, considered a reliable overview of real-life attacks against organizations around the world, indicates that more than a whopping 85 percent of all major attacks begin by targeting users. You can access the report at www.verizon.com/business/resources/reports/dbir.

Reducing losses by reducing risk

Just as people get themselves into automobile accidents despite advances in automobile safety, even reasonably aware users may fall victim to cybersecurity attacks. All cybersecurity countermeasures will eventually fail. Countermeasures include encryption, passwords, antivirus software, multifactor authentication, and more. Perfect security doesn't exist. Your goal in establishing a security awareness program is to reduce risk by influencing user actions.

REMEMBER

Don't expect users to be perfect — risk reduction isn't about eliminating risk altogether, which is impossible. Expect your security awareness program to reduce the number and severity of incidents, thereby reducing losses from the incidents.

Also, a more aware user knows when something seems wrong and knows how to react to it. If your users sense that they might have been compromised, they start taking actions to mitigate the loss. If they accidentally email sensitive data to the wrong person, they try to stop the message or have it deleted. If they end up on a malicious website that starts serving adware, they disconnect before additional damage can occur. They know how to properly report any and all potential incidents, so your organization can begin to stop any loss or damage in progress. In the worst case, at least they can launch an investigation after the fact to find out what happened.

In the ideal situation, even when a user takes no potentially harmful action, they report the situation to the appropriate party. They report details such as whether someone tried to follow them through a door, even if they turn the person away, because they know that the person might attempt to enter through another door or follow someone else through the door. If someone detects a phishing message, they don't click on it — instead, they report the message because they realize that other, less aware users may click on it, and then the administrators can delete the message before that happens.

As you can see, awareness requires more than knowing what to be afraid of — you also have to know how to do things correctly. Too many awareness programs focus on teaching users what to be afraid of rather than on establishing policies and procedures for how to perform functions correctly, and in a way that doesn't result in loss.

REMEMBER

The goal for awareness is for users to behave according to policies and procedures. Part of the function of an awareness program is making users aware that bad guys exist and that those bad guys will attempt to do bad things. But awareness programs primarily focus on making people aware of how to behave according to procedures in potentially risky situations.

Grasping how users initiate loss

At a cybersecurity conference where I spoke, I was in a buffet line at lunchtime. At one table that the line passed, I saw some stickers that said, *Don't Click On Sh*t!* The person in front of me was an administrator, and he grabbed a handful of stickers while saying, "I need a lot of these to give to my users." I then replied, "You must give your users a lot of 'sh*t' to click on."

The guy was confused and asked what I meant. I replied that the users would have no items to avoid clicking on if the systems he supported didn't pass the messages to the users. I then added that if he knows users will click on problematic items, he should be taking active measures to stop the inevitable damage. He was confused, but of course kept the stickers.

TIP

For more information on user-initiated loss, find a copy of my book, written with Dr. Tracy Celaya Brown, *You Can Stop Stupid: Stopping Losses from Accidental and Malicious Actions* (Wiley, 2021).

Users can cause only the amount of damage they're put in the position to cause — and then allowed to carry out. However, even after they make a potentially damaging mistake, or even if they're blatantly malicious, it doesn't mean that the system should allow the loss to be realized.

For example, a user can click on a phishing message only if the antiphishing technology used by your organization fails to filter the message. If the user clicks on a phishing message and ransomware is activated, the ransomware can destroy the system only if the user has permission to install software on the system — and then in almost all cases, you have no standard antimalware on the system.

REMEMBER

User error is a symptom of the problems with your system. Even if a user makes a mistake, or is even malicious, the resulting loss is a problem with the system providing users with potential actions and then enabling the loss.

In essence, users may initiate a chain of actions that create the loss, but the loss is a result of failings in the system as a whole.

Knowing How Security Awareness Programs Work

Unfortunately, there is little consistency in what is perceived to be a sufficient, organizational security awareness program. Some organizations just have *users*, or employees, sign a document. Many other awareness programs require employees to read the document once a year (or, increasingly, watch a video).

At the other end of the spectrum, when I started at the National Security Agency (NSA), my security awareness training actually began long before I started working there. After I passed the initial aptitude test, I was sent information to arrange for an interview. During that interview was a conversation about the special security considerations of working for the NSA. I was prepared for what would be involved in obtaining a top secret clearance, as well as the need not to discuss my potential employment. I was then invited to visit the NSA headquarters for further interviews.

My travel packet included a basic discussion of security requirements. Upon arrival, I was provided with another security briefing related to how to get into, and then behave within, the facilities. I met with counterintelligence officers, who provided a general overview of security requirements and then administered a polygraph exam. I also took a battery of psychological tests. During the technical interviews, I met with professionals who also discussed the job expectations, including the expected security-related behaviors. The NSA is a special case, of course — most organizations don't engage in such rigorous screening practices.

TECHNICAL STUFF

The goal of a security awareness program is to improve security-related behaviors. The goal is not to simply make people aware of an issue — the goal is to inspire people to behave appropriately to avoid the initiation of a loss and, ideally, to detect and respond to the potential for loss. Whether people understand how their actions promote security is secondary because the goal of an awareness program is to change behaviors, not just impart knowledge.

When I started working at the NSA, I took a 3-day security awareness class. Security awareness posters were hung on walls all over the buildings. Applicants received security newsletters and attended regular security-related presentations. These awareness tools were generally unnecessary, however. All I had to do to see how to behave was behave like everyone else. Everyone wore their badges, so I wore my badge. Everyone lined up to have their belongings inspected on the way out of the buildings. In essence, the entire culture was the awareness program. People lost their jobs because of security violations. I am not saying the NSA was perfect, because it clearly had some major failings, but for all the potential risk, the NSA experienced relatively little loss.

Clearly, few organizations in the world have the type of awareness program that the NSA has. Unlike organizations that prioritize profits, branding, and other deliverables, the NSA focuses on security. Security *is* the NSA brand.

A good security awareness program intends to change and improve security-related behaviors. You can incorporate many tools into an awareness plan to create that change. Chapter 7 defines a variety of tools that you can incorporate into your program. Some tools are more popular than others; however, no tool is absolutely required. The choice depends on your needs. At the end of the day, a *security awareness program* is essentially a set of tools, techniques, and measurements intended to improve security-related behaviors.

Establishing and measuring goals

The ultimate goal of a security awareness program is to change and improve security-related behaviors. Security programs are created to reduce loss. As an essential part of an organization's overall information security program, security awareness should likewise reduce loss.

In Chapter 8, I discuss some metrics you can use to judge whether your awareness program successfully reduces loss. Many security awareness professionals talk about the likeability of their tools, the number of people who show up to their events, and the quality of their posters. These metrics and general impressions are nice to know, but they're relatively useless from a practical perspective.

A metric demonstrating that you're changing behaviors in a way that reduces loss, or preferably improves efficiency and makes the organization money, is the most useful metric to show that you're producing value. This isn't to say that it's the only possible benefit of a security awareness program. Awareness programs also often provide intangible benefits to the organization. These benefits include protecting the organization from damage to its reputation, illustrating that the organization is committed to security, generating excitement and engagement among employees, and reassuring customers that your organization is actively protecting them.

REMEMBER

If your goal is to contribute to your organization's security effort, you must identify the benefits your program will bring to the organization. These benefits can't be that the program merely provides information. The program should improve behaviors. You must be able to show how the program returns clear value to your organization, and this value should ideally return clear value to the bottom line.

GETTING THE BUDGET YOU NEED

I developed a philosophy during my career in cybersecurity:

You don't get the budget you need — you get the budget you deserve.

Security awareness teams typically compete against other teams for budget funds and other resources. For example, the team may work under the cybersecurity, human resources (HR), compliance, legal, physical security, or another department within the organization. All these teams compete for funding and other resources. Even if your cybersecurity program has sufficient resources to fully fund all teams, including the awareness program, you have to show that you deserve the budget amount you're requesting. You need to financially justify your efforts.

You can have plans for the best awareness program in the industry, but if you cannot demonstrate that you deserve the appropriate budget, you won't get the budget you need to implement it. Chapter 8 details how to collect metrics that help you show that you deserve what you need.

Showing users how to "do things right"

For your awareness program to help create desired behaviors, the program must show people the proper way to perform job tasks, or "do things right." In other words, you provide instructions on how to do things properly by default.

When you consider most of the materials produced by vendors, and a great deal of the materials produced by organizations for internal use, these materials frequently focus on the fact that "bad people" intend to trick you. They tell you about criminals who will do harm if you fall for their tricks. This information can provide motivation, which can be worthwhile, but it's doesn't show users how to recognize suspicious situations as they encounter them.

When you teach people to focus on the ways bad people will exploit them, the training will fail when the bad people try a different trick. Expecting users to combat well-resourced, highly skilled criminals is a losing proposition. You cannot expect users to be consistently effective in thwarting such parties.

The better approach is for your awareness training to focus on the way that users can do their jobs properly. Ensure that users have an established process that they're familiar with and that they know how to follow. The process should account for the potential of bad people trying to game the system.

I once worked with a large online gaming company that had problems with criminals calling up the support desk to dupe the support personnel into changing the passwords on specific accounts so that the criminals could go into the accounts and sell the assets. I created a decision tree to authenticate callers. As long as the support personnel followed the provided guidance, no accounts were compromised and no one had to train the support personnel to handle each and every possible scenario that bad people would try. It didn't matter. We just told them the one way to do their job properly.

Though this strategy may not be feasible in every case, for every job function, your awareness efforts should generally focus on providing guidance in how people should do their jobs properly. This requires embedding security within job functions.

In many cases, you may find detailed procedures already defined but not well known or practiced. In this case, your job is to find those procedures and figure out how best to translate them into practice.

Recognizing the Role of Awareness within a Security Program

Awareness isn't a stand-alone program that the security team uses to deal with the *user problem*, as it's commonly called. Security awareness is a tactic, not a strategy, used to deal with the user problem.

As I cover in the earlier section "Reducing losses from phishing attacks," for a phishing attack to exploit your organization, your system first has to receive the email message on your server. Your system then has to process the message and present it to the user. The user has to review the message and decide how to act on the message. If the message contains malware, the system has to allow the malware to install and execute. If the message sends the user to a malicious link, the system has to allow the user to reach the malicious web server. If the user gives up their credentials on a malicious web server, the system then has to allow the malicious party to log in from anywhere in the world.

When a phishing attack succeeds, the user action is just one link in a fairly involved chain that requires failure throughout the entire chain. This statement is true for just about any user action, whether it involves technology or not.

Here are several concepts to consider:

>> The user is not the weakest link.

>> Awareness addresses one vulnerability among many.

>> The user experience can lead the user to make better decisions — or avoid making a decision in the first place.

>> Most importantly, to stop the problem, you have to engage and coordinate with other disciplines. See Chapter 5.

Dealing with user-initiated loss (after all, the actions can be either unintentional or malicious) requires a comprehensive strategy to deal with not just the user action but also whatever enables the user to be in the position to create a loss and then to have the loss realized. You can't blame a user for what is typically, again, a complex set of failures.

Though it's true that, as an awareness professional, you can just do your job and operate in a vacuum, doing so inevitably leads to failure. It goes against the argument that you *deserve more*. This doesn't mean that the failure wouldn't happen even if everyone cooperated, but operating in a vacuum sends the wrong message.

REMEMBER

Awareness isn't a strategy to mitigate user-initiated loss — it's a tactic within a larger security strategy.

The security awareness program isn't the sole effort responsible for mitigating user error. If you say nothing to oppose this idea, you give the impression that you agree with it. Worse, you give the impression that users are responsible for any loss resulting from harmful actions that you already anticipate they will eventually make, such as clicking on a phishing link or accidentally deleting a file.

You have a responsibility to reduce risk by encouraging secure behaviors. But you're also part of a team and you should work in concert to support that entire security team to reduce loss. In a coordinated cybersecurity department, each team determines their part in reducing losses related to user actions and takes the appropriate actions. Likewise, each team determines how best to support each other in the overall reduction of user-related losses.

As a security awareness professional, you can be the tip of the spear in coordinating a comprehensive solution to reducing user-related losses. Your primary focus is to create behavioral improvements that reduce the initiation of losses.

Disputing the Myth of the Human Firewall

The section heading might anger a lot of security awareness professionals, but I see the idea of the human firewall as a dangerous myth. The idea that users are your last line of defense (which is a catchphrase for many phishing simulation companies) is fundamentally *wrong*.

First, consider that users are *not* the last line of defense in any practical way. For example, if a user clicks on ransomware, the user environment can stop the user from downloading malware by not giving the user permission to install software. Even if the software is downloaded and installed, antimalware can stop the ransomware. To accept that the user is the last line of defense, you have to discount many useful technologies that are commonplace in organizations.

Michael Landewe, the CTO of Avanan, said it best:

> If a user is our last line of defense, we have failed as an industry.

Regarding the claim of creating a human firewall, in principle it sounds great, but any security professional knows that even technical firewalls will fail. Users are less reliable than technology. Creating a human firewall implies that you will create an entire organization of users who always behave appropriately and securely. That isn't possible, however. Though humans can consistently behave well, no individual (and especially no group of humans) in the history of mankind has always exhibited error-free behaviors.

Consider also that although other technologies do only what they're instructed to do, humans can have malicious intent. If you leave your users as your last line of defense and they're malicious, the results will be disastrous.

I want you to create the best security awareness programs possible, but you need to remember where you fit within the overall chain of actions. If you give the impression that the user has ultimate control of your systems, then the first time a user fails, you fail in your self-described mission, which can damage the credibility of your program. Consider that you don't even see people who manage firewalls imply that their firewalls will stop all attacks from getting in. If you spout off to management that you will create a human firewall to repel all attacks targeting humans, then the first time a user fails, your program has failed based on *your* statements. Everything else you do will be met with skepticism, including requests for budget funds, personnel, time, and other resources. Don't set yourself up for failure from the start.

The reality is that most people don't give users and security awareness programs enough credit. Every time a user avoids clicking on a phishing message, your awareness efforts are successful. Every time a user locks up sensitive information, your awareness efforts are successful. Every time a user protects their screen from shoulder surfers, your awareness efforts are successful. These successes happen all the time.

Your users are a critical part of your organization's system, and your efforts can significantly reduce loss. Aware users have helped organizations avoid disaster. I have personally been involved with users who have thwarted major attacks. Even when attacks have been reported after the fact, aware users responded appropriately, alerted the appropriate people, and significantly reduced the resulting loss.

The awareness programs you create can provide an immense return on investment. Just be sure that you set realistic expectations.

IN THIS CHAPTER

» Making compliance the goal — and nothing more

» Failing to compel compliance

» Overindulging in science with limited practical use

» Mistaking social engineering skills for awareness expertise

» Setting inappropriate expectations

» Valuing products more than process

» Buying into gimmicks that yield no results

» Overestimating the role of security awareness

Chapter **2**

Starting On the Right Foot: Avoiding What Doesn't Work

After working in the security awareness field for 30 years, I have learned the importance of knowing not only what works but also what *doesn't* work. In the security awareness field, knowing what doesn't work is almost *more* important than knowing what works.

This chapter helps you sidestep the problems I encountered throughout three decades spent working in security awareness. Your security awareness programs probably won't be perfect from the start, but being aware of the red flags can definitely help you steer your program in the right direction.

Making a Case Beyond Compliance Standards

Checking the box means that an organization wants to meet compliance standards and nothing more. In this situation, you will have a harder time garnering budget and management support for your efforts. To create a security awareness program that changes employee behavior, however, you need to make your case — and prove that awareness provides a real return on investment.

CHECKING THE BOX MIGHT NOT BE JUST FOR AWARENESS

Sometimes the Check-the-Box mentality extends not just to the awareness program but also to the security program in general. One of my friends was hired as a CISO of a credit union. One of his first acts was to have me submit a proposal for a security assessment. The proposal met his budgetary needs and he submitted it for approval. He called me up a few weeks later to tell me that they would not be proceeding with the assessment, because his management team thought they had only $10 billion in assets and believed that criminals would never go after such a small financial organization. He went on to say that he found out that the only reason he was hired was that the auditors told the board they could not pass an audit without a CISO in charge of information security. It was no surprise when he left the organization three months later.

Clearly, an entire security program based on the principle of Check the Box presents a major threat to an organization, and, more importantly, to its customers. I use this example to highlight the point that, although an entire program being a Check-the-Box effort is a clear danger, treating any element of the program as a Check-the-Box effort represents a major risk to the entire program.

TECHNICAL STUFF

Though standards evolve, at the time of this writing, the major industry standards regarding security awareness are vague. For the most part, all they require is that an organization has an awareness program in place. The standards imply that organizations should hold annual awareness training, but they don't specify what these trainings should entail or how to create them. As long as an organization can provide some form of confirmation to potential auditors that employees received some form of annual training, "the box is checked." Even though auditors sometimes require phishing simulations, the standards provide no instruction for creating the simulations or performing them effectively.

In Chapter 8, I show how you can justify your efforts, even to a tough Check-the-Box crowd, by using metrics to demonstrate the value of your efforts to your organization.

Treating Compliance as a Must

Security awareness programs fail when they treat security as a *should*-do task and not as a *must*-do task. Security becomes a mere should-do task when programs seek to influence people to behave securely. These programs attempt to influence users to do the right thing by providing them with more information. Security becomes a must-do item only when users appreciate the consequences of their failings.

Consider awareness programs for sexual harassment, financial compliance, and similar issues. These programs don't try to influence people to do the right thing — they inform users of their job requirements and the consequences of failing to meet those requirements. Failing to meet financial compliance requirements (such as properly filling out time cards, for example) can result in employees not being paid.

Compliance with a security awareness program that can prevent company operations from grinding to a standstill from a ruined computer network is something that, similarly, must be treated as, well, a must-do task. Security behaviors should be embedded within all business practices — not just added to the process. For example, when you're authenticating a user for a system, the security checks should be, not an addition to, but rather an embedded step within the overall practice. It isn't a separate function.

REMEMBER

Ruining the company computer network typically has far-reaching implications that are difficult to recover from. Yet desired cybersecurity practices continue to be treated as a should-do task. If you want your awareness message to be conveyed and followed, you need to portray your message as a must-do task. In other words, proper security-related behaviors aren't optional — they're required, just like all other business functions. Let me be clear: I am not saying that you personally should make the behaviors a *must*; good security practices are likely an organizational mandate.

Motivating users to take action

Awareness professionals naturally want to believe that if they inform a person about an obvious concern, that person will take appropriate action, just by virtue of having received the information. In my experience, this assumption too often proves incorrect. Gaining compliance requires much more effort than simply relaying information. You need a detailed strategy, specific to your circumstances, that involves enforcement and creating a culture where everyone implements the expected behavior by second nature as part of their normal job function. (I discuss these strategies in detail in Part 2 of this book.)

Consider how this dynamic plays out in the rest of your life. Most people know that eating healthy foods and exercising can improve their health. In some cases, they even know that they can face dire medical consequences if they refuse to eat well. Yet they continue to ignore the advice. Relating this example to security awareness, the trick is to ask people to do a few simple things differently that will reduce an organization's risk profile hugely and quickly, not make them into security experts.

TECHNICAL STUFF

BJ Fogg, a Stanford University researcher, developed many highly accepted concepts of human behavior. One of those behavioral concepts is the *information-action fallacy*, which is the belief that if you tell a person what they should do, why they should do it, and how it directly benefits them, they will do it. Just as this strategy doesn't work in fitness, neither does it work with security awareness, where the implications are less dire for the individual.

REMEMBER

When you implement your awareness program, you must dispel any belief on the part of yourself and the security team that, just because you inform people of an apparently critical issue, they will follow your guidance.

Working within the compliance budget

The *compliance budget* concept highlights how employees at work have a variety of requirements placed on them and their time. They have to balance how much time they use to satisfy various required tasks. The compliance budget accepts that users may well understand the importance of good security practices. It also acknowledges that users may consider other concerns to be equally or more critical. The more embedded security practices are within a job function, the more likely the practices will be implemented.

For example, if a user is running late to a critical client meeting, even if they know that securing the workspace is important, will they run even *more* late to the meeting to secure their computer and lock away sensitive documents? How do they determine which correct action takes priority? If you portray the security practices in your awareness program as a should-do item, you allow the user to ignore your guidance in favor of more apparently pressing issues. If your guidance is defined as a must-do item, however, it's much more likely to be followed and implemented.

REMEMBER

Users are typically balancing a variety of concerns, both personal and work related, and you need to consider how you're presenting your materials with regard to positioning security awareness, among all the other daily concerns across their work and personal lives. This is where nudges and other properly placed security reminders, as discussed in Chapter 7, can have an impact on diligent users.

Limiting the Popular Awareness Theories

This section is probably the most controversial one in this book, as I take on a lot of popular concepts that I consider specious. When I read articles written by seemingly well-meaning security awareness experts, I see them quote scientific studies on psychology and marketing, among other areas, and I hear terms like *mental models* thrown around. These studies present ideas that seem important, but at the end of the day, I consider these ideas not practical to improve behaviors across an entire organization. I'm not saying that they're irrelevant, but the focus on these sciences appears to be misplaced (as I discuss in the next section).

Applying psychology to a diverse user base

Yes, psychology can be a useful subject, and it defines the personality types of various people. At one level, by understanding various personality types, you should be able to understand the diverse thinking among your target audience. However, to properly implement psychology as a science as a fundamental part of your awareness program, it involves developing awareness targeted to individual personality types.

Consider that there is no single form of psychology. Consider that a psychologist works with each individual in a way that satisfies that person's individual needs. Just as some techniques work better than others for various types of psychological problems and personalities, it's the same for awareness.

WARNING

Many people confuse behavioral science with psychology. Likewise, they mistake organizational psychology for individual psychology. Psychology can be useful, but you have to understand its limitations. Psychology focuses on individuals, whereas you have to focus on impacting the *organization*. This is a numbers game. In Chapter 7, where I address a variety of communications tools, I generally recommend that you attempt to use as many as possible. The reason is that people will respond differently to various types of tools and messaging. You need to understand that some types of communications, such as an anime-style video, may intrigue some people and completely disenfranchise others. Though this statement seems obvious, it's easy to forget when you have your personal preferences.

Differentiating between marketing and awareness

Marketing programs create a mental hook in getting people to understand desired actions, and they influence people to take those actions. "If you see something, say something" is a great example of a marketing campaign that produced some noticeable results. (See the previous sidebar, "If you see something, say something.") Understand, however, that fundamental differences exist between the practical implementation of marketing programs and security awareness programs.

Here are three of the critical differences between marketing and awareness:

>> Marketing addresses completely voluntary behaviors; awareness behaviors are an expected part of everyone's job.

>> Marketing success can be achieved by minimal increases in desired behaviors; awareness programs intend to inspire as much of the user population as possible to practice the behaviors.

>> Marketing campaigns typically target specific segments of the population to change behaviors; awareness campaigns target as much of the user population as possible.

Marketing is a comprehensive effort to understand and convince a targeted audience to perform a specific action voluntarily. Consider the key points of the preceding sentence: *targeted audience* and *perform a specific action voluntarily.* Advertising campaigns target very specific audiences because they need to address messaging specific to the audience. Even individual soda (or pop, or soda pop, depending on your region) ad campaigns target specific demographics. Those ad campaigns then attempt to inspire people from those demographics to voluntarily buy soda. Though soft drink companies want everyone to buy their sodas, they know which age groups and demographics are the prime targets of their products. For good reason, Mountain Dew advertisements frequently feature extreme sports, for example, and advertisements for tonic water usually feature older actors.

You, on the other hand, are targeting your entire user base, which likely contains a multitude of demographics and job roles. Remember that the security practices you promote are must-do items and not should-do items. You're not marketing a voluntary consumer purchase that they wouldn't otherwise make. You're ensuring that all users are aware of the expected behaviors that will keep your organization functioning properly while protecting the organization and its customers.

Even more important, your goal is to have your users practice those behaviors. Marketing campaigns can usually declare success when they have single-digit percentage increases in their audience's practicing the desired behaviors. For example, if a pizza delivery service can persuade 5 percent more people to order pizza during a football game, that might mean a 100 percent increase in sales — and the pizza seller is delighted. On the other hand, if you persuade only 5 percent of users to secure their workspace, it's better than nothing — but you still have a massive security vulnerability.

Even the campaign advocating "If you see something, say something" hopes that they can inspire a small percentage of people to become more aware in reporting security exposures, in the hope that prodding one person out of hundreds to report something might prevent a major incident. Awareness programs need to create behaviors that are consistent across the organization. Again, though some aspects of marketing and advertising have applicability, such as understanding the best ways to communicate with your audience, you need to understand that, unlike in traditional marketing campaigns, you're addressing multiple audiences, with a message that should not be treated as trivially as choosing Pepsi over Coke.

You can, however, make use of marketing principles by realizing the limitations of traditional marketing, when you realize that you need to target multiple audiences, and you will likely need to create multiple streams of communications with different messaging. More important, your messaging should be treated as critically as other serious messaging, such as sexual harassment and fraud prevention. Part 2 of this book covers methods to achieve consistent behavior change across various subcultures.

Distinguishing Social Engineering from Security Awareness

This section is personal for me. I started working in the awareness field as a result of my performing social engineering simulations, and then companies inviting me to come in and present awareness programs that told people exactly how I messed over the company — so that people would know what to look for in the future. I entertained people with my stories that the *Wall Street Journal* referred to as ". . . alternating between hilarious and harrowing." The stories were definitely memorable. When I would later go back to my targets to measure improvements, however, they were small at best.

Consider that just because you can stab a person doesn't mean that you can perform the surgery to repair the damage you caused. It's unfortunately easy to physically harm a person with a knife; it takes infinitely more knowledge and skills to use a knife to save the person's life. It's a completely different skillset. Having performed social engineering for decades, I can state that it's easy to trick a user into giving up information. It's infinitely harder to train an entire population of users *not* to divulge information on a consistent basis. It's likewise a completely different skillset.

Social engineering is a broad term for nontechnical attacks to achieve, or support, attacks to access or otherwise target computers or information. Phishing is the most common example, but dumpster diving, shoulder surfing, and telephone pretext calling are also common social engineering attacks. The most iconic attacks are those where someone calls up a user and pretends to be from technical support to solicit their password.

To be good at what they do, social engineers essentially know how to be good liars. They know how to perform transactional influence. They manipulate a user to do a one-time act that they should not otherwise do.

Social engineering requires a skillset that's completely different from the one for awareness. A social engineer has to find one trick of influence at one given point in time to succeed. An awareness professional, however, has to create consistent behaviors on the part of users with whom they may never have a personal interaction. A social engineer might find holes that need to be fixed, but using an analogy, fixing a hole in a dam doesn't strengthen the dam as a whole.

Providing information showing that the threat is possible makes the information a bit more memorable, so users can remember it for a few more weeks. This can be valuable to increasing the Forgetting Curve, which is discussed in Chapter 3.

TIP

Though social engineers don't necessarily have transferrable skills for designing an awareness program, social engineering tests can be a useful way to gather metrics. Social engineering, when performed properly, can determine how people will actually perform when faced with a potential attack. However, don't fall into the trap of believing that social engineers are competent awareness professionals by default. Awareness is much more than telling people what tricks not to fall for. It's telling people how to behave properly on a consistent basis.

Addressing Mental Models That Don't Work

"Hackers are unstoppable geniuses."

"There may be computer crimes, but it won't happen to me."

"I am too unimportant to be a target."

These statements represent common mental models that I deal with in security awareness programs, and these mental models are both harmful and wrong.

Mental models reflect the way a person perceives their environment. For example, in most countries, the hot water faucet is on the left and the cold water faucet is on the right. Red usually means something bad or to stop, and green means safe or to go. When I visit a US airport, I expect that flights on a monitor will be listed alphabetically by destination. When I am in Europe or Asia, I generally need to know the departure time before I look on a monitor to find my gate. I can usually pick up a TV remote control and figure out how to turn on and use any TV. You might naturally assume that working with mental models with regard to security awareness would also be useful, but this isn't the case.

People's mental models regarding cybersecurity are both inconsistent and frequently wrong. This causes them to make bad decisions. Most computer criminals are opportunists who take advantage of bad *cyberhygiene* (basic computer practices), such as not installing antimalware software or not performing backups.

Your goal is first to understand the current mental models that serve as a barrier to positive security behaviors within your user base. Then you must create correct mental models to replace them with. You need to instill strong security practices as a habit.

If your users believe that hackers are unstoppable geniuses, you need to talk about how they are frequently caught and how someone in your organization thwarted attacks by practicing what you preach. If they believe it will never happen to them, talk about how the organization suffered attacks. Show people how theoretically unimportant targets were used to gain access to other parties. You need to understand and dispel the harmful mental models, not try to adopt them to your needs.

Chapter 5 discusses getting to know the users, which includes how they perceive security concerns. When you can understand how mental models are failing security awareness efforts, you can start to address them head-on and begin to change perceptions.

Making Perfection the Stated Goal

Perhaps the greatest form of self-sabotage you can commit as a security awareness professional is to overpromise what your program can deliver. For example, telling management to expect a *human firewall* to work — that your users will be both your first and last line of defense — sets you up for failure.

In the first place, nobody will believe you. Because no experienced security professional would expect perfection, you lose at least some of the credibility you may have had from the start. Then, the first time you have an inevitable security incident, the occurrence chips away at your remaining credibility.

As I discuss in Chapter 3, the goal of a security program is risk management. A competent CISO doesn't promise perfect security. They say that they're working to manage the organization's risk by implementing a security program. They don't promise to defeat bad people. They don't promise that incidents will never happen. They essentially say that they will *reduce loss*.

REMEMBER

Focus any and all claims you might make to be reasonable and based on the potential for risk reduction. To perform risk reduction, you must gather data and make reasonable and defensible claims of potential loss reduction.

Measuring from the Start

You should always collect metrics before you start rolling out an awareness program. These metrics are commonly referred to as *Day 0 metrics*, and serve to show the value you create.

Even if you want to strive for perfection, you need to figure out where you are beginning. Too many awareness practitioners start their programs without figuring out how to judge their success. With awareness, it's easy to see failure — but almost impossible to see success without proactively looking for it.

With all business processes, there has to be definition of success — and that is in the form of some metrics. I talk about various types of metrics in Chapter 8, but for now you need to understand that without knowing where you're starting from, you may never know the level of success you have.

REMEMBER

Even in the absence of perfection, by collecting metrics throughout the lifecycle of your program, you can demonstrate the real value you return.

Prioritizing Program Over Product

When people think of security awareness programs, often the first things that come to mind are computer-based training (CBT) and phishing simulations. When implementing a program, the person responsible for a security awareness program typically chooses a vendor and then determines which of the vendor's products to use. Awareness programs should be a strategy for effectively addressing the risk associated with user actions. Products are potential tactics, which may or may not address a piece of a strategy. Though some tactics are common, they are not a strategy to address user risk. If you want a program instead of a product, there has to be more than just a choice of which products to roll out.

Consider what you would say, when asked about a technical security program, if a security engineer said they were buying a firewall and antimalware. Clearly, both of those products are required, but they don't make for a complete security program, because attackers can bypass these products or find flaws in the implementation of the products. They leave too many other vulnerabilities addressed, even if they individually function perfectly.

With awareness, focusing solely on implementing products is also an incomplete approach. You need to determine how to roll out the entire program. You need to identify the components of the program and its metrics, the organization's subcultures, and more. As mentioned previously in this chapter, if you're incomplete in how you implement an awareness program, you will reach only a small population of users and in ways that may not impact them. Part 2 of this book covers the appropriate process.

If a system exists to simplify implementation of phishing and CBT, it represents the implementation of products and not the implementation of a comprehensive awareness program. If your goal is just to implement a Check-the-Box awareness program, however, product implementation is likely all you need.

Choosing Substance Over Style

When I worked for the NSA, it was clear that any mishandling of sensitive information could result in an employee's termination and, potentially, prison. The NSA allowed some gimmicks and creativity as part of its security awareness efforts, but providing entertainment definitely wasn't a priority. We employees didn't watch comical videos. We didn't play games where we sat around and won prizes if we guessed the amount of prison time we might earn. Violations are serious offenses and were portrayed as such.

Entertainment has its place. Contests are useful for engagement. Humor can enhance engagement. Giveaways are fun and can provide reminders of awareness messages. But the purpose of a security awareness program is to change and improve security-related behaviors. Your efforts should focus on those efforts and formats that contribute to behavior change.

WARNING

Though you want material that is engaging, you can walk a fine line between engaging and trivializing. Humor, when used appropriately, can enhance learning. Avoid using humor for serious subjects, however. You don't see humorous videos regarding sexual harassment. Humor can trivialize an otherwise important concept, and you need to ensure that people understand that strong security behaviors can prevent significant loss.

Unfortunately, I have seen many awareness efforts that lead with humor. The users like it, if it's done well; however, it doesn't mean that it has the desired impact, which is to change behaviors. You don't want to bore the audience, but you do want them to take your lessons seriously and apply the information.

There's nothing wrong with telling people sometimes that they have to do something because they simply have to do it. You're paying them to perform a function. In other departments, such as accounting and human resources, people know that they might be fired or that they won't get paid if they fail to do certain things, such as properly fill out a time card. You can do the same with security responsibilities.

TIP

To determine whether your awareness training is effective, ask participants what *they learned from it* rather than whether they liked it.

Understanding the Role of Security Awareness

Awareness is just one tactic within an overall strategy to reduce the risk associated with user-initiated loss. If you're in charge of your organization's overall efforts to mitigate user-related loss, you need to consider awareness as one tool in your arsenal. If you're responsible solely for awareness, you need to understand your place within the overall loss-reduction strategy.

Users can fail only if the technology around them provides them with the opportunity to fail. A user can't click on a phishing message, for example, unless all the antiphishing technologies in place failed to filter the message in the first place. Of course, technology fails significantly less often than users fail. For this reason, you need to either frame your efforts accordingly or work with the teams that provide the users with the environment.

Here are some ways other teams can help:

>> Work with the teams that provide the technical security environments to reduce the opportunities presented by the environment for users to initiate losses.

>> Work with the teams that manage the technology that anticipates harmful user actions, such as data leak prevention tools, to mitigate the harm from the actions proactively.

>> Work with the operations team to see how users' actions can be better defined to avoid the initiation of losses.

REMEMBER

Security awareness is just one tactic, among many, to mitigate damage caused by users. If you want to fail, portray your efforts as a strategy to deal with the entire problem.

IN THIS CHAPTER

» **Establishing common knowledge**

» **Seeing what safety science does right**

» **Borrowing from accounting practices**

» **Knowing the ABCs of awareness**

» **Applying group psychology to your awareness efforts**

» **Understanding how risk management works**

Chapter **3**

Applying the Science Behind Human Behavior and Risk Management

When you create a security awareness program, or any awareness program, you're attempting to influence group behavior throughout an organization. The success of your program depends on the reliability of the science and the theories you base your assumptions on.

As I say throughout this book, perfection and universal applicability are myths of the security profession; they don't exist. I have found, however, that the sciences described in this chapter work more consistently than other flawed but commonly held ideas, such as those that can cause the difficulties I cover in Chapter 2.

As you see in this chapter, you gain the most benefit for your awareness efforts by consulting sciences that influence (or attempt to influence) crowd and organizational behaviors. You need to understand the sciences of how people think and behave only to the extent you need to know to do your job properly.

Achieving Common Sense through Common Knowledge

The greatest criticism I seem to hear about security awareness is that it's all common sense. It's common sense to know not to click on certain emails. It's common sense to know that the tax service won't call you to persuade you to give them a credit card number to pay a bill immediately. And so on. Going back to my psychology lessons, the response that comes to mind is this: "You can't have common sense without common knowledge." To a large extent, security awareness is about creating *common knowledge* (stuff that everyone truly knows) so that users can exercise *common sense* (perceived good judgment in practical matters).

People within an organization generally assume that what is common sense for them is common sense for everyone. But within the group, people often lack the common knowledge required to share common sense understanding.

REMEMBER

Common sense is based on common knowledge. You can't have common sense without first establishing common knowledge.

In cybersecurity, people without a technical background definitely lack the knowledge that people within the IT or security professions possess. You need to account for this fact when building your assumptions. You must understand where common knowledge does (and does not) exist among the individuals within the group whose behavior you want to influence.

When you approach the design of your awareness programs, ask yourself, "Is this fact or idea common knowledge, and should it be?"

WARNING

Be sure to consider whether users lack the common knowledge required to act on your recommendations. Security awareness programs often tell users to create strong passwords, for example, or to check the identity of the sender for the email messages they receive. Even though most awareness communications require concise messaging, you must consider whether you must back up such guidance with instruction. If users don't know how to create a strong password or how to adequately verify the identity of an email's sender, the higher-level guidance is worthless. You must establish a base of common knowledge before you can require the common sense behavior.

Company leaders sometimes assume that technical workers, including security team members, have more common sense than the average users. In my experience, this assumption is often incorrect. A common tactic used by cyberthieves, for example, is to pretend to be another person, call an organization's Help desk, and persuade an unwitting Help desk representative to reset that person's password. As a test, I have personally convinced a Help desk rep within one of my targeted companies to send me a new computer during a social engineering exercise. During physical penetration tests, I frequently just walk into the security office and persuade the employees to issue me an actual facility badge.

Unless you *know* that a person in a given job function receives fundamental training that enables them to act on your guidance, you should assume that they lack the necessary common knowledge. This assumption should be embedded in every aspect of your awareness program, where you consider whether users have the underlying knowledge to enact the information you provide. You probably can't include every basic concept into awareness materials, but you need to design your messaging to accommodate a lack of common knowledge.

TECHNICAL STUFF

If you need to provide more detailed information than you can provide in a given communications medium, you might want to link to or refer to a more detailed information source, such as the knowledgebase I describe in Chapter 7. This way, you can provide your intended message *and* ensure that common knowledge is available.

Borrowing Ideas from Safety Science

Perhaps one of the most valuable sciences an awareness professional can research is safety science. To put it simply, *safety science* intends to prevent workplace injuries. Workplace injuries create tangible loss to an organization. Organizations must deal with not only the immediate cost of treating the injury but also lost productivity, medical costs, potential lawsuits, legal penalties, regulatory penalties, increased insurance costs, and other losses. Depending on the industry, operations may cease if an injury occurs.

Clear costs are associated with workplace injuries, so specific cost savings are generally easy to attribute to efforts that prevent them. Extensive resources, with sponsorship from top executives, are understandably put toward safety efforts. There is also the potential for regulatory requirements to drive executives harder. Security awareness efforts, on the other hand, provide benefits that can be more difficult to measure. When a user makes an error related to security, they may not injure themselves, but they can definitely cause damage to the organization. So safety science has to be adopted to cybersecurity practices.

Recognizing incidents as system failures

A critical philosophy adopted in safety science says that if an employee injures themselves, it's a failure of the entire system. The idea is that a user should never be in a position where they can injure themselves, and even if they are injured, the extent of the injury should be minimized.

TECHNICAL STUFF

Safety science identifies these three phases to an injury:

>> The environment that puts a user in a position where they can injure themselves

>> The action that creates the injury

>> The response to the injury

Safety experts first focus on creating a workplace that is less likely to cause an injury. For example, I spoke to the safety manager at a manufacturing company where I was creating an awareness program, who told me that the company had problems with forklifts hitting employees inside a warehouse. After studying a variety of alternatives, company leaders decided on the simple act of painting yellow lines down the aisles of the warehouse. Employees were to walk on one side, and forklifts were to stay on the other side. This strategy stopped approximately 90 percent of accidents involving forklifts.

Because you can never completely remove the possibility of injury, you must consider that users will be in a position to injure themselves. Safety science then studies the role of awareness, as well as what IT professionals call the *user experience*. If a user is operating a piece of equipment that is too big for them, for example, they can injure themselves. Likewise, if the user doesn't know how to properly use the equipment, they can injure themselves. Even if the user does know what to do, they might not do it as intended.

As I discuss in Chapter 1, you have to work with other teams to create a resilient environment, and when you know your environment, you can train people how best to use it.

REMEMBER

Just because a user is aware of what to do doesn't mean that they will do it. They may not have mastered the information. They might know what to do and not have motivation to do it. They might want to implement the awareness information, but they might be in a rush and take shortcuts. For many reasons, even an aware user might not follow awareness guidance.

Responding to incidents

Even with the best awareness, someone will injure themselves. You therefore need to put in place an environment that expects an injury and attempts to reduce its severity. This includes ensuring that first aid kits are in place, along with properly trained first responders, the ability to shut down operations if required, and other procedures. This also includes a *post mortem* (a post-incident review) of the injury to examine how similar injuries can be prevented in the future.

The root of the problem is not that a user takes an unaware action but rather that the user actions create damage. Safety science looks at the process holistically.

REMEMBER

Though someone should address safety problems in a cohesive way, awareness professionals seek only to create better implemented awareness programs. Understanding how your work as an awareness professional fits in with the overall loss reduction program is important. You can then work with the other security teams to coordinate your efforts *and* tailor your efforts to fit within their efforts.

Applying Accounting Practices to Security Awareness

A proper accounting program protects an organization from financial loss. Accountants study financial processes and determine where losses can occur and how to control them through processes.

In much the same way as safety scientists figure out how a person comes into the position of a potential injury and proactively tries to remove that potential, accountants try to put processes in place to proactively remove the opportunity for financial errors. This involves proactively tracking financial and tangible resources. It means that there is categorization of all resources. This is why there are so many annoying processes apparently in place in many businesses.

Likewise, a person has to endure many processes when they're in the middle of a financial transaction, and follow detailed operational guidelines for how transactions are to be performed. For example, when I travel and have to file an expense report, I have to meet specific requirements for the level of documentation required. In some cases, I can just ask for a flat amount for all meals. In other organizations, I have to categorize every expense I want to be reimbursed for and then provide a receipt for any charge. In one case, I left out the receipt for a $4.53 Frappuccino, and the complete expense report claiming more than $3,000 was rejected until I could find the receipt.

Though I of course cursed the accounting department, I recognize that they're just following the rules. Those rules were put in place because of the historical fraud that occurs whenever people submit fraudulent expenses. Clearly in this case, the organization expended more in lost labor costs between my time to redo the expense report and the time spent by someone in the accounting department to review the report thoroughly — twice. However, the processes were put in place to prevent what could become a large amount of fraud in aggregate.

Similarly, time tracking is critical for paying employees inside organizations. If people don't properly enter and certify hours worked, they may not be paid. Therefore, people enter their information accurately and timely.

TECHNICAL STUFF

Note how nobody argues about most accounting processes. Nobody argues that it's unfair to the user to not pay them if they don't complete the time card properly. Nobody argued on my behalf for my organization to pay my travel expenses without the required documentation. Essentially, these accounting practices are a must-do item, not a should-do item. When you want cybersecurity practices to be a must-do and enforceable, you can use these examples that the organization already penalizes employees for not following other critical processes.

After the user has satisfied their business responsibilities, accountants then have review and audit processes in place to ensure that information is accurate, with no discrepancies. For example, I worked in a fast food restaurant where they tracked the number of servings of expensive foods. The restaurant served fried clams, and because the point-of-sale system could track every order, the store manager had to count the available servings at the beginning and end of the shift, and they had to ensure that sales matched the difference in available servings.

Though the clams were a specific example, all mature organizations track just about everything in and everything out. The accounting process looks to ensure proper tracking of financial resources. Some of it is to ensure proper financial reporting for taxes and investors. They look for any deviations in expectations. The reason for deviations don't matter.

In cybersecurity, you have to apply these lessons and use behavioral analytics, review log files, and otherwise look for evidence of violations of security procedures. Though this is a critical response issue, reviewing this information can also tell you where user behaviors need to be improved.

REMEMBER

Much like an accountant's job is to identify deviations — whether the deviation is caused by error, accident, or malfeasance — when a user deviates from defined practices, the system should not care. It should be identified and investigated. Your organization should detect an action regardless of motivation. For example, if a user attaches a sensitive file to an email, it should be stopped regardless of whether it's an accident or the user has malicious intent.

Whenever a deviation occurs, the type of deviation drives the follow-up process. It's possible that forms, such as an expense form, will be returned for revision. If something valuable appears to be missing, it might inspire an investigation. In extreme cases, there might be a need for forensic accountants to complete a detailed investigation.

Applying the ABCs of Awareness

The mark of success for an awareness program is that people change their behaviors as required. For security awareness programs, these behavior changes should provide a return on investment and justify the awareness program, as Chapter 8 discusses in detail.

In short, the ABCs of awareness mandate that awareness influences behavior. Behaviors practiced consistently create the culture. Culture in turn provides awareness and drives behaviors.

The goal is for awareness to influence behavior. Then behaviors, practiced consistently, create a *culture* (or consistent behaviors practiced across the organization), and in the case of a security awareness program, they create a *security culture.* Your security culture then helps to drive both awareness and behaviors. Figure 3-1 illustrates this relationship.

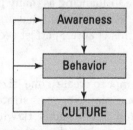

FIGURE 3-1:
The ABCs of awareness.

REMEMBER

Having awareness doesn't matter if users don't practice the desired behaviors. Most people know not to reuse passwords across multiple accounts, for example, yet you still face incidents unnecessarily because users reuse their passwords. In 2019, criminals published credentials for more than 3,000 Ring cameras in people's homes. They were able to hack in and interact with children, using passwords that had been stolen in hacking incidents and then sold on the dark web. Though the passwords were from various websites, attempts to use them to access the cameras were successful because the parents had used the same passwords on the Ring account as they did on other Internet accounts.

If behaviors are consistently poor, the security culture is weak. If senior employees choose not to wear their badges, a new hire walking into the organization will soon stop wearing their badge too, no matter what the awareness posters say.

TECHNICAL STUFF

Have you ever heard someone say that it's easier to stay in shape than to get in shape? In other words, if you're already fit, you can just continue to do what you're doing to stay fit. Otherwise, you have to change and improve something in order to become fit. It's the same for a security culture: If it's strong, it's easier to maintain a strong security culture than to strengthen a weak security culture. Just making people aware of what they *should* do won't change their behavior, because the culture reinforces the weak behaviors. You need to consider how to *change* the culture, and that takes more effort than just attempting to tell people what to do.

Benefiting from Group Psychology

Psychology that focuses on individuals is helpful to relate to people in intimate settings and in generalities, but if you're trying to change behaviors consistently across a large organization, the study of the individual has limited value. You need to influence an organization as a whole or, more specifically, you need to influence the security culture.

Clearly, to influence the culture, you have to influence the individuals within the organization. However, when you're trying to influence a culture, you're not trying to influence everyone — rather, you're influencing as many people as possible. For example, in the cybersecurity field, everyone *ideally* has strong and unique passwords. However, as I discuss later in this chapter, perfect security will never exist — only risk *reduction*.

In many ways, this may sound like an attempt to create a one-size-fits-all strategy. The reality is that you're creating a one-size-fits-*most* strategy. Again, ideally, you would be able to meet with all individuals and work with them to have them understand the desired behaviors and convince them to enact the behaviors in a style through communications that are best for their learning styles. Again, that strategy isn't practical, so you have to look at ways to influence groups of people, regardless of the individual learning styles. Admittedly, you will never get everyone — but, again, your goal is optimized risk reduction.

The ABCs of behavioral science

The *ABCs of behavioral science* are similar to the ABCs of awareness, but with important differences: The ABCs of awareness lay out a path, and the ABCs of behavioral science define motivation. (See Figure 3-2.)

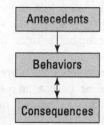

FIGURE 3-2:
The ABCs of
behavioral
science.

Here's how to break down the ABCs of behavioral science:

>> **A stands for *antecedents*.** In the context of this book, an antecedent is something that intends to influence a behavior. Antecedents in the security field are usually security awareness efforts. For example, users might see posters reminding them to wear their security access badges.

>> **B stands for *behavior*.** The B is the desired behavior that you're trying to create. For example, users may be expected to wear their badges at all times while in the building.

>> **C stands for *consequences*.** Consequences are the responses to the behaviors. Users may experience a range of consequences for their behaviors:

• *Negative consequences:* The user experiences embarrassment, inconvenience, or correction. For example, a security guard might stop someone who has forgotten their badge, or the person may be unable to enter an area that's protected by a badge reader.

• *Positive consequences:* The user is rewarded for the behavior.

• *Neutral consequences:* The behavior happens, and the user experiences no obvious consequence.

To apply this concept using clean desks as an example, consider how you tell people to keep a clean desk and lock computers and hard copy materials when unattended. You provide awareness to tell them what to do and what is expected. Combined with the awareness you provide, they also see what their coworkers are doing. They then either follow your guidance or not. They might partially follow your guidance as well, such as shutting down their computers but not securing hard copy materials.

If the employee fails to follow the guidance and you do nothing, that is a neutral consequence — and their behavior is likely to continue. If, however, a coworker or a supervisor speaks to the employee the next day regarding their failure to follow the clean desk policy, they will likely improve their behaviors the next day. If someone from the security department calls the person in and threatens disciplinary actions, they are most likely to improve their behaviors in the future. Though I don't advocate threats on the first occasion, any negative consequence is likely to improve behavior in this example. Again, the peer pressure of seeing how coworkers behave is likely to strongly influence the behavior as well.

TECHNICAL STUFF

Both antecedents and consequences influence behaviors; however, they don't influence behaviors equally. Antecedents have at best a 20 percent effect on changing behavior. Consequences have an impact of 80 percent or more.

In the ideal world, you can provide positive consequences for improved behaviors. However, providing negative consequences should not be out of the question, especially if the insecure behavior costs the organization money or other resources.

Consequences should be consistent across the entire organization. Some individuals may rebel against or ignore certain consequences, but your goal is to move the organization as a whole. This doesn't require everyone to adhere to follow your guidance — just most people.

TIP

Culture, from the ABCs of awareness, can serve as a form of consequences. Culture provides peer pressure. Peer pressure is one of the most effective forms of consequences and drivers for change. If you can improve the security culture, the culture provides all the consequences you need.

The Fogg Behavior Model

Dr. BJ Fogg is the Stanford University researcher and widely noted behavioral expert who created the Fogg Behavior Model. In the most general of terms, he studied what caused humans to exhibit various behaviors at different times. Although his model is based on the psychology of individuals, it explains many user actions. If you understand the model, you can design consequences that can impact the entire organization.

TECHNICAL STUFF

To read more about the Fogg Behavior Model, see Dr. BJ Fogg's website (https://behaviormodel.org). You can find his book, *Tiny Habits: The Small Changes That Change Everything* (Harvest, 2021) and other resources on his website, as well.

Fogg broke down the expectation of a desired behavior. The components of a probability of a *behavior* are *motivation*, *ability*, and *prompts* — or B:MAP, the acronym Fogg created. A relationship exists between ability and motivation. If motivation is high, a person will be more inclined to exhibit a behavior, even if the behavior is difficult. The example typically used to illustrate this idea is that of a mother taking heroic actions to save her child.

Conversely, if motivation is low but the task is simple, you're generally inclined to do it. An example is putting a dish in a dishwasher.

In the case of saving the child and putting the dish in the dishwasher, you have *prompts*, or indicators that an action needs to be taken. The prompt for the mother taking heroic actions is the child in danger. The prompt for putting a dish in a dishwasher is the plate being in the proximity of the dishwasher. The action line represents the theoretical point where the combination of the motivation, action, and prompt is likely to have an individual take a desired action.

Though the intent of the model is clearly based on individual motivation, you can consider this mapping at a group level to determine the abilities you need to create within the overall organization. *Abilities* are the skills your awareness program needs to create or encourage so that the users have the requisite knowledge to complete the desired behavior. Likewise, you can create consequences to create perceived motivations across the entire organization. Awareness can also make people aware of the prompts to better trigger the desired behaviors.

For example, food service workers are mandated to wash their hands after using the restroom. This task requires minimal ability, so all that's required is the appropriate prompt, or *nudge* (discussed in Chapter 7). The prompt is frequently a sign in the restroom stating that employees are required by law to wash their hands before returning to work. The prompt is simple, and sinks are immediately available. The motivation is a reminder that the workers can be punished for not washing their hands.

TIP

Prompts (or nudges) should be placed as close as possible to the spot where a behavior should be exhibited. For example, if you want people to lock their desks or computer monitors when their desks are unattended, put a reminder on their computers or desks — or at the exit to the office/cubicle area.

Relating B:MAP to the ABCs of awareness and behavior

Culture and consequences also have an impact on motivation and prompts. Peer pressure can be quite a strong motivator. The desire to avoid disappointing peers is a critical motivator, and if peers create a negative consequence for an individual not performing an action, it again incentivizes the action.

Also, if the culture regularly prompts the action, you will find the action much more likely to occur. This may include employees policing each other about sensitive subjects to avoid outside of the workplace.

At the same time, your awareness program should provide information and other resources to increase the ability of the individuals to perform the actions. This might be, for example, better instruction on how to detect and report phishing messages.

TECHNICAL STUFF

As an awareness professional, your job is technically to create awareness of the desired behaviors. You should also look for opportunities, however, to suggest technical tools that can be added to increase abilities and prompts. You will likely have to work with other teams to accomplish this task, but it's worth the effort. For example, adding a button labeled Report Phishing Message to an email client can increase the ability to report a potential danger — while also providing a constant prompt. This would likely involve working with the endpoint support team.

Though behaviors may be related to an individual's motivation and abilities, you can analyze the behavior at a macro level to identify how to improve the overall motivation and abilities of individuals. You can then decide on ways to improve prompting as well.

The Forgetting Curve

The *Forgetting Curve*, shown in Figure 3-3, describes the rate at which individuals forget information when it isn't reinforced in memory. Suppose that I introduce you to someone, for example — the longer you go without being reminded of the person's name, the less likely you are to remember it.

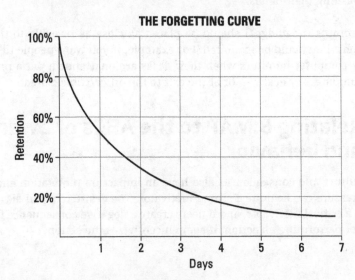

FIGURE 3-3:
The Forgetting Curve.

Security awareness programs naturally rely on users' retaining information, much of which may be new to them. Suppose that you show people a three-minute video and then administer a three-question quiz on the content of your program. If users have no reason to recall that content beyond the training session, their ability to recall the information declines quickly, until eventually they forget the information altogether. Fortunately, you can offset users' memory decline by building a reinforcement strategy into your program.

This list describes some ways you can try to "interrupt" the Forgetting Curve and slow the rate of forgetting among users:

>> **Reminders:** Provide periodic reminders to refresh and enhance users' knowledge. These can be posters, mouse pads, or any other "nudge" item that provides a frequent trigger for the information.

>> **Significance of information:** Convey the significance of the information you share in your communications. If users assign significance to what you're saying, they may automatically (like magic!) embed the information into long-term memory. This can include describing significant harm experienced, or, potentially, penalties for violating the procedures described.

>> **Memorable presentations:** Present information in memorable ways, such as by using humor, outside speakers, or unique formats.

>> **Show connections:** Tie the information to other memorable lessons, such as relating a past incident to how the application of your information could have prevented it.

REMEMBER

Reminders interrupt the Forgetting Curve and are more likely to result in long-term retention of the information.

Remembering That It's All About Risk

When I speak at various events, I sometimes ask my audience, "Who is a security professional?" Of course, everyone raises their hand, and I reply, "You are all failures."

I go on to explain that the dictionary definition of security is being "free from risk," and you can never be free from risk. Therefore, you will always fail when your stated goal is security. Supposed "security" professionals are charged with *risk management,* or determining risk and then mitigating that risk as long as mitigating the risk isn't more expensive than the risk being realized.

Risk can have different meanings in different professions. As I advocate through-out this book about the need to deliver and demonstrate risk reduction, the remainder of this section defines what I mean by risk reduction in a way that you should be able to share with others — especially those people whom you report to or need to show your return on investment.

Optimizing risk

When you create a security awareness program, you want to create the most risk reduction while using the least resources. To optimize your efforts, make it your goal to influence as many people as possible, but don't expect to influence every-one. You *can* potentially influence everyone, but that means dealing with everyone individually, and unless you're in a very small organization, this approach is impractical and too expensive. From a practical perspective, if you spend more on your awareness program than you save through your efforts, your program will be a hard sell to management.

To discuss risk, you need to have a working definition of risk that you can use to step your organization through the costs and the expected rewards. This should also include the definition of exactly what is at risk. The following sections should help with the process.

The risk formula

Risk is what your organization has to lose. Depending on your industry, risk can be a probability or a value.

To better understand how risk is defined, consider the visual relationship shown in the structure of the following formula, which I call *the risk formula*.

$$Risk = \left(\frac{(Threat * Vulnerability)}{Countermeasures} \right) * Value$$

As shown in the formula, *Risk* is the value you have to lose times the probability that loss will occur — which makes intuitive sense. For example, if your organiza-tion has a value of $100 million and the probability of loss is 75 percent, your risk is $75 million.

Value is essentially what you have to lose. The probability that you will lose that value is a function of your *Threats* combined with the *Vulnerabilities* that allow the *Threats* to exploit you. If you have no threat, you have no risk. If you have no vul-nerabilities, you have no risk. The reality is that you always have threats *and* vul-nerabilities, so unless you have no value, which is inconceivable, you have risk.

When you consider the formula, the only thing offsetting your risk are *Counter-measures*. Your countermeasures mitigate threats. You won't mitigate value, because you don't want your security program decreasing the value of your organization.

TECHNICAL STUFF

For a more thorough discussion of risk, see my book *You Can Stop Stupid* (Wiley, 2021), which covers the subject in detail.

Value

Value is what your organization considers an asset. It can be a monetary asset, a reputational value, an intangible value (such as morale), or an operational effi-ciency, for example. It doesn't have to equate to money specifically, but there will be a distinct asset that your organization wants to protect.

From an awareness perspective, you have to ensure that you clearly identify your organization's assets so that your user population knows what they need to pro-tect. This is one of the motivations to promote to your users to encourage them to more likely enact behaviors.

Threat

Threat is essentially the Who or What that can cause harm, if given the opportu-nity. Most people think of threats as malicious people. They are clearly threats. However, your awareness program is useful only if you believe that providing guidance to well-meaning users is valuable. And it is valuable, as well-meaning users are a more prominent threat. These people lack malicious intent but take actions that are nonetheless harmful because of ignorance, carelessness, or human error, all of which can be reduced by way of awareness. Well-meaning users cause exponentially more loss in aggregate than the malicious actors. The incidents can be significant, but more frequently the losses involve many small-but-frequent incidents that add up. For example, compromised credentials and lost devices result in losses that aren't significant individually. However, in aggregate, they add up to major losses.

Do you remember the old term "death by a thousand cuts," which refers to many small and seemingly inconsequential losses adding up to a major incident? It's easy to ignore the small losses, but preventing small losses can frequently save an organization more money than preventing a large incident. When you create a security awareness program, you must consider all threats and determine whether the frequency of a small loss becomes worthy of expending limited awareness resources (Chapter 8 discusses this process in greater detail).

DEALING WITH NATURAL DISASTERS

The types of threats that represent incidents resulting from non-human-related occurrences are events such as hurricanes, earthquakes, floods, and power outages. At the time I wrote this chapter, fires were ravaging California while two hurricanes bore down on the US Gulf Coast. These disasters will cost organizations billions of dollars. Even those organizations not directly affected by such disasters minimally suffer increased gasoline prices, which result in increased shipping costs.

Just as well-meaning people cause more damage than malicious actors, some threats result in more damage than most humans can imagine. Many of these threats are relatively small and localized, but more than enough are massive and have disastrous effects.

You probably can't provide any awareness of value regarding the existence of natural disasters, but you can use these occurrences to motivate people to implement basic countermeasures. For example, data backups and the use of uninterruptible power supplies are critical to mitigate the damage from natural disasters.

Vulnerabilities

Vulnerabilities are an organization's weaknesses — they allow a threat to exploit your organization. Someone may want to harm your organization, but they can't act on their intentions unless you provide vulnerabilities that they can exploit. Awareness is a countermeasure that addresses relevant vulnerabilities.

Here are the categories of vulnerabilities as I identify them:

>> **Technical vulnerabilities:** Weaknesses in technology that create loss.

>> **Physical vulnerabilities:** Allow physical access or otherwise allow for damage of physical resources to occur. For example, you can spill water on your computer and cause damage, or someone can walk into your office and steal the computer.

>> **Personnel vulnerabilities:** Involved in the hiring, maintaining, and separation of people. For example, you might hire people who are incapable of performing the job, or who may be criminals. Similarly, if you don't have the right legal documents in place, you're placing your organization at risk.

WARNING

Personnel vulnerabilities can involve direct employees or anyone with access to your information. Edward Snowden, for example, was not an NSA employee — but rather an employee of Booz-Allen, which was a contractor to NSA. His access allowed him to steal classified information and download that information onto USB drives that he carried out of the NSA facility.

>> **Operational vulnerabilities:** Involve weaknesses in how processes are designed and implemented. Do people do things that are secure or insecure? Are processes inherently secure or insecure? For example, some companies have posted too much information on websites. The now infamous Twitter hack of July 2020 involved a wide variety of operational weaknesses, where too many employees had access to the administrator tools, where employees gave up their credentials, and where it required only a single employee to reset passwords on accounts with more than 100 million subscribers, among a variety of other weaknesses.

TECHNICAL
STUFF

Awareness is useful for addressing all categories of vulnerabilities. Awareness can help people know how to secure their technology and counter technical vulnerabilities. Awareness teaches people how to use and enforce physical protections. Awareness highlights operational procedures to implement policies and otherwise behave.

Countermeasures

In the risk formula (see the earlier section "The risk formula"), countermeasures are what you do or implement to mitigate threats or vulnerabilities. Most organizations cannot mitigate threats, however. Unless you're a nation-state, you cannot stop terrorists, for example, from existing. You cannot stop a criminal from being a criminal. You cannot stop a hurricane from striking Florida.

Though you cannot address a threat, you can address the vulnerabilities that threats exploit. With a hurricane, for example, you might choose to locate facilities outside of hurricane zones. If you know that facilities might lose power from a wide variety of threats, you can address the vulnerability of nonresilient power sources by installing backup generators.

REMEMBER

The primary purpose of countermeasures is specifically to mitigate vulnerabilities.

As with vulnerabilities, I divide countermeasures into the following categories — these categories correspond to the implementation type of the countermeasure, not the vulnerability it addresses:

>> **Technical countermeasure:** Mitigates vulnerabilities by using technical tools. A software tool used to fix a technical flaw is a technical countermeasure. Multifactor authentication is a technical countermeasure that can mitigate an operational weakness of poor security awareness as demonstrated by users who don't know not to divulge their passwords. Awareness messages embedded in screen savers are also technical countermeasures.

>> **Physical countermeasure:** Uses physical tools, such as reminder signs, to mitigate vulnerabilities.

>> **Personnel countermeasure:** Involves tools that address the human resources (HR) process, such as a security awareness presentation into new hire orientation.

>> **Operational countermeasure:** Addresses how work is performed, which may also include the identification of governance. This may include how to properly identify callers asking for protected information.

Building a Security Awareness Program

Create a strategy to communicate your message and measure results.

Tailor your program to your organization's culture.

Choose program topics that consider business drivers and other factors that motivate users.

Pick the comunications tools that work best for the users you need to reach.

Integrate metrics that show how awareness benefits your organization.

Chapter **4**

Creating a Security Awareness Strategy

Perhaps one of my biggest frustrations is when I talk to well-meaning people who manage awareness programs and they say something like this:

"I contracted a CBT and phishing service, and I think I will phish people once a quarter, and here is my plan for which video I will push out each month. I was going to see how that goes for a few months and then figure out what else to do. What do you think?"

These questions reflect the common misunderstanding among many in the cyber-security world that you can run a successful awareness program by throwing the proverbial spaghetti on the wall to see what sticks.

Building a security awareness program requires having *strategy.* CBT and phishing services are tactics. Before you start buying anything, you should know how you intend to use it, and how it fits within the overall strategy of your awareness program. So often, people get ahead of themselves and buy the wrong tools for their needs, and then I have to work with them to figure out how to adapt these wrong tools for a job that would have been much more straightforward had they invested in proper planning.

Unless your goal is to just "check the box" (which is *not* a path to success; refer to Chapter 2), don't rush out and buy tools until you've devised your strategy.

Strategy before tactics, always.

REMEMBER

Identifying the Components of an Awareness Program

To create a security awareness program that works, you first need to know the three components of any successful awareness program. I define those components as the communications tools, the topics, and metrics:

>> **Communications tools:** These are the methods of communication you use to promote your awareness message. The communication tools represent *how* you communicate with your target population. These can be traditional tools, such as newsletters, posters, and videos. They can also include gamification and other, more creative efforts. (Don't miss Chapter 11, which covers the ins and outs of gamification.)

>> **Topics:** Topics are *what* you communicate through the communications tools. For example, topics might include phishing prevention, physical security, and other messages. (Chapter 6 highlights many more topics to choose from.)

>> **Metrics:** The methods you use to measure how well you achieve your goals are called *metrics*. In the ideal world, these metrics are the tangible savings that you create with your awareness program. (You can find much more on metrics in Chapter 8.)

Before you can bring together these communications tools, topics, and metrics, you must perform a thorough analysis of corporate culture, business driver, past incidents, and other factors to determine a strategy for your awareness program. Part 2 of this book shows how to perform such an analysis.

TIP

You can implement all the tactics you want, but you can claim that your program has the potential to succeed only when you have a defined strategy that enables you to measure how well your program performs. How well you bring together the communication tools, topics, and metrics of an awareness program is a huge part of its potential success.

REMEMBER

Choosing effective communications tools

An organization's culture tells you how the organization prefers to communicate. Keep this in mind when you choose communications tools for your awareness program. Step back and consider the organization's culture. Be strategic with your choices.

Chapter 5 provides ideas for how you can get to know the culture of an organization, but for now, understand that organizations often have preferred communications methods that are driven by their overall culture. Many organizations I deal with have an overabundance of internal newsletters, for example, and most people who work for these organizations just delete these newsletters before reading them whenever they receive yet another newsletter.

TECHNICAL STUFF

A big difference exists between a security culture and an organization culture. The purpose of a security awareness program is to change the security culture that exists within the organizational culture. So when you choose communication tools, you're seeking to communicate in a way that people expect you to communicate. Your ultimate goal, however, is to improve or change security-related behaviors, and — ideally — attitudes. You want to *drive* the security culture, not adhere to it.

When choosing communication tools, consider also that most (if not all) organizations contain subcultures within an overall culture. Each subculture, or subgroup, within the organization has distinct business needs and communications styles. A retailer like Walmart, for example, typically has at least four subcultures: headquarters, IT, store associate, and distribution center employee. Each of these subcultures must be addressed independently. Unlike some retail items, communication styles are rarely one-size-fits-all. For more information how best to work with the subcultures within an organization, see Chapter 5.

TIP

The easiest way to determine there is a distinct subculture is if there are unique communications styles for a given business unit — as well as distinct needs for different topics. In a retail organization, for example, the people who work in the corporate headquarters have ready access to desktop computers, perform most of their work on those computers, and regularly handle sensitive information. The retail associates are in an open store environment, have minimal access to computers, and have tactical access to information needed to assist customers and perhaps handle a financial transaction. Both groups have vastly different awareness needs and receive information in different ways.

Picking topics based on business drivers

Once you understand how to communicate effectively within an organization's culture, you need to figure out the concerns that are important to each culture within the organization (and it may have more than one). The *business drivers*, as I call them, are those operational concerns that the organization considers most important. When you consider topics to cover in your awareness program, ask this question:

What do people need to understand to do their jobs properly?

When you create a security awareness program for an organization where people work on personal computers and check email frequently, you clearly want to include, as a topic of your program, the proper use of computers. The business drivers differ when you're creating a program for a warehouse-based culture. In a warehouse, people probably use personal computers infrequently, so the topics you choose to cover might be geared more toward mobile device security and the importance of not sharing inventory details, which could reveal proprietary information and imply the organization's financial status.

Don't randomly choose one topic per month for 12 months to determine your awareness program content; create conscious intent for the program. As covered in Chapter 5, be sure you tailor the content for the needs of the culture you're addressing. You may find that you need to repeat important topics and ignore others. Your goal is to provide constant relevance to your organization and not choose topics just because they're ones that everyone else thinks your program should have.

WARNING

Avoid focusing on irrelevant topics, because users may perceive it as a waste of time. The topics you present should be either obviously useful to work life or applicable to home life. Presenting topics for the sake of presenting them isn't useful — and may even create backlash. During the COVID-19 pandemic, for example, an organization I contracted with required that I take monthly awareness training. One month the topic was travel security, which obviously wasn't relevant, because no one was traveling at that time. Including the irrelevant topic wasted time and promoted skepticism about the usefulness of all future training provided.

Knowing when you're a success

The last component of an awareness program is arguably the most important, and often the most overlooked: metrics. Metrics allow you to measure improvement, or a lack thereof.

TECHNICAL STUFF

Metrics should be collected as frequently as reasonable, given available resources and practicality. For example, if you want to use the number of malware incidents as a metric, in theory you can log in hourly to your antimalware system. The reality is that once a week might be reasonable.

Stop and consider that typical metrics involve the percentage of people who complete mandatory training. The typical metrics may also include the percentage of people who click on phishing simulations. Ensuring that everyone completes the mandatory training may hold some value for compliance efforts, but this metric doesn't tell you whether the organization has experienced an improvement in awareness or, more important, an improvement in behaviors. Likewise, phishing simulations tell you that people recognize phishing simulations, but this metric doesn't necessarily mean that people know how to recognize real-life phishing messages.

Weigh what you know about an organization's business drivers against what you know about its culture to determine which metrics are worth collecting. In terms of business drivers, pursuing important metrics that give useful results will justify support for the awareness program. An organization's culture, on the other hand, tells you what metrics can be reasonably collected. The metrics you collect should be both important and reasonable to collect, given available resources.

Awareness programs traditionally have a difficult time justifying their existence. If you can build in the justification from the start, you enhance your chances of success. Start now: Make metrics as important to your program as any communications tool you use.

GAMIFICATION

Whenever I hear the term *gamification* used in the security awareness world, I think of the popular meme that features Inigo Montoya from *The Princess Bride,* where he says, "You keep using that word. I do not think it means what you think it means."

Gamification does not mean "a game." Gamification is essentially a reward structure that rewards people for demonstrating appropriate behaviors. Frequent flier programs are a great example of gamification because they reward people for behaviors such as loyalty to an airline, staying at partner hotels, and using corresponding branded credit cards. In return, loyal frequent fliers receive upgrades and free flights.

Gamification is not a traditional awareness program, and may be part of a larger awareness effort. You still need to understand the culture and the business drivers, however. The business drivers tell you what behaviors you want to reward, and the culture helps you figure out appropriate rewards. Metrics then determine how you distribute the appropriate rewards. Chapter 11 covers gamification in detail.

TIP

Consider collecting metrics *before* you start your awareness efforts. By measuring behaviors before you implement your program, you can show how much things have (hopefully) improved due to your efforts.

Chapter 8 discusses how to determine metrics in more detail.

Figuring Out How to Pay for It All

Though it isn't necessarily a fundamental part of an awareness program, you must proactively understand how to acquire the funding and other required resources for your program. There are countless awareness efforts you can implement, but the most limiting factor will likely be your allocated budget and supporting resources.

TIP

You probably already have an assigned budget. However, you might be able to increase that budget by cooperating with other internal efforts, such as privacy and regulatory compliance programs. A great deal of synergy typically exists across these efforts, and you might be able to share in their budgets, if you help them achieve their goals.

Other resources might include staff to support your efforts, access to corporate communications programs that distribute communication within an organization, and executive support. Try to determine the ideal awareness program, and then examine what it might cost. For example, you might want to bring in an outside speaker. If you want to invite a prominent authority from the security industry, you must be able to pay their fee. To contain costs, you may want to consider a local law enforcement officer or an internal expert. And don't forget the venue: Before you can even enlist a free speaker, you need to reserve a place for the event.

As you bring together your plans, you should at least have in mind the general range of your budget. If you have metrics that demonstrate the value of your awareness efforts, it may increase the budget and the level of support you receive. In the meantime, as the saying goes, you can't have a prince's appetite on a pauper's budget. You can, however, become creative. Chapter 9 addresses budgeting, and potentially increasing your budget, in more detail.

Chapter 5

Determining Culture and Business Drivers

Often, when an awareness manager approaches me for help with their awareness program, they start off talking about the videos they chose. They describe how they thought the videos were funny or the right length or whatever else they considered when choosing them.

What these managers rarely tell me is how specifically the videos fit their organization's culture. They don't discuss, for example, which groups within the organization will watch which video.

To put together an awareness program that works for your organization, you must tailor the program — and that includes videos and any other aspects of the program — to the organization's culture and subcultures. You must understand the business drivers and how they affect the work done by each group within the organization.

Understanding Your Organization's Culture

If you want to put together an awareness program, your first step is understanding your organization to figure out what will *really* work. Even if something works for a lot of other organizations, you have little guarantee that it will work for yours. You need to understand what defines success for your organization and how to achieve it.

REMEMBER

You must consider the security culture *and* the general culture of an organization. An organization's *security* culture is how people behave with regard to security-related concerns; the *general* culture is how the organization behaves as a whole. When you create a security awareness program, you work within an organization's general culture to improve its security culture.

For example, an investment bank typically is a formal organization: People generally dress formally and act conservatively. You might assume that they would behave more securely, but frequently that isn't the case. I've found that investment bankers don't want to wear badges that will ruin their $5,000 suits. They don't want the aggravation of separate passwords. And they are frequently perceived as being their organization's moneymakers, so the organization typically doesn't enforce security policies on them.

Organization culture tells you how to communicate within the organization. You need to understand this point so that you know how to influence the people in an organization. In another investment bank I worked with, during an interview of their CISO to determine the best way to communicate with the employees, I asked him about posters. His response: "We're not putting up posters next to Picassos." In talking to him further, I learned that the CEO was held in incredible esteem among the employees — everyone even religiously read a daily newsletter put out by the CEO's office. My team was told that if you managed to have any content published in that newsletter, it would be embraced by just about everyone in the organization. Clearly, we did not use posters, and we strived to put our content in the CEO newsletter at least once a month.

As I describe in Chapter 3, *culture* is the combined behaviors of the organization. You see how everyone behaves and communicates. If an investment bank has fine art hanging in its lobby, you don't want to put up a cheap security awareness poster. You might put posters in certain bathroom stalls, but clearly not in a prominent place.

You can generally look around to see how your organization communicates in general. Consider how you know how to do your job. Consider how you find out about important information. How do mandates come down? What are the *musts* in the organization, and what are the *shoulds*? How does everyone behave in general?

TECHNICAL STUFF

When choosing the communication tools for your program, consider how they're otherwise used in an organization. For example, if you're considering using videos, consider whether videos are forced on people as a mandate. Consider these questions: Do people appreciate the other videos they're required to see? Do they follow the presented guidance? As you design your awareness program, you should consider whether what you're considering using is actually used and accepted throughout the organization. Though you might hear that something is part of a typical awareness program, you need to consider how it fits within your specific organization.

Culture isn't just a matter of looking at the walls — the overall work environment is a critical driver of culture as well. For example, if you work in a factory, your methods of communicating are limited, if not defined, by the factory's environment. Employees likely have no personal computers, which therefore might eliminate the ability to use screensavers or have them watch videos. Flight attendants and pilots have a limited ability to access information at work. Unionized environments frequently limit formal training hours, so mandating awareness videos would likely require eliminating other training requirements.

Though some nuances might not be obvious, such as limitations on training, communications mechanisms and styles are clearly apparent to even the casual observer. Though you need to delve into more than what's visible, by observing how the organization conveys information, performs on-the-job training, and generally operates — and on how its managers interact with employees — you can observe how the culture passes on information. If you see that information from the security department isn't adhered to or is generally ignored, you can observe how information that is well received makes it to the population, such as in the earlier example of the CEO's daily newsletter at the investment bank.

TIP

At the time of this writing, organizations are beginning to emerge from the COVID-19 lockdown. You need to consider whether the communications styles you see are transient or might be considered the new normal. Microsoft Teams might be the preferred communications tool, for example, or it might be a temporary solution that you can rely on only for the short term.

Before choosing a communications tool to be a part of your awareness program, find out whether the organization already uses the tool. If it doesn't, ask yourself why not. If you still want to use the tool, ask yourself why you believe it will be accepted, given that your organization has no experience with the tool.

TECHNICAL STUFF

If your organization has a corporate communications department, someone there might be able to provide you with invaluable guidance about the best ways to communicate. This person may have a biased perspective, but if they can provide statistics about the effectiveness of different communications tools and communications methods, their guidance can be quite useful.

Determining security culture

Security culture isn't directly related to the overall culture of the organization, but you must evaluate security culture whenever you study your organization's culture. In my experience, determining security culture is often easier than determining organizational culture.

I tell people that when I perform a *social engineering assessment* (by simulating a nontechnical attack to test for security awareness vulnerabilities), I know within the first 30 seconds the level of success I will have because — after taking a quick look around — I can usually determine an organization's security culture.

Do people hold the door open for strangers? Are desks left unattended with information and computers unprotected? Do people wear badges? Is any adherence to security policies apparent?

Whether or not there are policies or procedures is irrelevant. The only thing that matters is the common behaviors, or results of those behaviors, exhibited by the population as a whole. This becomes quickly obvious.

TECHNICAL STUFF

The existence of security policies, procedures, and guidelines in no way indicates that the governance is followed. The existence of documents is only useful for audits, unless the specified behaviors become a part of common practice within the organization.

As important, you find that if people are lax with certain security behaviors, they are likely lax with most, if not all, behaviors. I find that people who leave their desks unlocked are more likely to exhibit other weak behaviors, such as using their home computers for work purposes.

Likewise, people who exhibit strong security behaviors for one aspect of security typically exhibit strong behaviors across most, if not all, aspects of security. I find that the people who lock their desks are more likely to challenge strangers they see walking around the facilities. If you see enough of these people, they will raise the security posture of the entire organization.

You can use what you learn about an organization's baseline security culture to figure out a starting point for your awareness program. Remember, though, that although you always need to know where you're starting from, how you got there likely isn't the best way to move forward. You should use what you learn about your organization's overall culture to determine the best structure for an awareness effort moving forward.

Recognizing how culture relates to business drivers

I discuss business drivers in detail in Chapter 6, but they're also important to consider when examining culture. Again, culture determines your communications tools, whereas business drivers typically determine your topics. However, business drivers are frequently defined by the culture as well.

I mention previously, for example, how factory workers might have limited access to computers. This implies that employees will likely have to review critical communications on their personal computing devices and, most frequently, their mobile devices. Factory workers typically have more concerns with physical security.

TIP

Consistency of business drivers across the entire organization indicates whether an organization has a single culture or multiple cultures. Knowing what you're dealing with on this front is critical to designing an awareness program.

Identifying Subcultures

No organization of more than minor size is a monolith in any regard. That is definitely true of their security and overall organizational cultures. There are clearly many unique cultures within most organizations.

Consider Walmart. At the time of this writing, Walmart is the largest company in the world, and the company is primarily a retailer. Because Walmart is generally a retailer, you might think a single awareness program is all you need in order to satisfy the company's requirements. When you look more closely, however, you can readily see that Walmart is composed of many different cultures, each of which requires its own awareness program.

The Walmart headquarters operation, for example, deals with contracts, finance, land acquisition, intellectual property, regulatory issues, and a wide variety of other fundamental and complex business concerns. The headquarters' operation has mostly desk workers with regular PC access. These desk workers have regular access to valuable data.

Walmart also has an IT team, which keeps the organization functioning. IT employees likewise have regular computer access and possibly some intellectual property. Their access facilitates the operations of computers throughout the organization and overall operations, which includes facilitating the use of sensitive information throughout the organization.

Then you have the Walmart distribution centers. Workers in those facilities have access to computers only to assist with movement of goods. These computers are likely mobile devices. These workers have limited access to sensitive information, except that what they see and do has financial implications. If these workers see that items are out of stock, for example, they have information that could reveal the financial health of the organization or suppliers.

Then you have store associates, who have limited use of computers, except to facilitate transactions and stock shelves. These devices, especially the point-of-sales (POS) systems, have limited functionality but arguably provide the most critical function of a retail business.

Each of these business units has a unique culture, which means their communications style and business drivers are distinct. Consider that each business unit has workers with distinct skill sets and varying levels of experience with computers. In addition, the demographics between business units varies, and many other distinct characteristics exist. Also consider that each business unit has different levels of employee longevity, which affects training requirements. This doesn't even include the differing geographies where the company functions, which implies different cultural considerations. Ideally, each business unit should have its own awareness program because you need to use different communications tools and address different topics to meet the needs of each individual unit.

TECHNICAL STUFF

I am still addressing culture and the implications for communications tools in this chapter. However, the presence of distinct business drivers is still critical in the determination of whether you're dealing with a distinct subculture requiring a unique awareness program.

For example, consider that the executive team of a large organization likely has similar communications tools as the IT team. They primarily work on desktop computers and communicate via electronic means as well as have in-person discussions. However, they have very different business functions. The executive team deals with sensitive information and needs to secure the information from social engineering, accidental compromise, and the maintenance of basic computer security. The IT team deals with some sensitive information, but has other sources of concern from social engineering, computer access and maintenance, and potentially authenticating users asking for support. Though similarities exist between the two groups and I would use many of the same communications tools, I would choose different topics for each of the groups.

Interviewing Stakeholders

Although you can easily observe an organization's culture, generally, as you look around, keep in mind that observations alone are just a starting point. Observations can go a long way, but you also need to gather information about what isn't obvious and/or might be important to the organization.

The identity of the stakeholders varies by organization, as well as the interest among the people you approach. You might find that many people you want to talk to don't believe it's a good use of their time. Some people don't believe they have anything to contribute. Others might believe that being involved is an important task and demand to have input.

TIP Generally, I've found that though people may not be enthusiastic to meet with me, they do usually agree to give me at least 30 minutes of their time. Should you run into difficulty having people agree to meet with you, if you believe those people are critical to the success of your program, you can appeal to the people who mandate your program to reach out on your behalf.

TIP It's always a good idea to interview the CEO and other executives, as they make themselves available. It gives them a sense of ownership in the awareness program, which might lead to more access to other people. Most important, it makes it significantly more likely that you will receive visible support and participation from the CEO.

Visible support from the CEO will open doors for you and ensure that you find the support and access you need from departments and people throughout the organization. Ideally, this also leads to obtaining the funding you need.

Requesting stakeholder interviews

Here are the people I normally request to interview (I may not be the one to conduct the interview, but I at least request it):

>> **CISO (chief information security officer):** This person is responsible for the overall security program, and likely has oversight of the awareness program.

>> **Physical security manager:** This person likely has overlapping concerns with your efforts and may have both insight and budget to contribute. The person may also agree to have security guards and other members of their team participate in your efforts, such as to post posters during their rounds.

>> **General counsel:** The general counsel likely has guidance on what is important to the organization, and may also know constraints you're not familiar with.

>> **Compliance team:** This team may be able to offer guidance to what you should include in the awareness program. They can share their experiences in promoting compliance efforts in the organization, for example, or they might even have an interest in cooperating with your efforts and have resources to contribute.

>> **Corporate communications team:** These might be the most important people to interview. In many organizations, they are the gatekeepers to the employees. They control all messaging to employees. They frequently have standards you must meet in order to have your materials distributed. They can tell you what communications tools are most widely accepted by the organization as a whole, and they may have a regular communications venue you can contribute to. This team possibly has a graphics team that can help you create materials. These people are likely long-term partners for your awareness program. Early on, however, you need to understand their roles and requirements and determine how they want you to work with them.

>> **Human resources team:** The human resources (HR) department is critical to an awareness program. They manage personnel policies, know what type of training requirements and limitations employees may have, and maintain a general awareness of any privacy or other concerns you may not have considered previously.

>> **Training teams:** Many organizations have in-house training teams who create and manage training programs across the organization. This involves technical, compliance, and any other type of required training. They typically are involved with choosing an awareness training vendor, and likely have requirements for what type of training gets loaded into the organization's learning management system.

>> **Unions or other advocacy groups:** In some environments, there is strong union involvement in training and employment. For example, at an airline I worked with, union contracts limited how many hours of training employees could be required to take. Any awareness training required of employees would require removing other occupational training. You need to learn whether you face any potential limitations on your efforts, and try to win over support from people who can veto your efforts.

>> **Wellness team:** A security awareness program is essentially a behavioral change program. Though wellness programs might have different focuses for behavioral change, they likely have a great deal of experience in attempting to communicate with the employees, and they can share their experiences. They can likely tell you what has worked and what failed so that you don't have to

make the same mistakes they did. An extremely competent wellness team would collect metrics to show the success of their efforts, and they might provide critical guidance to how you can prove your return on investment.

>> **Sustainability team:** Many organizations also have a team devoted to promoting recycling, conservation, and similar efforts. This team often knows the most effective ways to communicate with the organization.

>> **Safety manager:** By nature, safety programs attempt to change employee behaviors and save the organizations money. If an organization has a strong safety program in place, the safety manager likely already knows what works to influence behavior throughout the organization and has a great deal to share.

>> **Chief officers (CXOs):** Each chief officer can provide information about what can make the awareness program valuable to their operations. If you can make them believe that you can satisfy their concerns and provide a benefit to their operations, they may provide resources, support, and so much more to assist your efforts.

>> **Geographic representatives:** If your organization cuts across many geographic regions, you need to understand the differences between the regions. It may seem obvious that differences exist between North America and Asia, but even within a region, you can find *significant* cultural differences. For example, New York City and Omaha, Nebraska, are located in North America, but these locations are almost certain to have different cultures.

>> **Influencers:** In my experience, every organization has certain people who know how to influence others in the organization. You find these influencers by asking others who they are. An influencer might be a department executive, an executive assistant, an office manager, or another person in a similar role. Influencers can tell you what it would take for them to follow your guidance, as well as what you need to do convince others.

>> **Representative employees:** I always ask my points of contact (POC) to arrange meetings with one or two representative users. Users, who are unafraid to speak out, frequently have input that you would never receive otherwise. They give you opinions about what will work and what won't. I make it a point to ask these folks what they think would work, and they respond with something they saw in the past that they believe had a significant impact. This can be some of the most valuable insight you can find. The representative users can provide overall attitudes about cybersecurity, describe impediments to adhering to cybersecurity guidance, and describe drivers that lead them to behave securely or insecurely, for example. In an ideal world, you stay connected with these people and use them as a focus group throughout the course of your program.

This is just a partial list of the people you may want to interview. You need to look into what is most appropriate for your organization and circumstances.

WARNING

Opinions are like noses: Everybody has one. Though you should assume the best from everyone, don't accept as the gospel truth whatever everyone else says. For example, one user told me that we should end phishing exercises because they make people feel bad if they click on a fake message. That might be true, but you cannot forego a basic component of an awareness program because one user doesn't like it (and claims that others who haven't spoken up feel the same way).

WARNING

After about ten interviews, I find that I tend to receive little new information from each additional person interviewed. Collecting information isn't the only benefit to these meetings, however. You can use these interviews as meetings to win over people who wield influence within the organization. When interviews start producing an abundance of repeated information, you might consider interviewing only those people you expect to possess unique insights or influence, or who help address political considerations.

Scheduling the interviews

As a consultant who designs awareness programs, I try to go onsite and schedule interviews to occur over two days. I schedule 30 minutes for each interview. When I have had to perform interviews remotely, organizations typically schedule the interviews over a longer period. I try to limit that period to two weeks.

If you're part of an internal team, you likely have unlimited time to connect with others. Try to limit the interview window regardless so that you can eventually move the project into the design-and-implementation phase.

Creating interview content

The primary purpose of the interview is to learn about the culture and business drivers of the organization so that you can design your program. Again, this would include the communications tools, topics, and metrics. To get to those points, however, you must ask a wide-ranging set of questions.

I have a questionnaire going into the interview, but the questionnaire is more of a formatted conversation starter. (Appendix A contains a sample questionnaire.) Some questions require a simple answer; other questions are open ended, intended to start a conversation. For example, I might ask, "What do you like most about the current awareness program? Why is that?"

TECHNICAL STUFF

When I perform these interviews, I frequently invite the CISO to sit in on the meetings. On almost every occasion, the CISO tells me how much they're learning from these interviews. Their primary purpose is to gather information that furthers the awareness program, but I end up collecting a great deal of information that is valuable to the organization's security program as a whole.

TIP

Ask "Why?" as much as possible. The answers to why questions tell you what works and what doesn't. I frequently find that things rarely work as intended. That isn't necessarily bad, because users frequently find value where none was intended.

Following are some general questions you should ask everyone you interview. You also need to ask questions specific to the person's job function and relationship or the influence they have to their awareness person:

>> What are the biggest problems you see?

>> What are the security strengths you see?

>> Do you have any specific concerns?

>> (If someone has been with the organization for a while) What has worked best within the company to change behaviors?

>> (If someone is new to the organization) Have you seen anything in your past organizations that you think would work here?

>> What have been the parts of the current awareness program that you like?

>> What did you not like?

>> Do you see other departments communicate well with employees? How do they do that?

>> Do you think the organization places importance on security?

>> Do you think your line manager expects certain things of you?

>> What happens if adhering to security guidelines causes you to take longer to do your job?

>> What prevents you from following good awareness practices?

>> How do you prefer to receive awareness information?

>> What information do you need?

>> What information do you want to see?

>> Can you offer any guidance to the awareness program?

REMEMBER

To check out a sample interview questionnaire, see Appendix A.

Taking names

As you gather information about the organization's culture, you want to make sure that you collect the contact information of anyone who is especially critical to the success of your program. Some of these people may be responsible to distribute information, such as the primary point of contact in the corporate communications department.

TIP

The interview process is part of the analysis phase of creating an awareness program. You should already have some ideas about what you want to learn or the feedback you want before performing the interviews. Keeping these ideas in mind when you meet with people allows you to assess the feasibility and difficulty of your ideas while also proactively helping with the implementation.

You may need to work with the physical security department, for example, to distribute non-electronic information, such as administering desk drops via this department or requiring the cooperation of the cafeteria manager to put table tents in the cafeteria.

WARNING

Identify the people who control the resources you need as early in the development of your program as possible. If you wait until later, you may find that some of your ideas are impractical. If you want to plan a desk drop, for example, you need to know the resources are available to print and then distribute the materials to every desk in the organization; without this assurance, you might end up developing a concept that you can't implement.

Partnering with Other Departments

As you analyze your organization, you need to figure out which other departments you need to (or should) partner with. Many of these departments are the same as those you should consider interviewing. (Refer to the earlier section "Interviewing Stakeholders.")

As you interview people from those departments, you need to determine which of those departments can offer you support, resources, or anything else that can further your goals. As the security awareness manager, your fundamental job is to create a communications program as well as distribute the communications. Other departments clearly have similar responsibilities in one way or another. Not only can you learn from them — they may be able to help you.

TIP

During your early conversations with the departments, try to highlight your mission and the support you have from management. This should help convince others to support you when you ask for their help.

TIP

To the best of your ability, research the efforts of other departments before you talk to them. Clearly, you won't know everything they do, but if you can at least have an idea of their efforts, you might have ideas for cooperation, the support they can provide you, and most important, the support you can provide them.

Some partnerships might be mandated. For example, I typically find that any organization of more than trivial size requires that the corporate communications department distributes all information to employees. Other departments may find that you have synergistic goals and agree to help you, assuming that you will help them achieve their mission. Be aware, however, that obtaining the desired support might not be easy — and you're asking potentially overworked people to perform more work on your behalf.

Here are some types of partnerships you might consider:

>> Joint events

>> Joint communications

>> Messaging in currently available communications tools

>> Printing and manufacturing contracts and resources in place

>> Distribution resources, such as security guards doing rounds

WARNING

Partnerships are great, but be wary of relying too heavily on partners. You have no authority over the partner departments, so you have no control if they reallocate resources. Their priorities might change, or they may choose to change their programs. The more you can obtain voluntary cooperation, the better.

Chapter **6**

Choosing What to Tell The Users

When security awareness professionals plan an awareness program, they consider how well their program accommodates an organization's business drivers. They create a custom program that gives users the information and tools they need to meet the security challenges that affect their particular organization.

Most accomplished security awareness professionals understand that a successful awareness program does much more than incorporate some standard phishing simulations and schedule monthly video presentations. These professionals know that in order to create a program that works, they must dig deeper to recognize an organization's particular needs.

This chapter shows how you can identify the topics that matter most to an organization. It also gives a rundown of the topics you see addressed by most security awareness programs.

Basing Topics on Business Drivers

To create an effective awareness program, or one that is even potentially effective, you must choose the content of the program based on an organization's business drivers. Choosing topics from a menu just because they seem interesting or relevant isn't enough — there's more to it than that. You want to create a *conscious* awareness program, which has a greater chance of serving the organization effectively, and Chapter 5 should start to point you in the right direction.

WARNING

Having a strategy is important, but resist planning any further out than three months at a time for the topics your awareness program will address. Certain aspects of your program are predictable, such as holding Cybersecurity Awareness Month in October, but predicting the most critical awareness topics a year in advance is almost impossible. Attacks that you can't predict may become commonplace and require focused awareness efforts. Consider, for example, the vishing attacks in the summer of 2020 that affected Twitter and other companies. Also consider how the pandemic created a sudden need for new work-from-home (WFH) requirements. You need to be able to be responsive, and planning out your program a year in advance limits responsiveness.

Business drivers come in many forms. A business driver may come in the form of a mandate by the organization, for example. The organization may mandate that employees be able to use their personal cellphones for work to save money that might have spent on company issued phones. Some business drivers are standing business drivers, such as phishing being an ongoing attack vector. Or an organization may incorporate new technology into its workflow, which can create the chance of new attack types occurring.

You need to examine what the topics are that would provide the most value to your organization and then determine the content that would best satisfy the needs.

Incorporating Personal Awareness Topics

Not every topic you incorporate into your awareness program needs to serve a critical business need directly. Sometimes, you can also benefit by offering information that helps users personally. For example, you may want to show users how to protect their home routers and how to protect their children on the internet. These topics can generate goodwill and enhance the overall security posture of the organization.

Personal security awareness is its own business driver, in a way. Increasing the security awareness, and therefore security, of employees *and* their families can increase an organization's overall security posture. An effective, or potentially effective, security awareness program considers employee well-being to be as important as any other business driver.

At a practical level, if an employee has a personal device compromised, including their home network, it inevitably puts business information in jeopardy. When an employee has their identity stolen, even if the incident somehow doesn't enable an attack against your organization, it impacts their focus at work and will also likely involve their taking significant time away from their workday to attempt to mitigate their losses.

More important, from an intangible perspective, providing information specific to the employee, as a person, makes employees believe that you value them beyond the employment relationship. It generates goodwill on the part of the individual toward the security program and likely helps generate goodwill toward the organization as a whole. From an organization's perspective, people will likely embrace something for personal reasons more than the sole benefit of the organization.

TIP

An awareness program can serve as an outreach effort for the entire security team. When you help people with personal and family issues, they're more likely to follow your security recommendations. They also become more comfortable with the security team, which makes them more likely to reach out to the security team with questions, and especially to report potential concerns. Employees' reporting of concerns can be an organization's most fruitful detection mechanism.

Motivating Users to Do Things "Right"

Awareness programs frequently focus on training users how to look for the hacker. The programs tell people that they should beware of a caller who asks for a password. They focus on the threat and their tactics. However, this type of training does little if an attacker attempts another pretext, such as talking a user into directly modifying the system's configuration rather than asking for a password.

There is no possible way to warn users about every possible attack. It is therefore critical to lay out as clearly as possible how users should do their tasks. Your organization should instruct users how to perform their job function properly, which doesn't lead to discretionary choices that allows users to be exploited. You must ensure that users know how to do things right.

WARNING

To tell users how to do things right, you need to review existing procedures and guidelines. You may have to essentially create the governance, if it doesn't exist. If the governance is incomplete, you have to flesh it out and create a best practice.

Here's an example of how this can work: I once worked with a large investment bank where a criminal contacted the Geneva, Switzerland, office and claimed to be the CEO. The criminal said that they needed a financial transaction to go out immediately. I was called in after the breach to make sure it didn't happen again. Giving users guidance on how to address the specific attack would have made the bank happy, but it didn't address the fundamental problem.

I didn't create an awareness program that told employees how to confirm the identity of callers; instead, I created a process for how to correctly perform any financial transfer. Though the bank clearly had processes in place to do so at a high level, there were no procedures for out of the ordinary transactions. I worked with the appropriate staff and refined the authorization procedures for all transactions. The process required specifying who can approve a transaction, and then the verification process for the transaction. We then worked together to determine whether similar processes existed where we could incorporate the lessons learned to prevent future incidents.

Though I used the incident in question as a footnote in the awareness training for motivational purposes, the awareness focused specifically on the new procedures and how to implement them. Why users were doing the right thing was irrelevant; the verification process, as presented, was simply a critical part of the job function. Just as they had to fill out time cards, they had to go through the established process when they performed transactions. It worked.

In the ideal world, all your awareness efforts focus on how users are to do their work properly. That clearly won't happen, but most of your efforts should focus on ensuring that your users know how to do things properly versus the threats of concern.

TECHNICAL STUFF

Case studies of past incidents and general information regarding the threats can provide useful motivation. For awareness to work, there has to be information about a solution — as well as the motivation to implement the solution. When tasks are defined as an expected part of a job function, they should be considered a must-do by users. However, when you cannot portray a behavior as a must, you can and should always reinforce the behavior with reasonable motivation, not unreasonable fear.

TIP

Admittedly, the difference between motivation and creating fear can be a fine line — the difference lies in how you empower the user. If you continually show how a hacker outwitted the best security protections, for example, you do little to inspire secure behaviors. If you highlight how a hacker took advantage of preventable vulnerabilities, and how adherence to recommended security behaviors could have thwarted the criminal, you leave the users empowered.

Common Topics Covered in Security Awareness Programs

In this section, I describe the topics covered in most security awareness programs. Each topic clearly has many offshoots, or subtopics. A complete list would be endless. Most of the topics that I cover in this section are pretty mundane, because they're representative and common. Plenty of topics are available to consider, and as you perform your assessments, you will figure out what your needs are.

TIP

Many of the topics presented here can and should be broken into multiple topics. For example, phishing is a critical subject, and with many nuances. Subtopics can be related to spearphishing, whaling, detecting phishing, reporting phishing, and more. Phishing itself is a form of social engineering, which likewise has many subtopics. Presenting a subtopic as its own topic is a viable method of constantly reinforcing a major topic while presenting new content.

TIP

I don't list reporting as a topic itself, but reporting should be addressed repeatedly throughout your program. Include the security reporting or Help line contact information in all materials you distribute to the user population. Make messaging available whenever possible, because your team is happy to talk to anyone at any time. The contact information should be reinforced whenever possible.

Phishing

Phishing is the most prolific attack used against users. You have many aspects to address regarding phishing, which include how to detect phishing messages, types of phishing messages, holiday message scams, whaling, spearphishing, and more. Phishing awareness can include information about ransomware, malware, and the like. It can also include information about malicious links and how to detect them.

TECHNICAL STUFF

Phishing encompasses a variety of potential delivery scenarios and forms of weaponization, and involves a wide variety of attacker goals. Phishing isn't properly addressed by a three-minute video. This topic is one that requires thorough discussion.

Social engineering

Social engineering is a term that has been usurped by the cybersecurity field over decades. The term once referred to the manipulation of society as a whole. Over time, the cybersecurity community adapted the term to refer to telephone pretext calls, where an attacker would call people to gain information that facilitated access to computers or information. The term then seemed to encompass any nontechnical attack by a supposed hacker.

Phishing is the most popular form of social engineering. But given its broad roots, social engineering awareness campaigns should likewise be composed of a broad range of topics. Again, the pretext telephone call was the initial form of social engineering, but you need to ensure that you address tailgating, dumpster diving, looking in facilities for unlocked information and unsecured computers, theft of equipment, lying to people in person, and more. The forms are endless.

REMEMBER

Talking about potential attacks can be helpful, but keep in mind that countless potential attacks fit under the social engineering umbrella. Users need to know how to properly respond to any request for physical access, computer access, information, or other resources. Establishing good fundamental behaviors is important, as is making users aware of those behaviors.

Texting and instant messaging security

Most people use mobile devices more frequently than personal computers or laptops. This leads to text or other instant messaging services becoming primary methods of communication. Some messaging services provide the ability to send full attachments, which can result in the transmission of malware. *Smishing* is essentially phishing via SMS (text message); these attacks send smartphone users malicious links in the hope that they'll open them. When employees use their mobile devices for both personal and business purposes, it can put your organization's information and systems at risk. Texting and instant messaging security is therefore a legitimate topic to include in your awareness program.

Physical security

Physical security can include principles such as not allowing tailgaters to follow you into controlled areas, locking up desks at the end of the workday, handling sensitive documents at home and in the office, watching for strangers walking around facilities, understanding the importance of wearing a badge, and countless other related topics. Security awareness programs almost always include topics related to, and integrated with, physical security.

TIP

Physical security is one of the best topics to consider providing specific guidance to specific subcultures. For example, outside sales representatives have completely external roles, and all their daily activities are in the outside world. People who work in laboratory facilities have to be careful about how they may dress to prevent static, contamination, theft of intellectual property, and so on. Working in office areas has its own concerns. Information relevant to one group might be completely irrelevant to the other groups.

Malware

Many attacks against users involve malware. *Malware* is typically introduced by phishing messages, unsafe or compromised websites, USB devices, worm-like attacks, or some other means planted by malicious people. Malware performs a variety of malicious functions that include keystroke/password sniffing, drive encryption, allowing remote access, compromising the entire system for complete remote access, and setting up the system as a bot to send out spam or be used in attacks against other systems.

As you can see, malware again overlaps with a variety of other awareness topics. Though you can include malware as a subtopic of phishing, web browsing, and other topics, as long as you include the relevant content, with the appropriate frequency, you should have sufficient coverage.

Ransomware

Ransomware is a type of malware that, once executed, encrypts storage on a device, rendering the device and its data unusable. If the device is connected to other systems and data stores, and if the user has permission to write to those data stores, those systems and data stores may also be affected (encrypted). The ransomware then threatens that if you fail to send the ransom payment, which is generally paid in Bitcoin, the data will forever be deleted. If you do pay, the attackers will send you the decryption key. In some variants of ransomware, the attackers threaten to release the information on the internet, thereby embarrassing the victim further while also possibly subjecting them to regulatory punishments.

Clearly, ransomware is a form of malware, so you might not need a separate topic to cover this form. Describing a ransomware attack can serve as extra motivation for users to implement the guidance you provide, however. Major companies and state and local governments have been devastated by ransomware.

Password security

Password security awareness involves informing users how to create and protect a password — and, possibly, how to use a password manager.

WARNING

In many organizations, password creation and storage, as well as mandatory use of multifactor authentication (MFA) is technically enforced. Even if the organization has such technical controls in place, don't ignore this topic. Address the concern of users reusing passwords across business and personal accounts. Personal accounts such as e-commerce, bank, and social media accounts frequently lack strict controls, and you need to emphasize good password practices across all accounts.

Cloud security

End-users likely fail to understand what the *cloud* is: It is admittedly a vague term that essentially means internet-based services and data storage. For most people, this is their primary computer usage; what is critical for them to understand regarding cloud security is that their information and computing activities are all possibly visible to other parties beyond their personal control. They should know that their data transits countless computers and is subject to monitoring. Likewise, they have no control of the systems, privacy policies, service reliability, or other factors that they regularly or casually use.

REMEMBER

Cloud use is one of those topics where you walk a fine line between making users aware of legitimate concerns and creating unnecessary fear. Your discussion of this topic should instill a sense of how cloud use should be implemented properly.

USB device security

Though USB drives (or *thumb drives*) were previously a more popular method of transferring files, they're still frequently used. If these drives can transfer files, they can transfer malware. Users must also be aware that any device they plug into a USB connection can contain malware. In countless incidents, criminals have compromised public charging stations (locations where people can recharge their cellphones) by manipulating the charging stations to load malware on cellphones whenever a cable is connected to the charging station.

Incidents have even occurred with digital picture frames that have been purposefully infected. When someone plugs the frame into a computer to charge the battery and download pictures, the computer is infected. Fans, cup warmers, lights, and other items are available that charge or operate off a USB port. Even cables can be configured with malware. Device owners need to be aware that they should avoid unknown USB devices or ports.

Internet of Things

Nontechnical people may hear the term *Internet of Things (IoT)* but be uncertain what it means. Though it might not be directly relevant to their daily job functions, users should be made generally aware that certain computers may connect to other computers over the internet and other networks — then they can make rational choices regarding proper maintenance of their household items.

Though IoT devices like refrigerators might seem innocuous and you may wonder, "What's the worst that could happen if a hacker finds out that I need more eggs?" you should know that it's a potential route into your house, network, and home computers. You have devices such as Amazon Echo and Google Home (and others) that are constantly listening for input — these devices are *listening*. And, if you have devices controlling home security systems, though the vendors may promise safety, I personally don't leave it to chance and blindly trust devices over which I have little control.

One aspect of a good awareness program is that it remains timely and relevant. IoT concerns, such as whether security issues exist with IoT devices, can be a helpful topic to roll out quickly.

Travel security

If any of your colleagues travel or otherwise spend a great deal of time working outside company facilities, you should have content available that is specific to travel security. It's a combination of mobile device security, USB device security, Wi-Fi security, physical security, issues specific to travel facilities such as navigating airport security, and other related topics.

Create a specific course for users who travel or generally work outside of traditional facilities. The COVID-19 pandemic in many ways rewarded those companies that proactively implemented travel and work-from-home processes. Having travel security materials available can provide a ready source of materials for repurposing.

Wi-Fi security

Wi-Fi security as a topic involves the safe use of Wi-Fi while out of the office. It has become extremely common for people to access Wi-Fi hotspots while away from home and the office. People access hotspots at coffee shops, supermarkets, airports, hotels, restaurants, and just about any other public area. These hotspots are subject to compromise and spoofing. In other words, criminals can either hack the hotspots or set up fake hotspots, both of which can intercept communications and potentially lead to malware installation. Users need to be made aware to avoid public Wi-Fi networks, and how to perform remote access securely.

TECHNICAL STUFF

VPN software is a technical solution that provides secure connections so that users can avoid potentially unsafe connections. Following the theme of telling users how to do things right, it would be appropriate for awareness programs to tell users how to implement VPN software properly.

Mobile devices

At a high level, *mobile* devices are any devices with computing capability that are easily transportable, such as laptop computers, cellphones, tablet computers, and special-purpose devices. They generally have all the risks of a normal computer, combined with the physical vulnerabilities. Clearly, overlap occurs with other common awareness topics, but you still need to remind users that their mobile devices are as valuable, if not more so, than their desktop computers, and must be protected as such. Again, though a certain amount of focus on the threats may be desirable, the primary focus needs to be on how to properly secure the devices.

Work from home

The COVID-19 pandemic made working from home commonplace. Even my former employer, the National Security Agency, implemented a work-from-home provision for many employees. Though a great deal of related awareness topics should have been known to many people, working from home clearly features many unique aspects. Some users even perform work-related functions on the same computer that their children use to attend online classes.

Again, other topics should account for many issues, but there is a need to reinforce the especially relevant topics to the users. You also need to ensure that your technical staff is especially aware of these issues, because a compromise of their systems and access can create extensive damage to your operations.

Basic computer security

No matter which topics you choose to include as part of your security awareness program, be sure to also address basic computer security issues, such as the importance of proper system configuration, patching, screen savers, regular backups, and other good cyberhygiene practices.

This is a useful topic for supporting materials. You can create checklists and links to supporting websites. Make sure that users know they should enact the counter-measures on their home and work computers.

TECHNICAL STUFF

Cyberhygiene is the term for performing basic cybersecurity functions that protect the computer while also helping to ensure that losses are mitigated should something go wrong. Typically, these functions are easy to perform, and just require enabling functionality that automates the tasks without manual intervention.

Insider threat

Though you typically don't want to provide information that primarily intends to inform people of bad news and, specifically, malicious insiders, doing so can help motivate users to implement your recommendations. However, too many people discount the insider threat, despite its status as the costliest of all threats. The Verizon Data Breach Investigations Report (DBIR) stated that 28 percent of significant incidents involved a malicious insider. Though no organization wants to create a sense of distrust, you need to ensure that you instill a sense of diligence.

Protecting children on the internet

Protecting children on the internet might not seem directly related to work, but helping users understand how to protect their children can gain your awareness program a great deal of support from your users. Not only that, users will more likely remember and embrace any information that happens to overlap with work-related cybersecurity issues. Providing information regarding how to secure their home computers, how to maintain personal privacy, how to browse the internet securely, and how to set parental controls on computers and other equipment show that you care about not just the organization but also the users and their families. This generates incredible goodwill for your program, and makes users more likely to come to you in the future with any questions.

Social media security

Social media security involves how users interact with social media sites, such as Facebook, LinkedIn, Twitter, TikTok, and Instagram. Users should be, for starters, informed about how to protect their privacy and organizational information and cautioned about posting personal information that can be used to steal their identities.

Devastating cases have occurred in which military operations were compromised because a soldier asked for prayers before a mission. Similarly, apps that tracked running routes gave the expected location of military troops in war zones. In another case, a US soldier posted pictures of helicopter reinforcements on Twitter, and the picture had a geotag that specified the exact location of the helicopters, which then came under attack.

Also consider the potential issue of embarrassment. Government Twitter accounts have been hacked. Companies have had embarrassing information posted to their accounts. Individuals have had people compromise their accounts to post embarrassing information. There is a lot of harm to protect against.

WARNING

Social media posts can also lead to potential fines and penalties. In one case, Reed Hastings, the CEO of Netflix, posted subscriber information on social media and then the SEC investigated whether he posted information into Netflix earnings, before official earnings were to be announced. Though many organizations are afraid to tell users what they should and should not post on social media, appropriate warnings should be issued as applicable.

Moving security

Moving security involves ensuring the security of information while your office location is moving. I came upon this topic when I was performing a physical security assessment of a Fortune 50 company and walked into an area with empty desks and a couple of big trash cans in the middle that were filled with papers. The first paper I pulled out of the can was a list of salaries. The second paper was a copy of a letter informing the recipient of a charge of sexual harassment against them. The next paper was a letter informing the recipient that their performance was unacceptable. I stopped looking and taped a large plastic bag over the top of the cans to cover them before hauling them to the security office. It turns out that this physical location was the former location of the HR office, which had recently relocated. The papers in the trash cans were intended for recycling but had been left behind before being properly discarded.

Moving security involves how to properly secure information, and potentially to switch computer systems. It should also tell users how to secure computers for transport and ensure that data backups are made should the computer be damaged or lost.

Compliance topics

As discussed in Chapter 2, many security awareness programs exist only to satisfy compliance standards. After evaluating just about all common standards, they seem to imply only that an awareness program exists. You get limited, if any, specificity about the content of the program. So, if your only goal is compliance, you can just use any general awareness course.

If you have a comprehensive awareness program that intends to go beyond compliance, however, you should still include information about the compliance standard itself. Basic information might include what the standard is, why it's relevant to the person's job, any unique aspects of the regulation, or any job requirements resulting from the compliance standard or regulation, for example. Essentially, the compliance standard or requirement becomes a topic itself.

Here are some compliance topics you often see mentioned:

>> **GDPR:** European data privacy regulation

>> **HIPAA:** US healthcare data regulation

>> **LGPD:** Brazilian data privacy regulation

>> **ISO 27001:** International cybersecurity standard

>> **PCI DSS:** International credit card processing standard

Chapter **7**

Choosing the Best Tools for the Job

O nce you decide on the topics you want to cover in your awareness program, you must choose how you want to communicate those topics to users. Many methods and tools are available to facilitate this communication, and your job is to determine which of those methods will work best for the organizational culture.

If an organization has people who work with desktop computers, for example, screen savers is likely one of your methods. If you're working with a manufacturing environment and the workers have morning meetings before reporting to the shop floor, you will want to supplement the content covered in those meetings with content related to your awareness program. Expect to build on the communications tools already used and, possibly, introduce brand-new tools.

This chapter describes some communications tools commonly used in awareness programs. Not all the tools I cover in this chapter are used by every organization. At the same time, this chapter doesn't provide an exhaustive list of every possible tool you might use. As you read the chapter, consider which tools seem like they might work best for the various subcultures within your organization. My hope is that you discover new tools that you can add to this list. Chapter 9 shows how to roll out the tools you choose.

Before you dive into choosing and rolling out tools, though, consider first identifying people who can perform outreach on behalf of the security team and its initiatives.

Identifying Security Ambassadors

Many awareness programs use employees from throughout their organization as an extension of their team. They find people who are willing to perform outreach on behalf of the security team to promote cybersecurity practices. These people are frequently called *champions* or *ambassadors*.

Depending on the culture of the organization, the ambassadors provide presentations and act as your local representatives. They promote your messaging. They distribute your materials. They organize local events. They take on the role that the local culture requires.

For example, in one manufacturing organization I worked with, many employees solely performed physical labor, and critical communications were provided verbally at weekly team meetings. The security ambassadors were sent talking points to present at the weekly meetings. The ambassadors comprised the only reliable way to convey awareness messaging to the teams.

Though ambassadors may not be critical to all subcultures within an organization, having a trusted person who is a member of the local team as your representative can increase the acceptance of your program.

Finding ambassadors

Finding a team of people who already have full-time responsibilities to do the bidding of the awareness program is obviously a fairly difficult task by itself. You therefore need to be creative in your recruitment efforts.

TIP

To make your job simpler, you need to find out what's available throughout the organization's culture and see, ideally, how to piggyback on those efforts. Many organizations have local safety representatives; some organizations have local HR representatives. In one organization I worked with, the administrative assistants had an established communications channel, and they were willing to serve as our ambassadors. Additionally, they had already earned respect and influence throughout their environments.

In the absence of an established group to draw from, you have to find people to recruit. They have to be willing to take on additional work, and be willing to be an enthusiastic promoter of your program. To find qualified people, you can solicit by way of internal communications channels. You might want to see whether you can offer some form of reward, such as providing bonuses or at least potential support for better raises, promotions, and evaluations.

Maintaining an ambassador program

To enjoy the benefits of having ambassadors to amplify your messaging, you have to invest in creating a communications and support infrastructure and in training the people who serve as ambassadors. You need to budget appropriately and understand that you will have to devote significant effort to maintaining the ambassador program.

WARNING

Once you find potential ambassadors, you must ensure that they have proper training. They need to be reasonably competent in overall cybersecurity awareness because they will likely be called on to make presentations and answer questions. They should also be reasonably good communicators and, hopefully, respected by their colleagues. You therefore need to create a much more detailed awareness program for your ambassadors and ensure that they score reasonably well on knowledge evaluations. This can be a major effort on its own.

Depending on the size and dispersion of your organization, you may face a major challenge to ensure the success of your ambassador program. You need to ensure that you have reliable communications and that you can, ideally, send bulk materials to ambassadors as needed. It's relatively easy to send softcopy materials via email. However, if you want your ambassadors to set up tables, sponsor giveaways, and take part in other similar initiatives, you need to ensure that they can get the materials they need when they need them.

Ideally, you will have the budget to bring your ambassadors together on an annual, if not quarterly, basis. You need to provide a consistent level of technical knowledge — consider providing training on how to give presentations and engage in overall communications. The reality is that people who volunteer to support you are well-meaning, but you have no idea about the skills they bring with them.

Again, if you have the advantage of working with an established group of people, as I did with the administrative assistants or when the organization already had a safety champion program in place (as I describe in Chapter 5), you can piggyback on top of that infrastructure. In the absence of having such an infrastructure already in place, you need to create it if you want to have a viable ambassador program.

WARNING

If you want to experiment with an ambassador program, keep in mind that you're expending not just your resources but also the time of the ambassadors, who have many other responsibilities. Though you might set aside some of your own effort and budget for experimentation, if a perception exists that you're wasting the time of the ambassadors, or otherwise using them poorly, that perception will generate a great deal of pushback.

Knowing the Two Types of Communications Tools

The distinction may seem small, but you need to understand the difference between passive and active communications tools. To many, an awareness tool is just an arrow in a quiver and you pull out the one that works best. The reality, however, is that you have to be mindful that passive and active tools aren't inter-changeable. They require different resources and different levels of buy-in from other parties. They require that you expend different levels of goodwill. That being said, here are the basics:

>> **Passive communications tools:** Available to, but not forced on, anyone. In short, these tools require no interruption of a user's normal activity.

>> **Active communications tools:** Require interaction from the user.

REMEMBER

The distinguishing factor for active-versus-passive communications tools is an action of some sort being required. You don't have to read a poster. If you send the poster, or its contents, via email, the user at least has to click on the email to delete it. Generally, active tools are more expensive to acquire. Probably most important, active tools require more time commitment from users, which should be considered the largest expense you incur.

The next two sections discuss how you can get the most benefit from using each type of communications tool. Both are valuable but have different types of costs associated with them. Passive tools function as subtle reminders, hopefully, at the right place and time when used in the right way. Active tools can be much more impactful and tend to immediately capture your audience's attention. They do, however, come with more costs, both related to monetary costs and, even more important, time costs.

Reminding users to take action

Passive communications tools can be reminders, but, if placed appropriately, they can function as a *nudge,* which is a tool that prompts someone to do the right thing at the right time. A common nudge is the reminder in restrooms for employees to wash their hands or a mouse pad on a desk that reminds someone to lock the computer when leaving their desk. At the National Security Agency, stickers were applied to all unclassified telephones to warn users not to talk about classified information on that phone and that the phones were monitored.

Given that passive tools require no effort on the part of the users, you can, if you're allowed to, add as many tools as is reasonable. An organization might restrict where you can place objects (imagine the aesthetics of placing a security poster next to a Picasso!). Organizations also often limit the design styles you can use. And, of course, the organization controls your budget.

REMEMBER

Design styles are typically mandated, or at least approved by, the corporate communications team. They will likely define what you can or can't do. They should guide you on the allowable "look and feel." They may also have some helpful templates and ideas for your own tools.

TIP

Consider your passive tools strategically. When you examine an organization's facilities, you'll probably see opportunities for nudges and reminders just about everywhere. Definitely consider all available options, but don't overdo it. If you take over all available space, you risk overwhelming users. I once turned on a TV show that continued playing the same commercial, back-to-back. Interrupting my TV show repeatedly with the same product just made me detest that product.

Requiring interaction from users

Active communications tools require interaction on the part of a user. With a passive communication tool, a user can choose to read a poster on a wall while doing something else in the area, such as waiting for a printer or photocopy machine. An active communications tool, such as a training video, requires focused interaction from users.

The level of commitment required by an active tool can vary greatly. If you send someone a security tip via email, they can choose to delete the email in less than a second. Reading it, however, may take three to five seconds. At the other extreme, when I started at the NSA, we had a two-day security awareness course. You can find personal protection courses that last more than a week.

THE HIDDEN COST OF SECURITY AWARENESS

When people think of the costs of your awareness efforts, they consider the hard costs of your program that comprise your budget, such as the cost to license training or run phishing simulations. They might even consider your salary or those of your staff and consultants. These are the obvious costs for your program.

Much more costly is the cost of the time the users spend away from their job responsibilities. For example, if you create a typical program that has a monthly CBT module with quizzes and a newsletter, you can estimate that users need to spend a mere 10 minutes on each module. Over a year, this totals about 120 minutes, or 2 hours of time. When the average worker, at least in the United States, works 2,000 hours a year, a couple of hours a year seem like a reasonable amount of time to devote to security awareness training.

For every 1,000 people, however, a similar calculation indicates that the equivalent of one person is devoted specifically to security awareness training. Perhaps the average compensation with benefits is $50,000. You need to determine what that figure is for your own organization. If an organization has 5,000 employees, it translates to $250,000 per year. If an organization has 100,000 employees, the cost is $5 million per year. As you can quickly calculate, the hidden cost of lost productivity can be significantly more than the hard costs of the awareness program.

Chapter 8 discusses this hidden cost in more detail, but for this chapter, you just need to understand that active communications tools require that they provide a return on investment that justifies the time invested in the provided training.

WARNING

Active tools can be considered a nuisance. Active tools go specifically to an individual, though a passive tool isn't specifically intended for anyone. If a user already knows and practices the guidance on a poster in a public area, they can rationalize that other people may not. If you send the same content by email, the user may be insulted that you think they don't know something that they actually practice every day. You therefore should carefully consider the benefit of any active tool to the potential for aggravation on the part of the users.

When used effectively, active tools can create a positive impression of your security program as a whole. You still need to consider the hidden costs of using those tools, however, to ensure a proper return on investment. (See the nearby sidebar, "The hidden cost of security awareness.")

Exploring Your Communications Arsenal

This section describes the communications tools most commonly used in security awareness plans — or, as I call it, your communications arsenal. With so many tools already widely in use, and more to be discovered as you gain experience, you truly have an arsenal of tools to choose from.

As you explore the descriptions of each tool, try to figure out what may or may not be applicable for your awareness plan. Consider these points as you assess each tool:

>> Is the tool appropriate for the corporate culture?

>> Are the resources available to implement the tool correctly?

>> Will it not be overly intrusive?

TIP Research communications tools from other types of communications programs for new ideas. As I've mentioned, safety programs, wellness programs, compliance programs — among many other types of organizational programs that intend to modify behaviors — likely have decades of combined experience in seeing what works and what doesn't work. Listen to their experiences.

The tools described in the following sections are passive communications tools. Examples of this type of tool include posters hung by the photocopier or printer, signs posted in the breakroom, or even a sign taped inside a bathroom stall. (Whatever works.) You make these tools available to users, but you don't force them to interact with the tools.

TIP As I describe in detail in Chapter 9, you likely will have to balance your choice of tools with budget, competition for resources among departments, and other organizational limitations, as well as a variety of concerns specific to your situation.

Knowledgebase

A knowledgebase is among the most useful passive communications tools and among the least spoken about. In short, a *knowledgebase* is a library of information regarding security topics. The library should be filled with articles related to security topics that users can search and read as they want. The articles are typically made available to the organization by way of the security team's internal website or an internal knowledge library, such as a SharePoint system. It can also be a web based system, like Wikipedia.

One benefit of a knowledgebase is that it provides a single place users can look to find detailed information on cybersecurity related topics when they want and need it. The articles in the knowledgebase offer a reasonably deep but user-friendly description of security topics. Providing a central repository allows for a comprehensive source of information with a consistent quality. Most communications tools cover awareness topics at a very high level and with little detail; knowledgebase articles provide more practical levels of information that help users understand and apply the knowledge.

TIP

You can embed links to knowledgebase articles into your other communications tools. If you send out a newsletter, for example, you might include links to the relevant knowledgebase articles so that newsletter recipients can find more detailed information.

Here's another example: You might tell users to secure their mobile devices in your awareness program. Though you can't provide instruction for securing all potential mobile devices in a 2-minute video, you can create a series of articles that walks users through the process of securing their mobile devices. You can create as many articles as required for securing iPhones with different versions of iOS, devices with different versions of Android, and so on.

You can create articles that walk users through more practical and personal topics, such as how to secure their home Wi-Fi or how to protect their children on the Internet. Unlike other communications tools, a knowledgebase usually has few limitations, as long as you can find a hosting system. The more robust you make the knowledgebase, the more useful it becomes, and the more users access it when they need information.

WARNING

Creating a knowledgebase obviously takes a lot of work; however, you must also realize that you're committing to the work of maintaining the knowledgebase and keeping the content updated. For example, if you describe how to secure an iPhone, you have to update the content whenever iOS is updated. Though that might be required only once a year — and some topics, such as how to choose a strong password, might rarely need updating — consider also all the other technologies you need to cover.

Posters

When used for a security awareness program, a *poster* conveys information on the topic of interest, such as phishing, physical security, or password protection. Of course, posters work only if users see them. Place posters in areas where they are allowed and will be seen.

WARNING

Though posters are straightforward in purpose, you still might have to work around some limitations. I worked with several companies where the corporate communications department specified a particular look-and-feel for all posters — which greatly limits creativity. Likewise, though all passive materials have the potential to become background noise, where they're less likely to be noticed. Similarly, if one poster has the same look-and-feel as the next one, I found that users are unlikely to notice when the content of posters changes. You likely want to make sure that your awareness program has consistent branding, but you must make sure that the posters you use have some noticeable distinction between them.

Hardcopy newsletters

Printed newsletters can be distributed to users throughout an organization, placed in common areas, or posted on bulletin boards or similar venues. Organizations tend to send newsletters by email in soft copy, which makes them an active tool. In environments where computers are used less prevalently, distributing printed copies is the best option.

I classify newsletters as passive because, even if a newsletter requires someone to read it, which is an active act, users can just ignore it and choose not to read it.

TECHNICAL STUFF

I find that newsletters usually have a discussion of one or more awareness topics. The discussion of a topic is typically limited to two or three paragraphs. Embedding links to relevant knowledgebase articles as they are available can be helpful. Additionally, newsletters frequently feature short news stories and tips. Newsletters should also tell users how they can contact the security team.

The general form of newsletters varies, but they're usually two or four pages long. Newsletters are usually released once per month. If you have the content and resources, however, you can consider releasing one every two weeks, if the corporate culture considers that a reasonable release schedule and if critical information needs to be conveyed.

Monitor displays

Many organizations have monitors in public and work areas and use them to provide information to passing employees. Monitors are frequently in cafeterias, in lobby areas such as elevator lobbies, and in any other place where users congregate for any period. Typically, the monitors scroll through a variety of information that relates to general organizational issues, statements from executives, promotion of wellness, and other information that organizations want to distribute to others.

TIP

Find out who controls the content that these monitors display, and see whether they will include your security content with the other scrolling content. As I mention in Chapter 5, you should talk to the corporate communications department, which likely controls this content, but other parties may be involved. Monitor displays are most likely of similar dimensions as any hardcopy posters you use, but in a 16×9 format. The content you can post on monitor displays is likely limited, so have a proactive plan. Consider modifying the monitor content as frequently as possible because users will stop paying attention to the content after they see it three times. Any content shown on the display can serve as a reminder, but it becomes background noise when users see it too frequently.

Screen savers

Screen savers are computer monitor displays that appear whenever a computer is locked or has been inactive for a specified period. Organizations often define the content of screen savers, which can be used to display your security awareness content. Because computer monitor sizes vary, and likely include laptops, you need to create graphics in dimensions that can work on any monitor. You also need to work with the appropriate teams to update the displays in reasonable periods.

Pamphlets

Everyone is familiar with *pamphlets* — those hardcopy materials that are frequently folded pieces of paper. Unlike posters that contain a simple and single message, a pamphlet intends to be a reference document and provides more detailed information.

As with newsletters, an active element is clearly involved in reading a pamphlet. Again, though, users can easily choose to ignore the existence of the pamphlet.

TECHNICAL
STUFF

From a design perspective, pamphlets are typically standard paper held in a landscape layout and then folded in half or thirds to provide for four or six pages. Though folding into six pages results in smaller pages, that may be desirable, given the amount or categorization of the content.

As enhanced references, pamphlets typically provide detail on a single subject. This is helpful for important topics, like how to handle information according to regulatory standards or how to secure information or types of technology. You have to anticipate not just the production costs, however, but also how the pamphlets are to be distributed. You can use them as giveaways at events. You might choose to make them available in public areas. If you want to distribute pamphlets to everyone within your organization, you need to research the logistics to get that done.

Desk drops

Any awareness tool that you distribute to each and every individual — usually, by leaving it on their desk — is referred to as a *desk drop*. Typically, the desk drop is an information card or pamphlet (or is similar to a pamphlet).

Some desk drops are more elaborate. In one case, I organized a desk drop that occurred during the Halloween season. It involved a small bag of candy that also contained information about the California Consumer Protection Act (CCPA) that went into effect in 2020. It was a notable way to attract attention to the importance of adhering to the requirements. It was, however, a logistical challenge to get the bags organized and distributed. The distribution was limited to the areas where users specifically needed to know about the CCPA.

TECHNICAL STUFF

All organizations have a mechanism to get physical information into the hands of all employees. These mechanisms are being used less frequently as electronic resources become available to both distribute information electronically and allow the provision of legal confirmation that the materials were received and acknowledged. If you can find out how to access these distribution mechanisms, you will likely need to justify the use of the resources.

Table tents

Table tents are self-standing information cards. You may imagine taking a sheet of paper in portrait layout and folding the top edge to the bottom edge. This provides for display in the two outside faces. You might find similar displays in restaurants highlighting menu items.

TIP

When I use table tents in an awareness program, I work with the cafeteria managers to place the table tents on cafeteria tables. There are frequently other common areas with tables where people eat, take breaks, or otherwise meet. In these cases, you may be able to persuade the maintenance staff to assist with proper placement of the table tents.

I once had table tents placed in meeting rooms as a nudge to remind users to ensure that sensitive information was not left behind in the rooms, on whiteboards, or on the meeting room computers used to display presentations.

Coffee cups or sleeves

Perhaps one of the greatest awareness opportunities I see companies overlook is the cups they provide for coffee. Many organizations discourage disposable coffee cups, but if your organization does use them, you can place awareness messages on the cups.

Another option is to put messages on the cardboard sleeves that slip over the hot cups to allow for easier holding (and to avoid being burned). The sleeves are less expensive than the cups themselves, but you can still print messages on them.

Before you choose to put messages on cups, check whether the people at your organization commonly use cardboard sleeves on their cups. If they do, your messages will be covered up most of the time.

Stickers

You can create a variety of stickers to serve as nudges and short awareness messages in general. The information on the sticker should be concise and appropriate to the purpose. I described the telephone stickers at NSA that warned users about not discussing classified information on nonsecure telephones. Stickers can be placed on computers to remind users to lock the computer when it's unattended.

Stickers can be created for any purpose to provide a nudge where it's needed. If the design is creative, users may want to collect them, which may increase engagement with the awareness program.

As you design your awareness program, consider where you potentially need nudges and whether stickers would be a good solution.

Mouse pads

Mouse pads with security messages make useful reminders for good security practices. The one critical issue to consider is that mouse pads aren't regularly refreshed with new messaging, so you need to ensure that any content on the mouse pad will remain valuable for an extended period.

Mouse pads work well for communicating the generic branding of the awareness program — which creates engagement. Or you might consider messaging for a problem that is common and will be a consistent problem for a length of time. The message can remind users to secure their desk, to browse the internet safely, to be wary of phishing messages, and more.

Pens and other useful giveaways

Every so often, I find myself using a pen, notebook, sticky note, or similar object that I picked up at some random event. These objects subtly remind me of a vendor, an event, or an organization that I worked with. And I admit that I have on occasion engaged the vendor on the giveaway.

These types of giveaways are useful reminders of your messaging. Clearly, any results generated by giveaways such as these are nearly impossible to measure, because you never know who did not initiate loss as a result of listening to the message. But if you have the resources to create these tools and make them available, you can at least generate goodwill toward the security program.

Camera covers

Perhaps one of the most useful passive tools you can provide are covers that users can place over the camera lens on laptop computers and other camera lenses. The lenses are typically slightly bigger than a pinhole, and the covers can be stickers or a slider that is permanently affixed to the computer and slides back-and-forth to open and close.

TIP

You can put a message on the cover. The message can be specific to the fact that computer cameras can be hijacked and remotely controlled, even if the light is off, or you can put other short reminders. You can even simply use the awareness program branding to provide an overarching awareness reminder.

Squishy toys and other fun giveaways

Not every communications tool has to be immediately useful. One of the most common giveaways I see at events is the squishy toy. Though the toy's initial intent is stress relief, if it's designed well, people often choose to keep it around and it can then function as a reminder of your awareness program.

You can easily find companies that sell fun objects, such as rubber ducks, and allow you to print messages on them. If you have the budget, you can potentially create small likenesses of your program mascot. Other examples of such giveaways are Frisbees, stuffed animals, small games, and other toys.

Active communications tools

Active communications tools are those tools requiring users to interact with them. A time commitment is involved with interacting with these tools. The time to interact with them likely requires users to take time away from other duties, or else it just adds to the workload.

WARNING

Earlier in this chapter, I describe the hidden costs of awareness, where many organizations do not calculate the time involved in required training. Some organizations, especially those with blue collar workers, are quite aware of these costs. Even if costs are irrelevant to the organization and its leaders believe that the time spent on awareness is well worth it, many employees will likely complain about being forced to participate in the training. Given the inevitability of pushback in some form, be judicious in the active tools you choose.

WARNING

In Chapter 8, I discuss in detail the critical difference between engagement and effectiveness. Active tools can be engaging in that they get users involved with the awareness program. However, it doesn't necessarily translate to effective behavior change. There is clearly an intangible benefit to inspiring users to engage with your awareness program; however, don't lose sight of the fact that as a business discipline, your awareness program should create a measurable return on investment, beyond just saying that people like your efforts.

Computer based training

Computer based training (CBT) is the video training that people have grown to love or hate. It's a recorded video that may or may not offer a quiz afterward. In short, it provides a fixed body of knowledge and probably checks for an acceptable level of immediate understanding of that knowledge.

WARNING

The CBT should be integrated with the entire awareness program. It is, however, where many awareness programs default to a check-the-box effort, where the printout of the completion of CBT becomes the goal of the program and the CBT is the *de facto* awareness program. Though it will satisfy compliance requirements, it's extremely unlikely that it will create a measurable impact in the improvement of security related behaviors.

CBT comes in many formats and styles, such as extended trainings where all information fits into a single session, and it can last for an hour or more. Sometimes users are fed one or two microlearnings per month, which are typically one to five minutes long and on a specific topic. It's also common to show one full annual training that is supplemented with monthly microlearnings.

The styles of CBT vary greatly. You have animations, clip art, live action, explainer videos, and anime style, for example. There are also different styles of delivery: CBT can attempt to be funny, or it can be intentionally stodgy, or it can be short and to the point. What's important to realize is that none of these style or themes is universally right or wrong. The style has to match the culture of the organization and be effective in getting the message across.

WARNING

Most people agree that making light of important subjects, such as sexual harassment or ethics, is grossly inappropriate. You need to consider likewise whether humor makes light of critical cybersecurity issues. I personally think that humor, if used in a responsible way to get a message across, can be useful. However, you have to walk a fine line between humor for the sake of humor and humor to enhance a message.

REMEMBER

Certain themed awareness videos also follow a supposedly engaging, ongoing storyline. Engagement can have some benefits, but you need to ensure that they produce a measurable impact on changing behaviors. You don't want to provide a video series where the only benefit is that users enjoy taking time away from their normal responsibilities.

Contests

You can implement a variety of activities that encourage users to learn by way of exploration and experience. They can take many forms and are limited only by your imagination. Here are some examples:

- » **Scavenger hunts**: You give users questions that have them search for cybersecurity related information based on technology sources, such as "What does *https* stand for?" You can also have them search policies to answer questions such as, "How many characters are required for a password?"

- » **Security cubicles:** Position a cubicle in a public place, and plant common security violations inside it. Then have users try to list all the violations. Examples are a printer with materials left behind on it, a monitor that isn't locked, and a sticky note with a password written on it.

    This type of event might be virtual using a picture of a workspace. Modifications can be, for example, a picture of an airport showing people exhibiting security violations, such as showing people looking at information related to workplace security within the view of others, leaving sensitive information behind, or leaving computers unattended.

- » **Escape rooms:** Put users in a closed environment, and have them engage in security puzzles that they have to solve. Examples are to guess common passwords, access a cellphone by guessing a passcode, and answer questions that lead to guessing a passcode on a lock. This activity, which should be timed and solvable, can have a limited number of participants. It also involves an extensive time commitment, but it might produce some engagement and possible behavior change.

Events

An *event* is where you bring people together at a given time. And, given remote work, the event can be held remotely. Most events involve presentations of some form on security related subjects. The presentations can feature some topic of general interest, such as discussions of news related issues, or they can involve specific subjects related to your organization, such as a rollout of a new security policy. Sometimes games are associated with the event, where you award prizes to users who participate in a game of skill, such as a ring toss, or who answer security related questions.

TIP

FINDING OUTSIDE SPEAKERS

Bringing in outside speakers can consume a lot of limited resources, but doing so can also impress the importance of your awareness efforts on your users. The fact that your organization is having them spend time away from work to participate in an awareness event can give the impression of the perceived importance of your efforts. You don't want to waste that perception by choosing the wrong speaker.

When choosing a speaker, consider whether the audience can relate to the content, the skills and charisma of the speaker, the relevance of the content, and presumably, the specific purpose of the presentation. Some speakers can also talk to multiple audiences and provide different levels. Though some speakers provide demos (or what I call dog-and-pony shows), you have to watch out for them being the equivalent of cyberse-curity parlor tricks: They look impressive, but to a knowledgeable eye, they're staged and wouldn't work in real life. Also, to an uninformed audience, these demos might give the impression that whatever a person does, a smart hacker will render their efforts useless — which is the opposite of what you're looking to convey.

When choosing speakers, choose the messaging you want to deliver. A fine line exists between discussing the threat and empowering your users to believe they can stop the bad guys. To that end, when you look for speakers, ask them for details about what they present and how they present it. Look at sample presentations and ask representative attendees what they think about the sample as well. Some speakers are willing to develop new presentations when requested.

Usually, the cheapest way to find speakers is to ask your vendors. They should find people within their organizations who perform evangelism work. In this case, the risk is that they might not be good speakers and they might provide too much of a technical perspective for end-users.

Law enforcement agencies frequently have people who perform outreach. These folks usually have acceptable presentation skills, and have presented to many audiences. The downside here is that law enforcement representatives primarily discuss the threat and don't focus on *prevention*. Neither will these agencies tailor their presentation to your specific needs. Saying that you have an FBI agent coming in to speak, however, can create interest for potential audience members.

You can find paid speakers via professional speakers bureaus. Speakers from this source generally cost from US$5,000 to $25,000 plus travel expenses. Though I cannot vouch for other speakers in that range, I sometimes negotiate my fees based on where and when the event is held, whether the people in the organization are personal friends, and whether other professional opportunities exist at the organization. You should expect a high level of professionalism from such speakers. Their content should be entertaining and informative. Likewise, their bios should generate interest from the prospective audience. My bio for speaking events is admittedly a little cheesy, but people who have never met me are intrigued by my being called "a modern day James Bond."

I also am approached by people who have seen me speak at conferences and other events. If you have seen a speaker at an event who intrigued and inspired you and who might have a message you want to share with your organization, feel free to reach out to them. It's always an honor to be asked to help, and the person might be willing to grant your request.

You can find people internally who can deliver the presentations, or you can bring in outside speakers. (See the nearby sidebar "Finding outside speakers" for tips on finding outside speakers who best suit your needs.) Internal speakers are good in that they know your environment and likely your priorities. If you can persuade an executive to present, it might add the sense of importance to the event and the message. Asking for the executive's participation may also help to obtain executive buy-in to the events — and your overall efforts as well.

MANDATORY OR NOT?

When you hold an event, you have to decide whether attendance should be mandatory. Making it mandatory will obviously cause a potential impact to operations, and you will likely face some level of pushback. I have personally been brought in by several organizations to give a mandatory presentation to all their employees, including major business units of Fortune 10 companies to small privately held companies.

WARNING

When you make attendance at an event mandatory, it has the impact of proving to the organization that they believe there is value in the event. At the same time, many users will automatically resent the event, claiming that they have obligations they absolutely cannot cancel or, if they can't, that the event will negatively impact their work schedule and/or quality. You can also expect many users to rate the event poorly by default. I therefore recommend that if you make an event mandatory, you also ensure that you have the support required to make it mandatory *and* that you truly expect to provide value either in content or achieving a corporate goal.

IN THIS CHAPTER

» **Recognizing the hidden costs of awareness efforts**

» **Fulfilling compliance requirements**

» **Assessing engagement**

» **Gauging whether your efforts are paying off**

» **Helping clients see the value of your program**

» **Testing with social engineering and phishing simulations**

» **Recognizing the value of Day 0 metrics**

Chapter **8**

Measuring Performance

As an awareness program proceeds, no matter what the awareness program involves, security incidents will occur — you can count on it. In response, people, including the managers who determine your budget, may assume that awareness has done little to improve security. At best, the manager may keep the program going just because awareness is "nice to have."

As I say earlier in this book, you get the budget you deserve, not the budget you need. You need to show that you "deserve more," and you do this by measuring how awareness benefits an organization.

Before you can measure whether an awareness program meets its goals, you need to do a great deal of planning: First you establish goals, and then you figure out how to measure them. Of course, some goals, such as those concerning actual behaviors, are both important and difficult to measure. Also consider that some people want metrics to be hidden, to avoid getting caught in wrongdoing.

This chapter shows how to mitigate these issues by embedding metrics into existing business processes. Accounting processes, for example, are designed to collect metrics proactively at all phases. You can — and likely will have to — work around processes already used within the organization.

Metrics are arguably the most critical aspect of your success as a security awareness program manager. You either figure out how to *deserve* more or you become a person whose value to the overall security effort completely depends on the personal opinion of your manager.

Knowing the Hidden Cost of Awareness Efforts

As you may imagine, awareness efforts have costs beyond the actual cost of running the program. These costs are likely higher than the cost of the program itself. Though I have run into a few leaders of organizations who are well aware of the exponential costs of training time, my experience is that these organizations generally employ mostly blue collar workers, where productivity is tracked by the hour. Otherwise, few people seem to consider the cost associated with the time required for users to participate in the program.

In some cases, the costs are obvious. In Chapter 5, I mention a program I created for an airline where the time for training was already calculated into contracts with pilots and flight attendants. We had to negotiate the topics to drop from the training requirements so that we could add cybersecurity training — and we had to resort to many passive tools. This is likely the case with many hourly workers. People are paid specifically for their time to perform a specific job, and training time is measured in a good organization.

Many awareness professionals fail to realize that their efforts begin by costing their organization money. Most people can anticipate the immediate costs of providing CBT and phishing simulations. For one thing, collateral materials must be developed or paid to be created, and any trainers brought in must be paid. But you also must anticipate the cost of lost productive time spent by employees taking awareness training.

REMEMBER

Assuming that you're in a white collar (or another type of) environment where time can be allocated as required, you must consider that employees have to swap out time doing their actual work for time spent completing training. This training time can add up. For example, if an employee spends a brief ten minutes per month on awareness training, it equates to two hours per year. For every 1,000 employees, that equates to the equivalent of one full-time person per year devoted to awareness training. The trick is to acknowledge this calculation and to find the justification for the awareness program. You have to show the *return on investment,* or that you're reducing losses that more than justify the time users spend on your efforts.

TIP

Though few organizations I've dealt with track the time required for awareness training, you must be ready to justify it. Though I don't recommend that you highlight it, in environments where time is tracked, you need to proactively address the issue. This is where a smart manager who isn't supportive of your efforts will challenge you. The way you respond is with metrics that justify the cost through reduced losses.

Meeting Compliance Requirements

Checking the Box is my term for all the actions an organization takes to ensure that it satisfies third-party compliance requirements. Those third parties' requirements might be government regulations, industry organization standards, customer requirements, vendor requirements, or other similar requirements. To prove that your program meets compliance standards, you may need to complete a self-assessment and document it for later reference. In many cases, independent auditors will verify compliance. The penalty for failing to meet compliance can vary greatly and result in a range of penalties that may include anything from a warning to fines or demands to cease operations.

For example, employment laws require that you post information regarding employee rights. Compliance just requires that the information be posted. Safety standards generally require some type of formal training, and people only need to complete the required training.

Security standards, such as Payment Card Industry Data Security Standard (PCI DSS), among others, have *vague* awareness compliance requirements, which in one way or another state that you need to ensure that employees complete awareness training. In this case, ensuring that everyone in your organization has completed assigned training is sufficient.

When an organization is merely trying to satisfy compliance requirements (Checking the Box), you may experience difficulty justifying more than the minimum budget required to provide training to employees. In many cases, auditors state that phishing simulations are best practice and require those as a condition of compliance. In these cases, phishing simulations are required.

Given the penalties at stake if an organization fails to meet compliance, you can easily justify the budget for efforts that work toward that goal. You also can use this factor to justify hidden costs associated with the time required for employees to take the training. Any awareness efforts that present a cost beyond compliance may require additional justification. To demonstrate the justification, you must use the appropriate metrics.

TECHNICAL STUFF

KEEPING YOUR EYE ON REGULATIONS AND LAWSUITS

At the time of this writing, Check the Box is just providing some form of awareness training along with proof that users completed the training. Standards and regulation don't specify anything else, except that the training *must* exist. As major ransomware incidents and data breaches (which have the general perception of being awareness failings) become commonplace, however, it's quite possible that regulations will become more specific.

At the same time, I personally believe it's inevitable that some future lawsuit will challenge the appropriateness of awareness training, questioning not only the existence of awareness training but also its appropriateness and effectiveness, given the threat. I could be wrong, but either way, as a professional, you should stay abreast of policy related issues.

Collecting Engagement Metrics

Metrics that are easy to collect tend to be popular. For this reason, Checking the Box, covered in the preceding section, is probably the most popular form of metrics. The next most common metrics are *engagement* metrics — for example, you can usually see how many people show up at events by tracking how many walk away with your complimentary squishy toys or otherwise tracking attendance.

TECHNICAL STUFF

Not only are engagement metrics easy to collect, but they also can make awareness programs seem like they're working. Though I see the merit of this bit of logic, and I do recommend that you collect these metrics, be aware that they do not show the effectiveness of awareness efforts. These types of metrics might show goodwill generated on the part of a security program as a whole, however. Then you may be able to use these impressions to motivate users to better engage with the security program as a whole.

Attendance metrics

Attendance metrics are generally straightforward. They can overlap with compliance metrics, assuming that a compliance requirement for attendance exists. How many people completed the mandatory training? How many people showed up for a given event? How many people watched an optional video? How many people opened up an emailed newsletter?

Frequently, organizations have a *learning management system (LMS)* that manages and tracks computer based training (CBT). An LMS, which is essentially the control system for a CBT effort, provides for storage of CBTs. It provides an environment to manage and schedule the distribution to all or parts of the organization. The LMS should allow for customization of the content. LMSes create reports that can show compliance and course completion. When you're tracking compliance, you clearly need to ensure that everyone takes all required training. Metrics may also include voluntary engagement with supplemental materials, such as when a user voluntarily takes extra awareness training or attends an event. If you provide an internal knowledge base, such as on a security portal, you can measure optional views of that content.

When you provide optional training, such as when you invite a speaker to discuss a topic where attendance isn't mandatory or you send out newsletters, the attendance or viewership implies whether you're reaching your intended audience. Engagement metrics should be examined to determine whether communications tools are being consumed beyond compliance. This strategy allows you to determine which tools can be dropped or should at least be considered for better delivery. For communications tools that have poor engagement, you either want to consider improving them or refocus your efforts into other tools.

WARNING

Some materials present a challenge for determining engagement. For example, it's difficult to know how many people read a poster or monitor display. You can place QR codes on posters, but you can't be certain that people will scan the code. For this reason, you may have to resort to surveys, if you believe that gathering this engagement is worth the effort.

When considering attendance metrics, keep in mind the hidden cost of awareness training — and the fact that every minute that employees are engaged with your program can be considered a minute that they weren't performing their primary job function.

Likability metrics

I don't recommend that you rely on likability metrics, but it never hurts to have people actually like your awareness program. You can ask people what they think of your program by asking them — typically, by way of a questionnaire that's delivered soon after training — how much they enjoy the content that's presented. Frequently, likability is collected on a *Likert scale*, which typically asks people to rate how much they enjoyed the materials on a scale of 1–5.

TECHNICAL STUFF

This type of metric has varying usefulness. Though you *of course* don't want to force unlikable training on anyone, the reality is that likability doesn't equate to effectiveness of training. If you have no other metrics to provide, however, likability is at least something with a positive implication.

Knowledge metrics

Knowledge metrics can show whether users have increased their knowledge about cybersecurity. Increased knowledge doesn't mean that you're getting the behavioral changes you seek, but it can indicate whether your messaging is getting across. Testing for knowledge level usually involves a short quiz covering the relevant knowledge.

TIP

If you test people immediately after they complete training, these quizzes can test their short-term memory, as opposed to actual knowledge a person possesses and may act on. You may want to also test people periodically to see how well they retain the information.

In the ideal world, you need to determine the essential knowledge required by an individual to perform their functions properly. You then develop a quiz that best tests for that knowledge. Typically, the quizzes are multiple-choice tests, which means that accuracy is reduced by 20–25 percent, depending on the number of answers presented. Multiple choice is the best option because grading and administration can be easily automated.

Measuring Improved Behavior

The goal of an awareness program is to improve security related behaviors. Metrics that actually measure behavior improvement are therefore useful to collect. Behavior is quite different from knowledge. Just because people know something doesn't mean that they will act on it.

To measure improved behavior, you need metrics that demonstrate the actual behaviors. Awareness programs sometimes include simulations of scenarios to test whether people behave properly. Collecting actual behavioral metrics can be difficult and expensive, however. You must be creative to come up with ways to do so that are simple and inexpensive.

To test security awareness in practice, for example, a company might hire consultants to make telephone calls to its employees and entice them to divulge their passwords. This method can cost a great deal of money and cannot be performed regularly. As an alternative, you can track security related calls to the Help Desk, which can be a sign of awareness, as more aware people detect and report more incidents.

REMEMBER

Behavioral metrics are among the most useful metrics. They show actual behavioral improvement, and not just specious indications of likeability. Even better is if you can combine the improved behaviors with monetary savings resulting from those improvements for a real return on investment.

Tracking the number of incidents

A key way to measure behavior is to track the number of incidents that are the clear result of a user action. Depending on the environment, this might include the number of injuries, system outages, malware incidents on a network, lost USB drives, or data compromises, among any other type of loss that can be created by a user. The most important phrase in this paragraph is *number of*. You are counting occurrences.

TIP

OBSERVING SECURITY BEHAVIOR

If a specific security behavior is immediately observable, you can consider it as a metric. Here are some examples of security behaviors you might track:

- You can track user adoption of security technologies such as multifactor authentication (when it's optional).

- You can also run a password cracker to examine password strength, beyond your organization's password policy.

- You can look to web content filters to examine bad web browsing habits.

- DLP software might be able to tell you the number of attempts to transmit sensitive data outside the company.

- You can look to websites such as http://haveibeenpwned.com to see whether anyone from your organizational domains has had credentials compromised on websites around the Internet.

- If you have access to dark web services, you may be able to also check whether your users reused passwords on other sites.

- If you find a compromised password, you can test it on your own systems to see whether the password is active and you are vulnerable.

- You can observe the number of people walking around your facilities who aren't wearing badges.

- You can count the number of unsecured desks during specific periods.

Examining behavior with simulations

Simulations are something to consider when you want to examine behaviors. Some simulations are more realistic than others. You can perform USB drops, pretext phone call simulations, tailgating simulations, phishing simulations, and more. You need to track these over time to measure improvement.

Phishing simulations, covered in Chapter 12, have become common for security awareness metrics. The one problem with this metric — and all simulations, for that matter — is that such simulations can be manipulated to mislead. You can create a false impression of tremendous success by testing first with highly complex simulations, and then later, testing with simplified simulations that make detecting phishing attempts a bit easier. Also, people sometimes learn to detect the simulations.

When you perform a simulation, you want to force a diverse sampling of your potential victims. Though phishing simulations are relatively easy to reach all users, the reality is that your limited resources mean you can test only a small percentage of your organization. You therefore need to ensure that your sampling is representative of the organization as a whole.

If you try pretext phone calls targeting only the IT staff, for example, you might (hopefully) feel a false sense of security in that they are more aware by default. Likewise, certain geographical areas are more trusting than others. Assuming that you have no experience in performing random sampling, you minimally need to be aware that you should purposefully seek out and study whether different cultures, locations, departments, and types of workers, for example, have different responses and vulnerabilities.

TIP

TURNING SIMULATIONS INTO TEACHABLE MOMENTS

It's possible to incorporate awareness into simulations. In general, a simulation is a metric. You are performing them to specifically measure behaviors. If you interrupt the simulation to tell people that it's a simulated attack, it can impact your results, because users will likely tell other people that a simulated attack is being conducted. It's just human nature. So you should consider incorporating awareness into your simulations carefully.

However, a simulation can provide quite a valuable teachable moment. When I perform simulations that I want to convert to teachable moments, I determine the most effective ways to do so and then decide whether they have the potential for rewarding people. For example, when I present tailgating simulations, I sometimes take both red and green cards with me. If someone stops me, I give them a green card indicating that our interaction is part of an awareness study — and it has a $5 bill taped to it. If they do not stop me, I give them a red card, which tells them that the interaction is part of a study and that they should have stopped me — and that, had they stopped me, I would have given them $5. In this case, I hope that the participants will tell all their coworkers about the simulation so that word-of-mouth becomes a helpful awareness tool.

For pretext phone calls, I might attempt to persuade users to visit a would-be malicious website. If they go, they instantly receive a lesson in awareness. Again, users are likely to tell their friends about this type of experience.

When users tell others that they were duped by a simulation, it's useful info, given the available resources. Again, simulations are expensive, and if users warn others that a simulation may be occurring, more users will be more aware and more likely to report incidents, fearing that *they* are potentially the victim of a simulation.

WARNING

Simulations can be expensive, if you use an outside contractor. They can be somewhat resource intensive, if you do it with your own resources. Some phishing simulation companies provide USB simulation capabilities along with their other services. Either way, simulations, when done properly, can be useful metrics. Doing them well can be challenging, however.

Tracking behavior with gamification

Chapter 11 shows how you can apply gamification within your security awareness program. In the truest sense of the word, *gamification* involves rewarding desired behaviors, and it can be one of the best methods for tracking behavioral change. To implement gamification, you have to identify the desired behaviors to track and set up a tracking system.

Demonstrating a Tangible Return on Investment

Demonstrating a tangible return on investment (*ROI*) is the most effective way to prove that you deserve more. When you can provide a specific monetary amount of loss that's reduced based on your efforts, you can use the information to demonstrate why you deserve more resources to further improve your work.

Here's an example of how you can determine the cost savings associated with behavioral changes. In the safety field, if the average injury costs the organization $50,000 and you demonstrate that your efforts have reduced the number of injuries from 20 to 10, you have saved the organization $500,000. In the security field, if you consider that the average data breach costs an organization $1.3 million, and if you can demonstrate a reduction in data breaches, you can demonstrate a significant ROI.

TECHNICAL STUFF

Though you want to see losses decrease, if your business is growing or certain types of crimes are proliferating, an increase in losses is inevitable. For example, if you increase your staff by 25 percent, you can assume that user-related incidents may go up by 25 percent. You must measure improvements in relative terms in that case. So, in this case, if user related incidents that you track increase by less than 25 percent, you are reducing losses.

TIP

Certain organizations and industries have a better understanding of measuring user related costs than others. Using Six Sigma-like methodologies, they obtain data to understand exactly what potential losses are and where they can arise. You can conceivably look into similar organizations and look at the possible costs of incidents they suffer. Depending on your field, you may be able to find readily available studies on the costs of incidents.

Recognizing Intangible Benefits of Security Awareness

Not all awareness efforts can be expected to have a clear tangible benefit. Some aspects to consider are cultural. For example, in one company where I implemented a security awareness program, I incorporated a security awareness knowledgebase within the corporate knowledgebase. The phishing article was the most-read article in the entire corporate system. This metric was a source of pride within the organization because — although there was no specific reduction in loss — the CEO believed that it was a critical indication of the awareness program's contribution to the organization.

TIP

I usually recommend providing awareness training specific to home and family needs. Some organizations initially think doing so is a waste of limited resources, but I explain that people are more likely to pay attention when something impacts them personally. If they behave securely at home, they will take those behaviors to work. It also generates goodwill.

To understand what might have intangible benefits to the organization, you need to understand the organization's culture. You need to talk to stakeholders and to people running other behavioral change programs to determine what they believe is valuable, other than the obvious. In some cases, you might find that the intangible benefits are easy to achieve and are even more valuable than some tangible benefits to the organization.

In many cases, your organization might track intangible benefits and assign a value to them. For example, brand value might seem to be an intangible, but many organizations do track it. Major cybersecurity incidents, such as those at Target and Sony, significantly harmed brands and produced intangible harm — you might want to work with your corporate communications department to see whether someone can offer any guidance on intangible value.

Knowing Where You Started: Day 0 Metrics

To signal that your awareness program deserves more resources, you have to show that efforts are making a difference. What many people forget to do is collect metrics before they start implementing the awareness program — these starting metrics are known as *Day 0 metrics* (said as "day zero metrics"). If you don't know where you started, you can't determine how much you've improved. This is especially true with behavioral and ROI metrics, which are the metrics that provide the most benefit for your awareness program.

TECHNICAL STUFF

Specifically, you need to first determine which metrics you intend to collect throughout the year of the awareness program — ideally, including behavioral metrics. You then collect the metrics before initiating your program. This is the Day 0 metric.

If you already have an awareness program in place, you can use Day 0 engagement metrics to measure the improved perception of your awareness efforts. Clearly, improved engagement is a secondary concern to improved ROI, but such metrics can be useful for a variety of reasons, as described earlier in this chapter, in the section "Collecting Engagement Metrics."

By collecting Day 0 metrics, you can then determine the impact your program had on the desired behaviors. In the ideal world, this will demonstrate the ROI provided by your efforts. If there is no improvement, you can at least be alerted to that fact and make changes as quickly as possible to improve the situation.

TIP

When you collect Day 0 metrics, I recommend resisting the urge to use the opportunity to promote awareness, because doing so can taint the metrics collection. If you tell someone they did or did not click on a phishing message, for example, they might warn others that phishing simulations are occurring. Though you might consider it a lost opportunity to deliver a just-in-time awareness message, a pure Day 0 metric is more than worth the lost opportunity.

If I am collecting the number of malware incidents, I can ask the administrators who administer the antimalware software to pull statistics at almost any time. I would ask for the statistics before beginning any awareness efforts. I would also request statistics again after completing a round of phishing simulations, and then again after completing training on safe web browsing, given that malware generally gets on a network by way of phishing and unsafe web browsing.

3

Putting Your Security Awareness Program Into Action

Gain the funding and other support required to implement your program.

Improve your strategy based on performance metrics and changing circumstances.

Determine whether gamification is right for your program.

Reduce risk by using phishing simulations.

Chapter **9**

Assembling Your Security Awareness Program

E arlier chapters of this book describe what goes into an awareness program and explain why these programs work; this chapter shows you how to turn theory into practice.

If you've already read all of Part 2, you found out in Chapter 5 how to understand the culture of your organization; you saw in Chapter 6 different potential topics to cover in your program; and you found ways in Chapter 7 to convey those topics. In Chapter 8, you saw how to determine whether what you implemented is having the desired impact. To this point in the book, I've laid out the building blocks of a real program, and now it's time to implement it.

Knowing Your Budget

In an ideal world, you would put together a program and then determine the budget you need. You would then approach management and whoever else you need in order to get the budget allocated for your program. Unfortunately, you probably will not have this luxury, especially if you're taking over an existing security awareness program or creating and managing a program from scratch. Most often, you're allocated a budget that you must work within.

BENEFITING FROM AN INCIDENT WINDFALL

As a person who gets called in to investigate and mitigate cybersecurity incidents, especially those that were initiated through an apparent awareness failing, I see a hidden blessing when incidents occur: Incidents can prompt executives to increase the security budget.

When an incident occurs, you must be proactive and claim your piece of any increase. The organization's first priority will be to mitigate the damage and clean up the computer systems. This work can be intensive and costly. Even though chances are good that such incidents are caused by awareness failings, awareness continues to be an afterthought for most organizations when allocating their budget.

Even when an organization understands that awareness must be improved, any perception that an awareness program consists of merely computer-based training (CBT) and phishing simulations can limit budget increases. You have to state specifically how you want to improve security awareness. As I proceed through this chapter, I can tell you that you need to be realistic about what you can afford, and focus on that. At the same time, you need to consider what you want to include and its potential cost.

I tell people that only fools and liars tell you that perfect security (often pitched as "the human firewall") is possible. I can promise that only imperfect security exists, and that some form of incident will occur. Be prepared to exploit the inevitable incident. Have a business case for desired awareness efforts readily available. When people ask what could have prevented the incident and how can the next incident be prevented or limited, you will be ready to propose the additional awareness tools you want to implement, along with the required costs of doing so.

Figuring out your budget involves more than simply running with a number that's been given to you, however. To determine your *actual* budget, consider these three sources:

>> **Any funding you can get from other sources,** including executive team and other departments

>> **Must-have items defined by the organization,** including existing vendor contracts and other requirements that must be met

>> **Discretionary spending,** or what's left over to spend

The following sections cover each of the preceding items in detail.

REMEMBER

If other programs underspend, or if an incident causes more money to flow into the awareness program, you may consider seeking additional funding. Keep in mind, however, that your budget was likely determined six months before the current fiscal year. You will likely have to make do with whatever you get.

Finding additional sources for funding

Your budget might be set, but if you're creative, you may be able to find additional sources for funding. You can often find people throughout an organization who are willing to support you. You just have to know where to look.

Securing additional executive support

It's possible that if you're creative, you can go to senior management and ask for additional budget amounts. Clearly, you have to go in with a plan. You need to know what you want to say, with clear business intent. Later in this chapter, I cover gaining management support (see the later section "Gaining Management Support"); for now, keep in mind that executive management may provide *additional* funding, if you can provide the right influence and if funding is available to be had.

WARNING

When you approach executive management, you must be mindful of any internal politics. You clearly need to keep members of your management chain involved when you approach their managers, or parties outside of your chain of command. Your managers may have information that can help you, such as knowledge of any hot button issues that will help to gain support for increased budget. During a recent engagement, for example, executive management expressed a major concern about ransomware, and tying a budget request specifically to preventing ransomware incidents facilitated a major budget increase. Also know that you might alienate other parties competing for budget. I have a friend who was CISO of a

Fortune 50 company. He told me that, although he always received more money when he asked for it, he asked rarely. He didn't want to alienate his peers, whose budgets potentially lost money whenever he received it.

Coordinating with other departments

As I describe throughout this book, a good security awareness program overlaps with a great deal of other organizational efforts. You should coordinate your effort with the relevant departments. If enough synergy exists across departments, you may be able to team with them on a variety of efforts.

For example, you may be able to embed your security awareness efforts within other departments' programs. Their efforts may not align perfectly with yours, but they should cost you relatively little, if any, of your budget. This can save your program a ton of money. Alternatively, if you incorporate another department's messaging into your efforts, you may be able to ask that department to contribute to your efforts.

WORKING WITH CORPORATE COMMUNICATIONS

In most organizations, the corporate communications department, or a department of a similar name, is either your greatest ally or the bane of your existence. The corporate communications department is generally responsible for the distribution for all materials to the organization. They maintain distribution lists. They create standards for materials to be distributed inside the organization. They set rules for distribution, such as types of materials that can be distributed and how frequently items can be distributed over certain channels.

This department is frequently constrained by its own resources, and would have to fit your requests into their workflow. Despite these limiting factors, however, they can significantly help your awareness program. They might have a graphics artist at their disposal. They know how to distribute your information to everyone inside the organization. They usually know which outreach efforts work and which ones don't. They know which newsletters get read and which ones do not. They often have suggestions for how best to reach various subcultures throughout the organization.

Their team can also supplement your team. They might integrate into your team and take on many of your responsibilities. Though corporate communications can be a burden to your effort, you will likely be required by your organization to work with that department and adhere to its mandates. You need to accept this fact and incorporate them into your plans.

TIP

You need to proactively determine how you want to work with the other departments and then provide them with a clear value proposition. These other departments likely have the same resource challenges that you do. If they're smart, they won't give up their resources in a way that is less effective than their currently intended plans.

You must be able to lay out specifically what you want and what you will provide. At the same time, you shouldn't make the proposal sound like a formal negotiation. The other department should feel that you see them as a friend and partner, not as a business transaction. You may encounter periodic competition for resources and attention from end-users, but the departments you partner with likely face the same problems you do. You should attempt to work with them whenever feasible.

Allocating for your musts

Having the freedom to allocate all funds from a budget that's dedicated exclusively to your awareness program is a best-case scenario. When you receive the budget for your security awareness program, however, you may find that a portion has already been allocated to other contracts. For example, your organization may have already entered into CBT and phishing simulation contracts that are charged against your budget. Also, many vendors that provide secure email gateways sometimes bundle in CBT and phishing training, so you don't have to allocate from your own budget for those tools.

When you encounter such situations, you need to adjust discretionary spending to accommodate budget constraints. If whatever software or services are already contracted overlap with any of your plans — well, at least for the short term — you don't have to spend time evaluating vendors.

You may also have regulatory or compliance standards that require you to implement a tool you didn't necessarily want to implement. For example, a standard you must meet may imply the use of CBT. In this case, you need to allocate the budget for CBT.

TIP

If a contract is already in place with a vendor that impacts your budget, you may be able to negotiate out of it to free up funding. Many vendors in the awareness field provide software and other services, such as antimalware products and secure email gateways. The awareness components of the contract are usually the least expensive part of the contract. Sometimes, you can get them to bundle awareness services with the larger contract, which can reduce or eliminate your costs for the awareness tools.

Limiting your discretionary budget

After you consider your allocated budget, all the potential funds you might receive from other sources, and then what you have already allocated, you have some idea about what you have left to spend. As you continue with the rest of the program, you can start to figure out which potential communications tools are feasible.

REMEMBER

Though you don't necessarily want to limit your imagination to just those items that cost little money, you have to be realistic about what you can accomplish. As the saying goes, you don't want to have a prince's appetite on a pauper's budget. You can be creative and possibly gain more support as time goes on, but you have what you have.

Appreciating your team as your most valuable resource

Money is an important resource, but don't forget that you need people to implement your plan. I mention a little earlier in this chapter how the corporate communications department might be able to supplement your efforts; however, you need to balance all your spending plans with the staff you have available to implement those plans.

TIP

If you need to bring on additional expertise (because you're short-staffed or for any other reason), you might consider outsourcing to specialists. If outsourcing is part of your plan, you have to budget for any contractors accordingly.

Without enough staff, you may have to limit efforts you can otherwise afford. Some communications tools, such as newsletters, don't generally require a significant financial or work effort to implement. Other communications tools, such as holding events, require extensive planning and logistics. Running phishing exercises, even with some of the more robust tools available, requires several days of effort. You need to plan, design the phishing messages, schedule the exercise, upload email addresses, troubleshoot problems (such as advancing messages through spam filters), interpret results, retest as required, and so on. (See Chapter 12 for a full description of phishing exercises.)

REMEMBER

Before you choose a communications tool, think beyond the cost — consider the manual effort that implementing the tool will require. Also consider that paying for additional support will eat into other aspects of your budget. You can implement some incredible awareness effort with the appropriate funding, but without the people to support the implementation, doing so is impractical.

Choosing to Implement One Program or Multiple Programs

Most organizations contain multiple subcultures, each with its own business drivers and communications style. Accordingly, you may find that each subculture warrants its own awareness program.

TECHNICAL STUFF

Subcultures can be classified by roles within an organization. For example, executives may be located across many geographies. Although different geographic regions often have distinct cultures, executive jobs may be similar enough across geographies to warrant a common awareness program. This might be true for many other job functions, such as researchers, factory workers, or cashiers. Many organizations therefore implement what is referred to as *role-based awareness programs*, which are designed for different job functions, such as executive or warehouse workers.

Ideally, you should consider creating multiple awareness programs so that each subculture has a program tailored to meet its needs. Unfortunately, you may barely have the resources to implement a single awareness program. Even so, you can usually find creative solutions within the scope of the available resources to meet the needs of the entire organization.

TIP

Many CBT and phishing simulation tools allow you to customize materials for various groups within an organization. You can use these tools to ensure that people who work in the accounts payable department, for example, receive phishing messages and CBT modules that have been tailored to their needs. Keep in mind that although you can use these tools to tailor content by subculture, they don't add new communications tools to those that are already available.

If you have the resources to implement multiple programs, for different regions or business units, or role-based awareness programs, you should go for it. Reaching different parts of an organization around the world with unique programs can be logistically complex. Doing so is worth the extra cost in money, effort, time, and people, however, if you can manage it. It provides for a much more targeted effort to make an impact tailored to the targeted populations.

TIP

You need to figure out how many subcultures or roles you can support. You won't have unlimited resources, and you must consider those efforts that will likely create the most benefit. I recommend that you implement programs that address the greatest losses, or where the cultures differ significantly. For example, cultures may differ significantly for an organization that has teams that communicate almost exclusively by email, and teams that don't even have computers at their workstations.

Managing multiple programs

When you implement multiple awareness programs, whether implemented via subcultures or role-based, you need to design the programs *to be* independent entities. You can, however, design the programs one at a time, or simultaneously design the multiple programs.

Aspects of the programs may overlap. For example, you will likely use CBT and phishing simulations for most programs. This can allow for a more cost-effective use of materials. It also simplifies administration of the program.

Each program will also have unique aspects. Consider how the communications tools you use in the program vary depending on whether workers work primarily on a computer issued by the organization or must access email and other communications from their personal devices.

Beginning with one program

Even when I personally intend to implement programs unique to subcultures, I frequently start by implementing a single program for the entire organization. The reason is that it reduces risk while simplifying the rollout of the program.

WARNING

You always encounter issues with an initial rollout. Approvals from stakeholders come slower than expected. You encounter logistical issues when sending materials among facilities. You run into issues with suppliers. People might not read your newsletters. Promised support might not come to fruition. Now consider managing these issues while rolling out multiple programs simultaneously.

TIP

I start with the base program that encompasses the most concerns simultaneously. After seeing how things go during the first quarter, I begin adding the aspects of the program that are specialized to various subcultures and roles. To limit risk, I usually add just one or two new subcultures per quarter, depending on the available resources.

Some subcultures warrant unique awareness programs sooner than others. This may include executives or high-risk groups, such as accounting or human resources. Even if you don't intend to implement multiple programs for multiple subcultures, you might consider separate programs just for high-risk groups. The cost of assigning special attention to these groups probably isn't so great that it can't be done.

TIP

If you want to address specific subcultures with a single awareness program, you can simply provide special components for those groups. In many cases, I created special in-person briefings for executive management on concerns specific to them. I worked with the executive security team to provide specific guidance on how to secure their home Wi-Fi networks and home computers. The executive managers were otherwise subject to the same awareness program as everyone else.

Gaining Support from Management

Though many awareness managers have the true support of their management and their management believes in the value of a well-implemented security awareness program, many awareness programs, unfortunately, are considered Check-the-Box efforts. Management authorizes and funds the program like it's in place only to satisfy external requirements. If you're reading this book, you clearly believe otherwise, as do I. Whether or not your management team believes in the true value of your efforts, this section intends to gain you as much support as possible.

Perhaps the greatest indicator of the likely success or failure of your program is the level of senior management support you have for it. If senior management supports your efforts, you will get the support from the departments you need. You're more likely to get a reasonable budget. You're more likely to get management to ensure that users spend the required time on your training and other efforts. Though you can't expect to get everything, it's a big start.

If you're lucky, your senior managers see security awareness for the actual value and understand that the awareness program is a critical risk-reduction tool. Sometimes, awareness is a pet project of management. Management may support your efforts for a variety of reasons.

WARNING

You should go to management with a clearly defined plan, but be aware that this support might be limited or burdened by preconceived notions. For example, some managers might state that they think awareness is critical, but believe that awareness is specifically CBT and that phishing simulations and other efforts are not necessarily. Some executives might have heard a speaker they like and then want you to spend a large portion of your budget on bringing in that speaker. So, despite some support, you might have to fight for efforts you find more critical.

Assuming that you lack full management support of your efforts, it's worth the effort to try to increase the level of support. As I mention earlier in this chapter, you might want to increase your budget — and management support can provide that increase. Even if you're satisfied with your budget, you need to ensure that you can gain the support of the other departments, as well as the guarantees that users will be required to devote the relevant length of time to your efforts. As I mention in the discussion of the hidden costs of awareness programs, the length of time required for the awareness efforts on the part of the users is the most costly aspect of your program.

This is one aspect of culture where you definitely need to understand the organizational culture and business drivers, to ensure that you can improve the security culture. You need to understand what will allow you to obtain and keep that support. This might include any preferences or hot button issues that will attract support. The more you understand what motivates your management to support any effort, the more likely you'll know how to gain that support for your efforts, so do your research.

TIP

Here are some questions to consider when you seek support for your awareness effort:

>> Are any projects top priorities for the organization?

>> Which efforts have support, and can you associate with them?

>> If similar efforts lack support, why?

>> Do you know the managers personally?

>> Do you know their attitudes on security awareness?

>> Is a particular person more sympathetic?

>> Can you demonstrate the value of your efforts to gain further support?

>> Which incidents have occurred in recent memory?

>> Did any data breaches take place?

>> Were any fines levied? Why? How much?

>> Were the adverse audit findings?

>> Have there been studies about customer perceptions relevant to cybersecurity? What were the findings?

>> Can you align your program with the organization's stated value and mission statement, and can you demonstrate that alignment clearly?

These are just a few considerations, and your circumstances likely provide for other considerations. You can ask your coworkers, and any executives to whom you have immediate access, what might best influence other executives — or at least those managers who matter in providing support.

CREATING AN EXECUTIVE AWARENESS PROGRAM

I stated previously that a part of your awareness program might focus on the needs of executives. Depending on how much success you're having getting support for your awareness program, you might want to start with the executive team.

Normally, you want to work out the kinks in your program, before launching programs specific to executives. You want to put your best foot forward. However, if you need to increase the level of support to increase visibility, funding, access to stakeholders, and/ or resources in general, you likely want to start with the executives in an attempt to impress them and demonstrate the value of your efforts.

Though you can potentially put together an entire program just for executives, as I say earlier in this chapter, you can just create high-value tools. Either way, you want to pull out all the stops to demonstrate how much value a good awareness program can provide. For example, you don't have to subject executives to off-the-shelf videos on generic topics. Focus on topics and tools that are personal to the intended audience. For example, you can discuss how to protect home networks. Securing mobile devices and personal computers is likely to be of specific value. Also consider one-on-one sessions and other highly personalized experiences to ensure that the message is clear.

Phishing simulations can be a double-edged sword. If you can put together highly tailored spear phishing messages, and the executives click on it and appreciate the warning, they can become major supporters of future efforts. On the other hand, if they're offended for being "tricked," they can pull funding or other resources. Personally, I have seen executives appreciate simulations, with none who complain. This may not be universal, and as discussed earlier, you need to know your audience — especially the executives.

If you're going to create a program for executives, you need to do it well. If it's perceived to be a waste of time by the executives, you might lose the support you already have. You need to ensure that every aspect of your program is as tight as possible. If a communications tool is poor or questionable, you should strongly consider holding off on the delivery — or cancel it.

Devising a Quarterly Delivery Strategy

One of the biggest mistakes I see in awareness programs is that they're designed as annual programs. In other words, the program is scheduled a year in advance. You would think that annual planning would allow for a well-thought-out and well-rounded program, but in reality, you can't know what issues will crop up a year in advance.

The COVID-19 pandemic, for example, radically changed awareness needs. Many programs didn't adjust well. I contracted with an organization at the time that had to ensure that I took mandatory awareness training. In December 2020, for example, I received a link to watch an awareness video on international travel. The lack of relevance is obvious. Awareness programs all over the world suffered from the same problem, as awareness professionals set delivery schedules for their programs a year in advance.

Many awareness professionals are surprised to find that creating an annual schedule that you update as extraordinary events occur isn't actually the best approach. For example, when events such as the COVID-19 pandemic hit, many awareness topics became irrelevant and others became critical. Then there are data breaches that can impact your industry, or internal incidents. Just as important, I don't want to move off an important topic unless I know that the desired behavior change has occurred.

Here are some shortcomings of annual programs:

>> Insufficient behavior change may occur for the perceived investment.

>> Awareness failings are perceived as incidents occur throughout the year.

>> Lack of reinforcement occurs when a topic highlighted by the program changes too quickly.

>> Employee turnover causes new employees to completely miss topics that are addressed by the program before their start of employment.

>> World events can disrupt the program.

>> Missed and important topics are not revisited for more than a year.

To account for these issues and more, I strongly recommend that you lay out a program only three months in advance. This short period provides for a great detail of versatility and allows you to focus your efforts. A program scheduled this way isn't a set-it-and-forget-it program, which is what many organizations seem to want.

Having a program that you adjust every quarter provides built-in versatility to adapt to changing circumstances and new requirements. It also enables you to examine improvement over the course of the program. Being creative is much easier when you put your focus into a short period with a small set of goals. You can focus on the trees instead of the forest.

Ensuring that your message sticks

A critical principle in all learning is *reinforcement*. People need to see a message several times over an extended period for it to sink in and then to become practice. The model I propose here is designed to provide enhanced reinforcement beyond what most awareness programs usually provide.

In the typical awareness program strategy, an awareness manager looks at potential topics and assigns a given topic for each of 12 months of a year. These topics are all too frequently driven by which topics are in the library of videos provided by the CBT vendor. Then the awareness manager determines the other communications tools they will distribute each month. So a person will be pushed a video and perhaps be exposed to a companion poster and newsletter for that topic. The users then watch the mandatory video, maybe they see the poster someplace, and maybe they open and read the companion newsletter. At that point, the Forgetting Curve (discussed in Chapter 3) kicks in, and unfortunately, users will not be exposed to that topic again for a year or so.

An awareness program also typically has a phishing campaign that may or may not be integrated into other aspects of the awareness program. A good awareness manager usually schedules events as well. All these components form common awareness programs.

When you plan for quarterly programs, you can be more creative with how awareness materials are distributed. I find that the most effective structure for a program, as opposed to working with one topic a month, is that you work with three topics simultaneously over three months. This way, each topic can be reinforced over the entire three months of the program.

TECHNICAL STUFF

No matter whether you manage a CBT-focused awareness program, a role-based awareness program, a multi-culture awareness program, or another type, you can implement multiple topics simultaneously. Doing so reinforces multiple topics constantly over a specific period. You can implement the delivery of multiple topics simultaneously with any format of scheduling or delivery.

Distributing topics over three months

Most traditional marketing formats flood individuals with information on a specific subject, in multiple formats, all at once. This tactic appears to make sense. Providing information in multiple formats can help reinforce memory retention. Although the information is reinforced to a certain extent, the Forgetting Curve still kicks in immediately.

Imagine if McDonald's said something to the effect of, "I had a TV commercial, a social media ad, and put up a poster along a highway for a month. We are done for the year." Clearly, that isn't how any commercial organization implements its marketing campaigns. It provides constant reinforcement of messaging, even if it's running multiple promotions.

Though many awareness professionals espouse the importance of marketing concepts, they don't implement the same methodologies as marketing professionals, which involve constant reinforcing over an extended period. Again, the concept of one topic per month is an arbitrary use of time and an implementation methodology.

All this leads me to recommend the methodology of choosing three topics and distributing information on those three topics simultaneously over three months. From a structural perspective, you choose the communications tools you want to use each month and intersperse the topics across the communications tools each month.

For example, over the three months, if you're going to use videos, newsletters, and posters, the video in Month 1 would be on Topic 1, the newsletter would be on Topic 2, and the poster would be on Topic 3. In Month 2, you can then rotate the topics across the communications tools. You then rotate the topics again in Month 3.

Figure 9-1 shows how you might intersperse topics across a quarter. The awareness program shown in the figure intends to educate people on USB drive security, social engineering prevention, and travel security. Those topics are rotated among most of the communications components listed. In addition, some active components, such as the monthly event and the roadshow, use random topics. As you see, the topics rotate and are reinforced over an extended period.

Figure 9-1 shows just a sample of an awareness program. You can add or delete as many communications tools as you want. The sample program shown in the figure doesn't include phishing, for example. Given resources and the likely limitation of engagement that you can have with employees, you will likely rely mostly on passive engagement tools and strategic active engagement.

REMEMBER

Your goal is to provide as much reinforcement as reasonable over the course of the program.

Tool	Month 1	Month 2	Month 3
Computer-based training	Social engineering	Travel security	USB security
Poster	Travel security	USB security	Social engineering
Featured article	USB security	Social engineering	Travel security
Newsletter	Social engineering	Travel security	USB security
Lunch and Learn	Travel security	USB security	Social engineering
Table tents	USB security	Social engineering	Travel security
Event	Kick-off booth	Security cubicle	Speaker
Roadshow	Human resources	Information technology	Marketing

FIGURE 9-1: A sample quarterly awareness program interspersing topics.

ACCOMMODATING DELAYS WITHIN A QUARTERLY SCHEDULE

Though the ideal is to have a program execute consistently within a quarter, I find that it's frequently difficult to have a program released exactly on that time schedule. It's admittedly tight, and you need your material created and reviewed for dissemination. A dozen or so people might have to approve the content of your program, which can take more time than you hope for.

Additionally, you might find that certain events can slow down a program, or you might want to delay part of your program. For example, in many cultures, the month of December is a bad time to try to establish engagement. Many people are away from work for a week or more, and even when people are supposedly engaged, many personal issues are distracting. People are rushing to complete work before they leave for the Christmas and New Year's holidays, because they have parties and events to plan around. If you have a critical message to share, there are times to avoid it and perhaps, just for an example, to extend content from November into December. You might also have the timing of organizational events to consider or work around. For example, in one case, I recommended holding off the launch of a program to coincide with the launch of other security efforts.

The time to measure results and create a new program based on the findings from the previous program may also create a delay. You need to either plan ahead or work off Month 2 metrics.

For these reasons and more, you might want your quarterly programs to happen over more than three months.

In the ideal world, you will develop a separate program for each subculture you're responsible for. There might be total or complete overlap between programs for different subcultures, and that's okay. You just need to remember that they're a distinct subculture when it comes to the next round and evaluation of metrics. You can also likely reuse materials between different subcultures. However, you should define programs for each subculture, even just to acknowledge that they're distinct subcultures that will require a reevaluation for each quarter.

TIP

There is typically no reason that guides you on which topic to start with in a given format. If there's a subject you want to focus on, you can choose to give it a little more exposure than the other topic. For example, you can use posters for the same topic over two or more months. You would use two distinct posters, but they can be on the same general topic.

Similarly, if you want to truly focus on a topic, you may just decide to use the one topic for two of the three topics you use. Much like I contend that there's no reason to focus on one topic per month, there's no reason that you can't consciously choose to have a single topic doubled up.

Deciding Whether to Include Phishing Simulations

Let me be clear: Despite what seems to be the status quo, a phishing simulation isn't a requirement for a security awareness program. Phishing is perhaps the most common attack targeting awareness failings. To a large extent, however, basic phishing attacks are filtered out by email servers, and phishing simulations don't provide perfect awareness against more advanced attacks.

Phishing simulations *can* raise general awareness, however. People may become more aware as a result that they can be hit by an attack. This is no guarantee of perfection, but as I repeatedly say, any reduction in risk can be helpful.

Chapter 12 discusses how to perform phishing simulations; for now, you just need to decide whether you want to perform regular phishing simulations. You might have access to a phishing service as a result of another service you have, such as an antimalware service. You might earn a discount for insurance if you use a particular awareness service that includes phishing simulations. So you might already have phishing services available to you.

On the other hand, incorporating these simulations into your program can be a major expense to your organization. The service might eat up most of your anticipated budget. If this is the case, strongly consider whether you want to spend that amount of money on a phishing simulation service.

WARNING

Free alternatives, such a GoPhish, are available, but you have to be technically adept to configure the software and run it yourself. Also consider the time required to create and run the simulations. A homegrown solution is possible, but these solutions have limitations and can require significant resources.

Planning Which Metrics to Collect and When

As I stress throughout this book, metrics are as fundamental to an awareness program as videos, posters, or phishing simulations. They must be embedded within the program at every possible phase and level. *Metrics are the difference between being a valuable business function and being the unwanted appendage of the security program.*

Chapter 8 gets into the nitty-gritty with regard to metrics. You get ideas for how to track engagement and improved behavior. The upcoming sections in this chapter focus on how you might implement metric collection within your awareness program.

Considering metrics versus topics

The natural inclination in the choice of metrics is to choose metrics that match the topics currently highlighted by your program (in a given quarter, for example). This isn't typically the most feasible way to do it. You want to track for continuous improvement, and as topics change, you want to measure something that is representative of overall awareness. For that, you need metrics that are easy to collect consistently.

TIP

Engagement metrics are relatively easy to collect, if they're available. These, again, are critical to know if you want to continue with a given communications tool. Collect these at all opportunities.

You should, however, try to collect behavioral and incident metrics that are consistent and available. Ideally, these metrics should be available throughout the course of a year, and be somewhat independent of outside influence. If they can represent common awareness, it would be ideal. Phishing simulations are one example; however, they might not be representative of actual phishing awareness.

REMEMBER

When you determine which metrics to use, don't consider as your primary question whether the metrics represent the short-term goals of your awareness program. The primary question you should ask is, "Which metrics are representative of awareness, and will I have consistent access to them?"

Choosing three behavioral metrics

After you have all the possible metrics to consider, I recommend that you find at least three behavioral metrics to track. These metrics can be for a variety behaviors and/or incidents. Though the more metrics you can collect provides a fuller picture, three typically provides enough to create a substantial dashboard, especially when combined with engagement metrics.

TIP

If you can easily collect more relevant metrics with little cost, such as by asking for the number of security-related calls to the help desk or the number of blocked web queries or malware incidents, for example, you should. You don't have to report all of them, but you will be able to make better decisions and provide better information.

Incorporating Day 0 metrics

I have already stated the importance of taking Day 0 metrics. This advice cannot be understated. You should begin designing your metrics collection program as part of your overall awareness program. You can collect the metrics while you're designing the program. The initial data collection doesn't have to take place immediately before the program rollout.

Scheduling periodic updates

Obviously, you need to update your metrics periodically. How frequently you update the metrics depends on their availability, the ease of collection, and the resources required to collect them.

WARNING

You should minimally attempt to collect metrics once per quarter, or during whatever period you've defined as your awareness cycle. At most, you should collect metrics once per month. If you collect them too frequently, you may find normal deviations that can give you false results. You need to see the trends *over time*.

TIP

As things change, periodically consider whether you want to change your metrics. It can be due to logistics, resources, or change in business needs, for example. A better source of metrics may arise. Just realize that you might need to change metrics and that is okay.

Biasing your metrics

When I complete penetration tests or am otherwise asked to collect metrics, if I believe that there's a need to have dramatic results, I can produce a high failure rate. In other words, I can tailor the attack so that people will fail. If I want the program to look successful, I can create easy attacks.

TECHNICAL STUFF

You might find some reason to bias results, such as showing very poor awareness on Day 0 metrics, so that you can show improvement for your program over time. For example, I can use a very high sophistication email message that will be extremely difficult to detect. If I want to show strong awareness, I can use blatant phishing messages. If I am doing a tailgating exercise, I can have someone dress like they clearly don't belong at the facility. Alternatively, I can have someone dress like a maintenance worker with a proper uniform. There are many ways to tailor the results as you see fit.

Branding Your Security Awareness Program

Awareness is a marketing effort. So, whenever you create a security awareness program, you must consider basic marketing concepts and the importance of *branding*. This involves tying a unique and recognizable identity to the program so that it's recognizable across the different components of the program.

In general, when users see something from your program, they should know it's part of your program. Successful branding makes this happen.

Creating a theme

When you work with an organization that has a mission statement and aligns many efforts with it, consider devising a theme that aligns with that organizational mission statement. Doing so will likely provide you with additional support and allow your awareness efforts to be included in other efforts that demonstrate alignment with the mission statement.

If the organization has mission statement, you can still create a theme to assist in the branding. Tie it to service to customers, employee well-being, protecting family, or whatever else suits your needs. A theme isn't required, but it can be useful to attach a higher purpose to cybersecurity.

Maintaining brand consistency

Every program should have some sort of theme and consistency to it. Though your program materials should not look so alike that they fade into each other, the materials should appear similar enough, or have some common branding, to reflect that they belong to a coordinated awareness program.

Iterations of passive materials, such as posters, need to be noticeably different from one iteration to the next while also showing consistent branding. If you put up a poster in a common area, for example, people might see it at first but, after a few visits to that common area, stop noticing it. If you then change the poster but use an overall look that is too similar to the original, people might not notice the change. Fortunately, maintaining branding can be as straightforward as using a logo or catchphrase on all your program materials.

Coming up with a catchphrase and logo

Your program should have a *catchphrase,* or slogan, that attempts to keep security concerns in people's minds. Try to come up with a catchphrase that highlights the mission of your program.

Over the years, I have helped develop many catchphrases: company and me; cybersecurity is my job; securing our patients' IP is our lifeblood; it's a jungle out there. Some of these catchphrases were synergistic with other corporate efforts. Some, at an organization's request, highlight responsibility to its customers. Some were just created because someone thought they sounded good. There's no consistent driver in themes or messaging.

A logo can also be useful to tying all the materials together. It can reflect the slogan or be used independently of one. A visually catchy logo can be quite useful.

Promoting your program with a mascot

Having a mascot can be extremely helpful in promoting your program. When used properly, a mascot creates excitement for your efforts. People frequently want to pose for a photo with the mascot. Mascots also make great giveaways — potentially, as a stuffed animal or a squishy toy.

The mascot doesn't have to be directly related to the theme for your program, although it can help. If the mascot isn't related to your theme, it should at least be endearing. If the organization already has a mascot, you may be able to get permission to use a version of the organizational mascot for your program.

Creating a mascot takes a little more creativity than your typical graphics efforts. You may therefore have to reach out to a good graphics artist who is more creative or has experience with mascots. Try to create a mascot that is reasonably well liked. Don't expect that it will be universally loved, however — some people dislike mascots altogether. A mascot can be limited to a graphic that appears in the corner of posters, or it can mean persuading someone to wear a costume. Depending on what you want to do with the mascot, it can be quite useful and versatile — and it can also be costly.

A mascot can become quite a visible symbol of your awareness program. The right mascot can greatly support your efforts. At the same time, just make sure to take your organization's culture into account because it can trivialize a program in more formal organizations.

IN THIS CHAPTER

» Getting the logistics in order

» Securing approvals for your program materials

» Collecting Day 0 measurements

» Showcasing your progress with well-designed reports

» Assessing your program

» Planning each subsequent cycle

» Factoring in recent news and incidents

Chapter **10**

Running Your Security Awareness Program

Planning a security awareness program is pretty difficult; however, running the program is where things get real.

When you run your program, you will discover that any planning was insufficient, incomplete, idealistic, and more. Even if your planning was mostly correct, you will learn some humbling lessons when you run the program. What you thought would work, doesn't. Promises are not kept. Incidents happen. Funding can be lost. Deliverables are late. You need to be able to adapt and improve your program as circumstances dictate.

This chapter doesn't cover every possible situation you may encounter, but it describes the critical operational issues you often find when you implement an awareness program. Running an awareness program, in large part, involves general project management. Books and resources are available to find out about that discipline. Some issues may seem like common sense, depending on the common knowledge you have as part of your awareness management experience.

Nailing the Logistics

The broad term *logistics* refers to the detailed coordination of a complex operation. For an awareness program, you have to work with suppliers, distributors, partners, and a variety of other vendors. During the planning phases, you should have identified all these parties, but the reality is that you will miss a few. It's impossible to plan for all possible situations that can come up with regard to working with outside parties.

One client informed me during the implementation of an awareness program that they would prefer that I arrange for the printing and shipment of posters to their offices worldwide because their internal resources could not offer the quality they wanted. Accommodating this request led to a logistical nightmare: I had to either pay hundreds of dollars in shipping costs or find local sources for each office to print and drop-ship the posters. These situations happen, and you have to try to proactively plan for them as best you can.

As you determine all the communications tools you intend to implement, you need to determine where you'll acquire them and their cost and required development resources. Document these resources so that you can identify any logistical issues that arise.

Determining sources or vendors

For each communications tool you use — and I am using the term *communications tool* broadly to mean any component of your awareness program — you should identify where you intend to get the tool. That can be from an internal source, such as a graphics department. Or you might create the tool yourself. It can also be from an external source, such as a vendor.

REMEMBER

Your organization may dictate that you use certain vendors. For example, you may have phishing and CBT contracts already available via your secure email gateway vendor. Or your organization may have a requirement that all posters be created by the internal corporate communications department. So, depending on whether the source is good or bad, you may have the blessing or curse of having a large portion of your work already accomplished.

The communications tools you choose must match the culture of your organization. A "funny" video series might be appropriate for a high-tech company, but it's likely to be inappropriate for an investment bank. Similarly, videos that feature cartoon characters aren't appropriate for all environments.

TIP

You need to determine the amount of money you have available. The budget determines which vendors you can use. You might want to create your own videos, for example, but few awareness programs have the resources to do so. Many vendors try to be competitive from a pricing perspective, but some may be more expensive than others. For example, many of the more established vendors lack competitive pricing for organizations of fewer than 1,000 people.

Scheduling resources and distribution

Remember to build in time for delivery from vendors and internal sources. I have personally found that internal resources can be slower than external sources. Unless it's already built into your schedule, corporate communications is unlikely to have people sitting around waiting for a new project, and they have to work your requirements into their schedule.

You may also face distribution considerations. If you want to send a newsletter to all employees, you're likely competing with a variety of other efforts for such a broad distribution. A smart communications team doesn't want a constant stream of random information fed to all employees — or else it all may become background noise. A typical organization has critical human resources information to periodically distribute, wellness information, executive communications, and other necessary information. Adding in a regular security awareness communication could require waiting for an appropriate opening in the schedule. Corporate communications, assuming you have such a department, likely has guidelines on how and when you can send different types of information to different levels of distribution.

Contracting vendors

If you will deal with external vendors, find out about the organization's contracting processes before you begin to approach potential vendors. You need to know the requirements for having purchase orders issued, the criteria for potential vendors, and the forms required by your organization to initiate the onboarding of vendors and ensure that the legal department provides a timely review of contracts. After you identify the vendors you want to use, start the contracting process as soon as possible.

Recognizing the role of general project management

Running a security awareness program has as much to do with basic project management as it does with awareness. Your skills in scheduling, budgeting, tracking, negotiations, and other tasks will likely be as important, if not more so, than your security awareness skills.

You need to set your expectations properly. I am passionate about improving security behaviors and reducing losses from human actions; however, this cannot happen if I don't implement the awareness program as a formal program that is well managed. A great event cannot be executed unless I schedule it, budget for it, ensure the availability of the appropriate resources and people, advertise for the event, arrange refreshments, and so on. The content of the event is clearly critical, but it will never have a chance to succeed if I cannot bring together the event as a whole.

TECHNICAL STUFF

It may be helpful to invest in taking a project management course or looking for people to join your team who have project management certifications, such as a PMP, or similar experience.

Getting All Required Approvals

Many organizations have a department that approves all materials released to the organization. Ask about the typical turnaround time for these approvals. The review process may seem burdensome, but it serves several purposes:

>> **Quality control:** Organizations try to ensure that distributed materials properly represent the organization. Spelling and grammatical errors are not only embarrassing but can also decrease the effectiveness of the communications.

>> **Legal review:** Given the litigious nature of the business environment, there's a need to review for basic concerns, such as using appropriate language and not violating labor agreements.

>> **Branding standards:** Reviews help ensure that any materials you distribute meet organizational branding standards. For example, I have had to adjust content to include new logos, appropriate color schemes, and gender-inclusive wording.

WARNING

Many people believe that the review process required to secure approvals is burdensome and unnecessary, but issues of poor taste and questionable wording do come up. In December 2020, for example, GoDaddy was heavily criticized for running a phishing simulation that told employees that if they clicked on the message, they would receive a holiday bonus. In response, many people stated that they would not do business with the company in the future. Though some people claim that criminals may use such a tactic, so it's fair game to run such a simulation, the backlash from employees and customers damaged the GoDaddy brand.

TIP

Work with the team that provides reviews proactively. Typically, the first time you put content through review, you may see several rounds of requested change because you're unfamiliar with the organization's standards or requirements. I strongly recommend allocating twice the expected turnaround time on your first rounds of program materials. As you become familiar with the review process and the evaluation criteria, you can expect the normal turnaround time.

Getting the Most from Day 0 Metrics

You must collect Day 0 metrics before you begin your program (see Chapter 8). By this time, you should have already determined the metrics you intend to study throughout the year. You can collect those metrics at any point before you begin the program. (In my experience, it generally takes at least two months from the time you start planning an awareness program until the formal launch of the program.)

TIP

Collect Day 0 metrics as soon as possible to get a head-start on your efforts. Some metrics, such as the number of security-related calls to the help desk, may appear easy to collect, but simple tasks have a way of becoming more complicated than you anticipate.

For example, you might find that the help desk doesn't categorize calls to the level you require. You may not have authorization for some data that you wanted for some reason. With phishing simulations, you may find that your technical team is slow in implementing required whitelisting of domains. (*Whitelisting* in the technical term for allowing messages through email filters that would otherwise be blocked because they appear to be phishing messages. See Chapter 12 for more details.) Certain people might not be readily available because of illness or leave.

As part of your planning, you should have identified three or so metrics that you intend to track over the course of the program (see Chapter 8). If you have the time and resources, you should collect all potential metrics reasonably available to you as part of a Day 0 effort. Collecting these metrics on an ongoing basis may be impractical, but if you have the initial metrics, you may be able to use them as a starting point to compare with metrics you collect in the future.

TIP

ADAPTING PHISHING EXERCISES FOR METRICS COLLECTION

A phishing simulation is an extremely common component of a security awareness program. When you perform a phishing exercise for metrics collection, however, you need to approach the simulations a little differently.

Most phishing simulations include training messages that inform users who fall for the message that they clicked on a phishing simulation. The messages tell the user how they could have performed better. If you incorporate these training messages into a simulation intended for metric collection, you increase the odds that users will warn other users about the simulation, which undermines the usefulness of the metrics you collect.

When you're doing a metrics-only phishing simulation, such as a Day 0 metrics collection, you should not provide any training or messaging that informs users of the simulation. If the phishing message simulates sending users to a link, provide generic content or a simple 404 message stating that the web page wasn't found. If the message intends to persuade users to give up their logon credentials, allow them to enter the credentials and move on. You have an extended period to train them after you collect the metrics, and in this case, collecting accurate metrics is more important than any increase in awareness you might possibly gain.

When you examine phishing metrics, be sure to consider the percentage of people who properly report the messages. This metric is more important than the number of people who fall for the message compared with the number of people who don't. The proper response to a phishing message isn't just not to click on the message but also to report the message.

Reporting the messages is so important, in fact, that you might consider rewarding users who do so. Chapter 12 covers this topic in more detail.

REMEMBER

Collect any metric that's available on Day 0. If you can collect malware incidents, do it. If you have the time to sit outside a door to see how many people, if any, stop tailgaters to ask for a badge, do it. If you want to test for yourself, try to tailgate people on their way in and count how many people stop you to ask for a badge. Walk around your facilities after hours and determine the percentage of desks that are left unsecured. If you have free time, do these things as experiments to get a feel for the overall security posture of your organization. If you later need a supportive metric, you may be able to return to these metrics.

Creating Meaningful Reports

A theme of this book is that you need to deserve more. You only truly deserve more, of course, when you can demonstrate that you deserve more to the appropriate executives in your organization. This means that you can provide metrics in a meaningful way.

You may need to create reports for your direct manager and your manager's direct manager. You need to find out what reports you need to provide, and the type of information they require. Some reports will probably be status reports to inform management how you're spending your time and budget. Management will want to see that the program is being managed well. These reports will likely be standard reports for all people running other projects in your department or another group. If your organization doesn't provide report formats, you can create whatever your management is comfortable with.

Perhaps most important is a report detailing your measurable results. This report should be simple and focus on improvements that can be attributed to your efforts. By this point, you should have chosen the metrics you want to collect and use to prove that you deserve more resources and support. Ideally, these metrics define a return on investment. If not, the metrics should define measurable improvement in behaviors. You can resort to compliance, engagement, or likability metrics, but they should imply some intangible benefits.

Presenting reports as a graphical dashboard

Reports that are to be provided to executive management should be concise. I recommend presenting them as a graphical dashboard. You should have each of your three or so metrics portrayed in graphical form. The graphical format should show before-and-after metrics so that the improvement you create is clear. This can be a bar graph, line graph, percentage change, or whatever gets the job done. Your choice of display should match the data.

Figure 10-1 includes a comprehensive index score, where I normalized the five metrics that we chose to collect. It simultaneously shows all improvements in the metrics.

Figure 10-2 portrays the number of lost or stolen mobile devices. In this case, a line graph is most appropriate because it allows for the depiction of the lost device over time. Note that we *did* add a note about when the awareness program began. In the case of this client, I experienced the fact that increased awareness results in more accurate reporting on behalf of the users. Users who are more aware are likely to report concerns more frequently.

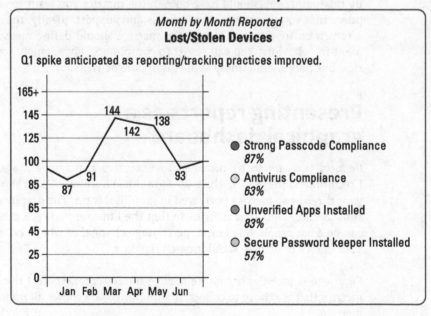

Secure Mentem Information Security Awareness
Corporate Index Overview

Index Factors		Comprehensive *Awareness Index Score*
Password Security	+30%	
Social Engineering Scam Identification	+13%	**6.4**
Communication Device/Server	+55%	
Patch Compliance	+33%	*SM Index Score*
Corporate Policy Rollout	12%	

FIGURE 10-1:
Consolidated
metrics
dashboard.

Mobile Device Security

Month by Month Reported
Lost/Stolen Devices

Q1 spike anticipated as reporting/tracking practices improved.

- Strong Passcode Compliance
  87%
- Antivirus Compliance
  63%
- Unverified Apps Installed
  83%
- Secure Password keeper Installed
  57%

FIGURE 10-2:
Mobile device
loss.

In this case, the diagram could have been more effective if I incorporated the likely financial loss associated with the lost devices. The client informed me that they did not have the financial costs associated with the loss, however, and they did not want to use industry estimates that they could not confirm. The number of lost devices was clearly important to them.

Figure 10-3 uses a bar graph to show different measures of phishing susceptibility between the calendar quarters. Though the results are less dramatic than you would normally hope, it was only a single quarter to obtain progress.

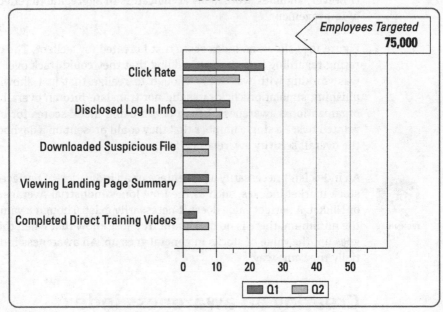

Employee Susceptibility Over Time

Employees Targeted
75,000

- Click Rate
- Disclosed Log In Info
- Downloaded Suspicious File
- Viewing Landing Page Summary
- Completed Direct Training Videos

0   10   20   30   40   50

■ Q1   ■ Q2

FIGURE 10-3:
Phishing results bar graph.

TIP

Though constant progress would be great, it is both unnecessary and unlikely. Not all categories are expected to show constant improvements. Results that are negative or neutral are a sign that things can be improved. Don't promise constant improvement, but rather efforts that will adapt to circumstances as they arise and will improve as you refine the program over time.

The reports you choose to provide are up to you. Different organizations have various preferences for reporting. Some organizations have established reporting templates and protocols because of quality control efforts like Six Sigma. (*Six Sigma* is a set of techniques and tools for process improvement and is a common business process that's implemented in many organizations.) Though you will likely need to provide, to different levels of management, some reports that detail the types of efforts and resources expended, I again strongly recommend that you create summary graphics that show some quick wins. Ideally, some low-hanging fruit will allow you to demonstrate early progress.

Adding index scores

An *index score*, such as the one shown in Figure 10-1, is essentially an average score you create that incorporates metrics. You basically create a formula that combines all the metrics into a single number. Some awareness indicators can go up. Some can go down. Others can remain neutral. Individually, it's a sign of improvement. However, an index score looks at indicators in aggregate to reflect an overall sign of improvement.

Figure 10-1 shows an index score that I created for a client. The client asked for a rating regarding how they were doing that they could track over time. The CISO I was working with was savvy enough to realize that just showing that reduced phishing simulation click rates did not translate into an overall improvement in organizational awareness. I then began using index scores for other clients who wanted to see a single number that they could present on a dashboard to represent the overall security awareness effort.

TECHNICAL STUFF

An index isn't necessarily a percentage or an indication of perfection. Consider the stock market indexes, such as the Dow Jones Industrial Average, NASDAC, FTSE, or Nikkei. A perfect value doesn't necessarily exist. Though a value of 0 is possibly the minimum, there is no maximum. You just know that when this mythical value goes up, the value of stocks in general goes up. An awareness index works essentially the same way.

Creating an awareness index

To create an awareness index for an organization, you need to determine the metrics that you can consistently collect. Like the Dow Jones Industrial Average, you can periodically change the components of an index, but it changes the index score to a certain extent. To start, you should have your metrics set so that you can create your index.

The number and range you choose are arbitrary. In Figure 10-1, the index score is 6.4. It was intended to be on a scale from 1–10. It could have easily been 64 on a scale of 1–100. It seemed better not to have it appear to be a percentage at that time.

TIP

Here are the basic steps I follow to derive an index:

1. **Give a weight to the different metrics.**

If you have three metrics, the default would be to give each one 33.3 percent of the index value. If you think one of the metrics is more important, you might perhaps break it out as 50 percent for the most important metric and 25 percent each for the remaining two.

2. **For each metric, determine a rating system.**

For example, for a phishing simulation, you may say that the percentage of people who didn't click on a message is the score. So, if 80 percent of the users did not respond to the metric, it would be an 8 (for a scale of 1–10). If you study unsecured desks, and 65 percent of desks are secured, that would be a 6.5. If you also want to include the people who completed awareness training, and 90 percent of people completed the training, that would be a 9.

3. **Calculate the index.**

If you then want to create an index based on the numbers in Step 2 and you believe that all values are equal, the index score would be (8 x 0.33) + (6.5 x 0.33) + (9 x 0.33). The index score would then total to 7.755 or rounded to 7.8.

You can modify the weights for each component of the index as appropriate. As long as you collect information and perform the calculations in a similar way, the index represents an overall awareness score that takes into account fluctuations in the metrics collection process.

Reevaluating Your Program

You need to evaluate regularly how successful your program is. Though you should be collecting individual metrics as they are scheduled, you need to evaluate the entire program at predetermined intervals. If you follow my advice and implement your program in quarterly cycles, the end of every cycle is a regular checkpoint. Even if you implement your program on an annual cycle, reevaluating your program every three months is likely prudent.

As I mention throughout this book, metrics are the most critical aspect of your awareness program. Again, you have to show that you deserve more — more resources, more funding, more support from management. You have to show that you're providing a return on investment. Other people will consider this, so you want to consider it first.

You should be more aware than anyone else with regard to the areas of success and failure within your program. You need to consider where you're fundamentally adding value, where you're failing, and where progress is uncertain. You need to take an honest accounting of the results of your efforts.

WARNING

If your program draws positive feedback from users, this doesn't guarantee that the program is a success. You need to find metrics that prove your efforts provide value to the organization. Try to see the less successful aspects of the program more readily than the apparent successful ones. I can promise that other people will, especially those who approve your budget.

Likeability is good. Positive comments are good. But providing metrics that state there is improved behavior and ideally a tangible return on investment is best. If all you have are likeability and participation metrics, make the most of them. You have to be able to frame these metrics in the best light possible, however.

Your goal at this point is to accept the honest metrics to determine how to better move forward. If you identify clear returns on investment, you need to continue that improvement. At the same time, find the deficiencies — and you will find deficiencies.

REMEMBER

Embrace your successes. Tout those successes. You do need to sell yourself and your efforts. Just be aware of the reality of the situations, both positive and negative, so that you can constantly improve your program.

Reconsidering your metrics

You should have chosen your metrics to be sustainable, reasonably easy to collect, and relevant to the organization and your program. This section applies to your first time through a program. You can, and possibly should, reconsider your metrics periodically, but for the first run of your program, you need to consider whether the metrics you chose to collect fit your purposes, and were as easy to collect as you anticipated.

Metrics that initially fit your purposes may stop working for you as circumstances change. You might lose resources to have a social engineering test performed every quarter. You may have pushback on your phishing program. You might find that responses to questionnaires are inconsistent. A change of management may cause support to fluctuate for aspects of your awareness efforts.

TIP

Here are some questions to ask when you assess your metrics:

>> Is the metric producing apparently consistent results?

>> Is there legitimate pushback to the metric?

>> Was the metric actually meaningful to the organization?

>> Was the metric as easy to collect as anticipated?

>> Is the metric producing meaningful results that aren't similar to other metrics?

>> Is there another metric that might produce more meaningful results and be easier to collect?

If you do achieve results, you may receive an increased budget, which would allow for more costly and time-consuming metrics collections. For example, you may gain the resources to add a USB drop, which can be expensive. So you can change metrics for good reasons as well as bad.

Evaluating your communications tools

Your communications tools are your awareness program. You need to consider how they're performing, in both the number of people that engage with the tool and their actual effectiveness.

In one case, I interviewed a security awareness manager to evaluate his program. He told me how he spent most of his effort and budget on a quarterly newsletter. The newsletter was translated into 20 languages and sent to email boxes around the world. I asked whether he had metrics for how many people opened the email. Though I don't recall the exact number, it was in the range of approximately 750. I then asked him the number of people in the company, and he replied 163,000. When he saw me cringe, he mentioned that there were a lot of factories and similar environments, and he believes that more people read the newsletter than I would think, because he assumes someone in the factories prints it and puts a hard copy in the breakrooms. Without data to back up his beliefs, the newsletter was an apparent waste of effort.

Though this case is extreme and obvious, your cases might not be so obvious. This being said, you need to determine whether you're getting the expected return on investment from each of your communications tools. Though the level of resources required depends on the communications tool, there is always an investment on your part. Even if there's no financial outlay, there is time required to distribute it and create it, goodwill cost to get people to approve it, and the potential waste of a limited distribution channel.

In some cases, the usage is obvious. If you hold an event and it's standing room only, it's seemingly a well-attended event. If few people show up, and if you record the event and few people watch the recording, clearly the event isn't worth the effort. With newsletters, you might be able to track how many times they are read. You might be able to count clicks on links in the newsletter. Again, if there are few clicks, it likely isn't worth your efforts to continue to create the newsletter. Other forms of communications tools should have their own ways of measuring engagement with the tool.

Engagement metrics are not a great way to judge the effectiveness of an overall awareness program, but you should collect engagement metrics for the tools you use. You don't use these metrics to prove how well you're changing behaviors. You use engagement metrics to determine how to allocate your limited resources moving forward. For example, if few people read a newsletter, discontinue the newsletter and use the funding and effort on other tools that have been shown to be more accepted by the users.

While considering engagement metrics, you want to study a breakdown in demographics. Are certain regions engaging with different tools than others? Are people in given job functions engaging with certain tools? For example, you know that people who don't regularly use computers likely won't engage with computer-based tools, but is there a trend in what they do engage with? You may, for example, find that relatively few people look at your mobile device content, but it's the only content that factory workers engage with. You therefore may want to continue to use it because it's the most reliable way to reach that demographic.

Clearly, there will be cultural differences across the world. This is expected, and you want to address the cultures. You may however need to make some hard choices. You may determine that though some cultures prefer one communications method, it might not warrant the overall effort given the competing resources.

Measuring behavioral changes

As I mention in Chapter 9, in your first cycle (or whatever previous cycle you were on), you should have had three topics of focus. Those topics represent your learning goals for the cycle. As you end a cycle, you should determine whether your goals have been met.

Keep in mind that you may not know whether you have met your goals. Your metrics are unlikely to equate directly to the topics you're running in this cycle of your program. Phishing is likely to be one of those metrics, but it might not be a formal topic in your current campaign. This is okay.

Throughout a cycle, your reasonable hope should be that people pick up some information and begin to apply it. For all the reasons I discuss in Part 1, it's likely that there will be, at best, some memory of what you present and a more frequent application of that information. You cannot expect much more than that, and that is okay. Even small improvements are a start, and if you can consistently build on small improvements, you achieve major improvements over time.

If your program addresses a critical need or behavior with a properly defined metric, you can make a fair determination. For example, if ransomware is a major concern and you're collecting ransomware statistics, you can make a fair determination of your success. For a broad topic, like social engineering or mobile device security, you probably can't determine whether or how much improvement has occurred without appropriate metrics.

As you consider the success of your behavioral modification goals, you can look to your overall metrics, or you can look to small improvements in your goal. In the worst case, consider that you won't always be able to measure success.

REMEMBER

You need to determine whether behavior change differs across the various demographics throughout your organization. For a variety of reasons, some areas might have seen more success than others. IT departments will likely respond to different behaviors than others. If the awareness program is in the IT organization, for example, you will likely have more support and adherence from your own department. You may also find that you created a theme that resonates more with one age group than another.

I once dealt with an organization that used the *Seinfeld* reference "Master of Your Domain" as a theme for its awareness program. That was rather catchy for Gen Xers and baby boomers, but did not resonate at all with younger generations.

In the end, you need to be honest with yourself about whether the topics were well addressed and you achieved the desired goals. If not, you have to examine whether there were perhaps inconsistent results across the organization. Inconsistencies are perhaps the most telling, because they can provide clues to why your program is or isn't working.

Redesigning Your Program

After you evaluate how you did (or are currently doing) in the cycle you're finishing, you can consider what you should be doing in the next cycle. Ideally, you've had reasonable success and the program flowed and executed well. If that isn't the case, you have some problems to address. Even if everything went perfectly, you can still look to make enhancements.

TECHNICAL STUFF

I find that awareness programs are generally evolutionary. Rarely are there radical changes. Some things are added, and others are eliminated. Even successful efforts are enhanced and improved as you learn more and can at least do things more efficiently.

Anything stand out?

There might have been something you wanted to do in the previous cycle that you didn't have the time or resources to implement. You might have wanted to start out conservatively, and add more aspirational efforts after you were comfortable that everything was going reasonably well. Now is the time to consider adding to your program.

Assuming that the resources are there, and that you have the bandwidth, you should consider adding what you can. This doesn't mean that you cannot or should not remove other communications tools that no longer fit, however.

Adding subcultures

It isn't uncommon to start your awareness program as a single program, and adding programs for subcultures is a logical stepping stone. As you become more confident in your program and abilities, it's time to consider creating unique programs for the appropriate subcultures.

REMEMBER

As I mention in Chapter 9, subcultures can be defined by geography, business role, department, function, and/or any other distinct and reasonable categorization. If you choose to create a unique program for a specific geography, you don't have to create a unique program for every geography. If you choose to create a special program for call center operators, you don't have to create a program for all other job functions.

TIP

As you consider adding subcultures, you should determine how much extra effort and other resources you have available. For example, you will likely send phishing messages to all employees. If you have unique awareness programs for some subcultures, you should create unique phishing campaigns for the subcultures and the creation, management, and reporting of unique campaigns might require significant effort. If you're using different posters in different geographies, you will still have the about the same level of effort to distribute the posters, but there is extra effort and cost in designing the posters.

You will likely be able to use a lot of your materials from your main campaign for chosen subcultures. Therefore, it isn't a linear increase in cost and resources for subcultures, though you do however have to determine what aspects will be unique to the subcultures. The goal is to determine what will make the program for the subculture more effective. Though it isn't necessarily out of the question to design a completely unique program for a given subculture, it usually isn't necessary. There should normally be overlap in the use of much, if not most, of the material used, saving you significant resources.

As you determine the subcultures you want to target, and then determine the resources required, you can identify which if any subcultures to add.

Adding, deleting, and continuing metrics

The previous section discussed metrics and how your chosen metrics might have been shown to be inappropriate for your needs. For these reasons and others, you might consider adding or deleting metrics.

TECHNICAL STUFF

If you have been using some metrics for your dashboard or incorporated into an index, you have to just accept that there is a fundamental change in the basis for the overall awareness metrics. You might need to annotate it for management when you submit the metrics for reporting. In all likelihood, you won't get a question as good management will understand the inevitability of periodic changes. There might be basic questions as to why and what will be the impact, but these are questions that are straightforward to address.

Adding and discontinuing communications tools

Based on an evaluation you perform after your running your program's first cycle, as described in the earlier section "Evaluating your communications tools," you may decide to change which communication tools you use in your program. Most likely, though, you will reuse the same tools across cycles. This section helps you plan accordingly.

TIP

I usually recommend that awareness managers start conservatively and limit what they do in the early cycles to see what works, and what doesn't, and then add things as they become comfortable enough to add more. In the planning stages, there should have been a variety tools you considered but chose not to use. During every review, consider which tools you might want to discontinue and which communications tools you want to add.

Your metrics might be able to tell you where you need more engagement from different populations. Are there additional tools that would better reach different populations? Are there tools that are apparently reaching some populations and you want to increase the usage of those tools?

If you learn that the events you held were well liked and seemed to have made an impact, you might want to hold more events. On the other hand, even if the events were reasonably well attended, you might find that the events were resource intensive. In this case, you may decide that they aren't a good use of limited resources and look to other tools that could prove a better use of your time.

The following list presents some more aspirational tools to implement as your program begins to mature. These tools require more effort, so you likely want to make sure that the basic program is running well before adding them. These tools are usually more appropriate for some subcultures. Even if you believe that they can and should be implemented throughout your entire organization, you likely want to start implementing the tool within a subculture or small part of your organization to work out any problems on a smaller scale:

>> **Gamification:** A rewards structure where you create positive consequences for desired behaviors. Gamification is a good tool to consider adding to an established program. For details on integrating gamification with your awareness program, see Chapter 11.

>> **Experiential engagement:** Contests, security cubicles, scavenger hunts, speakers, event tables, and so on. See Chapter 7 for more suggestions for experiential engagement.

>> **Security ambassadors:** Users you entrust to perform outreach within their own communities. They function as your local hands, eyes, and ears in their organizations, as described in Chapter 7.

You can consider which tools you're comfortable to add to the current program. Again, you want to use everything possible, but at the same time, as with all cybersecurity efforts, you have limited resources and you need to determine the best balance for your needs.

Revisiting awareness topics

The natural inclination for most awareness programs is to address 12 topics over the course of the year, changing the topic monthly. In Chapter 9, I discuss why I recommend otherwise.

TIP

I advocate that, for every cycle, you need to determine which three topics are your most critical awareness needs. What I recommend that is different from most other awareness practitioners is that you should consider the three current topics as potential topics to feature in the next cycle. In other words, the driver for the content of your awareness program at any given time is your business needs, as described in Chapter 6.

This doesn't mean that you completely ignore what topics you had in the previous cycle. If it's a generic topic where you aren't necessarily collecting relevant metrics, such as travel security, you can move on to other subjects. However, if it involves common and concerning topics such as phishing, malware, or secure workspaces, you should definitely consider the topics for any cycle, even if it was used before.

If you choose to rerun a topic, you still need to create fresh content. Showing the same content from one cycle to the next makes the topic come across as background noise. With phishing, for example, you can discuss basic phishing one cycle, cover spearphishing in another cycle, choose web link safety for the next one, and so on. There are many ways to keep a topic fresh.

TECHNICAL STUFF

If you're collecting metrics regarding specific topics and the metrics come back bad, you want to rerun a topic and attack it in a different way. It should not even be an option to remove the topic until you see improvement. Again, this isn't the way many professionals approach the problem, given that they have mapped out their program a year in advance, but it should be the way you do it.

In essence, with the exception of the likely elimination of less relevant topics from the previous cycle, every topic is viable in every cycle. You then take the three topics and place them in the matrix, as described in Chapter 9.

Considering Breaking News and Incidents

When choosing topics for the next cycle, you must consider any incident that your organization, your industry, or the general public experiences. If you have a significant phishing loss or a ransomware incident, for example, you should incorporate it into your program and address it in your program in the coming cycle.

If incidents occur in your industry and you receive warnings from relevant Industry Sharing and Analysis Centers (ISACs), you should incorporate the incident and the relevant topics into your awareness program. (There are ISACs for many industry sectors, including the financial sector, state governments, and healthcare.) For example, even cybersecurity companies were informed that North Korean hackers were targeting security researchers using what amounts to catfishing tactics via Twitter. Though it's unlikely that any random individual would be targeted, incidents such as this one make the threat real to an organization and an industry.

When a cyberattack becomes a major headline, try to make it relevant to your users. In the Twitter hack in 2020, a hacker was able to social-engineer login credentials out of a Twitter employee, and then use those credentials to change the passwords of notable Twitter users and sell access to the accounts. The lessons to promote based on this incident included social engineering, vishing (voice phishing), phishing, multifactor authentication (which is vital), password security, and many others.

Widely publicized malware incidents, such as Wannacry, which had a massive impact around the world, are a great time to promote the importance of running antimalware software and system updates, and other issues.

TECHNICAL STUFF

When COVID-19 began to have an impact around the world and created an environment where work-from-home became the default when at all possible, many awareness programs were sent into a scramble. My clients, who followed my strategy, had no problems adjusting to the circumstances from a strategic perspective, because they already anticipated creating a fresh program on a regular basis.

COVID-19 was unique in that not only were topics affected but delivery methods were also somewhat changed. People still had email and online access to watch computer-based training. Posters, in-person events, desk drops, and the like were no longer useful. Likewise, many metrics were no longer relevant. Phishing simulations, for example, were still potentially valid, but tailgating tests and clean desk counts were no longer possible.

THE COVID-19 IMPACT

COVID-19 presented challenges for most professions, and the awareness profession was no exception. In hindsight, there could have been months of planning, but the reality is that it was like the proverbial frog in boiling water, where it was a slow progression until there was a universal tipping point, where office work just stopped and everyone who could work from home was told to do so. The tipping point seemed to happen on or about March 16, 2020, and most people seem to have their own story of their sudden realization that things had changed.

A good portion of the impact to awareness professionals depended on their organization. If they were responsible for awareness for a large organization, many different cultures were affected differently. Retail operations might have shut down completely, or at least had significantly reduced operations. If factories remained open, besides social distancing, minimal operational change occurred in general. Desk workers moved to working from home.

It's possible that security awareness professionals were pulled in to work on awareness regarding COVID-19 prevention and to inform people about updated safety and work protocols. They probably created mandatory mass emails that were critical to operations. Rules were likely developed that required approvals of top-level management. In this case, awareness was focused on what I vehemently recommend: how to do a job function properly for the circumstances.

The reality was that security was a secondary concern for work from home. It became a case of "Just make it work." Then reality set in. Many people lacked work computers, so they were doing work on their personal computers. This computer had to frequently be shared by the entire family. Computers handling sensitive data were used for attending classes, social networking, games, random web surfing, watching porn, and every other activity that people use their home computers for. Even work computers were being used for nonwork purposes, and organizations could do little to stop it. People had no choice because everyone in a household likely had to use a computer simultaneously. Organization-owned computers were easier to control, but when your employees use their own computers for your purpose, you have no authority over how the computers are used.

Organizations could roll out technical controls, if they could afford it, but awareness had a renewed importance. Criminals were quick to take advantage of employees working from home. Phishing schemes thrived on it. Criminals targeting specific organizations knew they had incredible opportunities as people were checking personal web mail accounts on computers outside of their organization's security controls that had access to corporate networks. Besides, of the generic attacks that happen to users on the internet, criminals realized that they could specifically target individuals by way of personal resources to gain access to the organization.

(continued)

(continued)

Topics had to be rolled out immediately, and organizations that planned their program a year in advance were left scrambling. The required topics generally presented themselves. They included securing your computer, phishing prevention, safe web browsing, web meeting security and safety, securely configuring a web meeting, securing your personal workspace, and talking to your children about Internet security, among countless other topics.

Delivery methods and metrics became the major challenges. It was unlikely that metrics were configured for remote work. Many organizations had remote workers, but it was far from universal. In large part, metrics weren't even a consideration, and despite my focus on this, it was completely understandable and acceptable given the circumstances. Some metrics, such as phishing simulation click rates, were reasonable to continue. You weren't going to get metrics specific to considerations such as physical security, however.

Communications tools were limited. Email and other forms of online delivery were usually acceptable to continue. However, you could not guarantee that all employees had the bandwidth to watch videos, especially with the likelihood of multiple people in a home streaming video simultaneously.

Some awareness programs created online events and training specific to the topics. Given the importance of home-based cybersecurity, many awareness programs were able to create awareness sessions for employees that were mandatory for users to watch live or the recording of the session.

I worked with some awareness programs that created work-from-home security kits. These kits included instructions for downloading and updating antimalware software for home computers, cybersecurity tip cards to share with families, and locks for laptop computers, along with mouse pads, stickers, and other tools that could be used for nudges. Getting these kits out to users took significant resources, but it was especially worth it for high-risk users. When resources were limited, the kits went distributed to high-risk users only.

If the awareness programs planned their programs in quarterly (or some other short) cycles, it was much more cost effective. For example, the annual programs commission the printing of materials in advance. They plan out the communications tools long in advance. COVID-19 showed the risk that comes with overplanning an awareness program, beyond the overall lack of responsiveness to the normal dynamic circumstances that security programs encounter.

IN THIS CHAPTER

» **Knowing the difference between a game and gamification**

» **Defining gamification**

» **Determining whether gamification can work for your organization**

» **Implementing a gamification program**

» **Getting the word out about your gamification program**

Chapter **11**

Implementing Gamification

I n Chapter 3, I introduce the concept of behavioral science and describe how consequences are four times more effective in creating desired *behaviors* than providing information via traditional awareness campaigns. Gamification is essentially a formalized process used to build meaningful consequences into your awareness program, and therefore should be four times more effective at achieving desired behavior changes than your other efforts.

It is therefore worth your time to consider putting a significant portion of your efforts into implementing gamification. It doesn't mean that you should — it means that you should consider it. However, be aware, before you continue reading this chapter, that the benefit comes with implementing actual gamification and not just a game, which is explained throughout the chapter.

Understanding Gamification

To most people, the word *gamification* implies that games will be a part of your awareness program. After all, the word gamification starts with most of the word *game*. The words, however, differ in meaning.

The definition of gamification is the application of typical elements of game play to encourage engagement with a product or service. I discuss those elements later, but the important issue is that it isn't a game. Considering the ABCs of behavioral science, discussed in Chapter 3, the encouragement is accomplished by providing positive consequences to the desired behaviors.

As an example, consider businesses that want to encourage salespeople to sell more of a particular product or service. You might think that salespeople should not need to be incentivized to sell more, because they already earn greater commissions based on how much they sell. That is true, but businesses frequently want to encourage even greater sales of certain products and services. So businesses created sales incentives. Many companies have a President's Circle for salespeople: The top salespeople receive special bonuses and trips, and people become extremely competitive to win the trips. Despite the fact that salespeople already earn commissions, enhanced rewards for selling more and selling specific types of services and products focuses them to hit targets beyond the minimum goals.

Consider, however, if these businesses did not give out trips for top salespeople and instead created a game to see who could name the features of a product. The game might be fun. Some competition might exist to be the person who knows the most about the business's products. In the end, though, while salespeople knowing more about the product "should" perhaps generate more sales, in this example, properly implemented gamification should reward and encourage sales, not knowledge. Encouraged by gamification, salespeople become even more competitive to win the trips and the acknowledgment. The game may be fun, but fun doesn't pay the bills.

TECHNICAL STUFF

Other examples of gamification include frequent flier programs, grocery store frequent shopper programs, and credit card rewards. Frequent flier programs reward customers with upgrades and preferred boarding for being a loyal customer, getting the airline-branded credit card, and other actions that increase the airline's profits. Grocery store rewards provide cheaper prices for customers who essentially allow themselves to be tracked so that the store can sell the information to vendors and better market to the customers. Credit card companies give cash-back bonuses or frequent flier miles to people who use the credit cards, which encourages people to use their credit cards more frequently.

The simple way to tell whether you have actual gamification or just a game is by going back to behavioral science, as described in Chapter 3. Essentially, awareness influences behaviors. Behaviors generate a consequence. Consequences then reinforce or discourage behaviors. If your gamification program quizzes people on information to encourage learning, you have a game. If your program rewards people for practicing the desired behaviors in a real environment, you have a true gamification program.

For security awareness purposes, consider a common game where you have users look at a password and determine whether the password is weak or strong. They might logically learn more details about password strength, and they can have fun doing so, but there is no indication that they will then create a password. You have essentially provided awareness, not consequences. Though it might help users lengthen the Forgetting Curve, it has no bearing on actual password strength. This is a game.

On the other hand, suppose that you run a password cracker against the master password file. You reward users who have passwords that cannot be cracked, and you force other users to change their passwords. That is gamification. It is dealing with actual passwords and reinforcing actual security behaviors. This strategy has a measurable impact on improving password strength.

Even if you consider that someone may enjoy the game so much that they're encouraged to go back to their computer and immediately change their passwords, it's a one-time event and they may or may not change their passwords back after having had to remember complex passwords for a time. Either way, everyone knows that just because someone knows what they should do, it rarely means that they will do it when there is nothing else to encourage otherwise more difficult behaviors.

Gamification, however, captures people exercising the appropriate behavior and rewards them for it. It generates positive consequences for demonstrating the desired behaviors. So a person who is rewarded for having good passwords, or who suffers a negative consequence of a weak password, is much more likely to not have weak password now and in the future.

Gamification uses rewards to create a positive consequence that reinforces behaviors as they are demonstrated. If you're just trying to make learning information fun (providing an antecedent), that is a game, not gamification. There is some scientific proof that people might retain information slightly longer (slow the Forgetting Curve), but there is no proof that it actually creates increased and consistent behavior change, which is what actually provides value back to the business.

Identifying the Four Attributes of Gamification

Gamification is a commonly used business process. A great deal of research has been done in the field, and standardization exists for the field. This is good news because you can use defined attributes for gamification to determine whether you're implementing it properly.

Perhaps the best and most commonly referenced set of attributes are those defined by Jane McGonigal in her iconic book *Reality Is Broken* (Penguin Books, 2011). I strongly recommend that you read *Reality Is Broken* for the definitive descriptions of the four attributes of gamification, but here is my quick summary:

>> **Goals are clearly defined.** You need to let users know the rules. They need to know specifically what it takes to earn the rewards at given levels. There are frequently levels or rewards that grow progressively more difficult to achieve as someone rises through the levels.

>> **Rewards are desirable to the participants.** Users should want to earn the rewards. The rewards need to be something that would be considered valuable and worthy of effort to the targeted audience.

>> **Goals are achievable.** If a person does want to achieve the goals, the time and effort to do so must be reasonable, given the potential reward. For example, if you want to reward people for reporting phishing messages, you don't want the basic reward level to require the reporting of 1,000 messages. The lowest tier might just require reporting a single message. Additionally, you would want to provide phishing simulations and counting the reporting of the simulated phishing message to ensure that the user has an opportunity to earn the rewards.

>> **Participation is voluntary.** If people don't want to actively engage in your gamification, they shouldn't have to. They might unintentionally earn rewards along the way, such as reporting a phishing message without the intent of being part of the gamification program. However, they should not be forced to intend to earn rewards. But when a person begins to earn rewards, it just might encourage them to intentionally engage with the gamification program.

To design a true gamification program, you need to incorporate each of these attributes. For the most part, it just makes sense. I will break down this topic further, but, for example, if nobody wants your rewards, nobody will try to achieve them. Ensure that each attribute is embedded within your gamification program.

TECHNICAL STUFF

Your awareness program is attempting to reduce your overall risk related to user-initiated loss. Your efforts cannot be limited to only those who want to be made more aware. That said, you can implement gamification for everyone and let people opt in for as much of the gamification as they choose. For example, you can send phishing simulation messages to everyone, and if they report them, you can reward them per a gamification plan that rewards people for reporting potential phishing messages. You can offer points for attending events that help people increase tiers in the gamification program, but they don't have to attend. They're more likely to attend, though, if the rewards are worth it.

The purpose of security countermeasures is to reduce organizational risk. The return on investment (ROI) of any countermeasure is that it reduces more loss than it costs to implement the countermeasure. As awareness training may have minimal obvious ROI, and gamification has the potential to be four times more effective than traditional awareness, even if you have a chance to reach only 25 percent of your users, you will likely have a higher ROI with gamification.

Figuring Out Where to Gamify Awareness

Generally, when you implement gamification, you don't target the entire organization. That approach likely isn't practical. For example, if you're in a manufacturing organization, factory workers, who don't use computers as part of their jobs and rarely access corporate email, won't likely be great candidates for gamification. People who regularly use computers are better candidates.

WARNING

Gamification does take some effort to implement, and the larger the target population, the more effort it takes to implement and manage the program. Therefore, picking and choosing where to implement gamification isn't based just on where it will have impact, but rather on the level of resources you can put toward the program. You need to choose wisely which subcultures gamification is appropriate for. If you try to include too large of a group of users, it may quickly become extremely costly and labor intensive — and impractical.

When you choose a target population for gamification, you need to understand the subcultures. Which subculture within the organization is more likely to be appropriate for gamification? As important, which subculture also has business drivers that are appropriate to target via gamification and are valuable enough to implement a resource intensive program?

TIP

Those subcultures that had awareness-related losses are the primary places to consider. Because there are potentially valuable rewards and promotions at stake, cultures that have a great deal of business value can be easily compromised because of failings related to security awareness.

You can bring gamification to the entire organization, and you perhaps should, with phishing reporting, for example, but you do have to account for the resources, which includes the technology to implement and track the program, the expenses or organizational capital for the rewards, the effort to promote the rules, rewards, and successes, and the people to run the effort. I know this sounds almost ironic, but you need an awareness program to promote the gamification program.

Examining Some Tactical Gamification Examples

I realize that many awareness managers are overworked with their awareness programs as is, let alone adding a resource-intensive effort that will drain funding. Many might believe that gamification sounds like a great addition to your program, but a full gamification program is too resource intensive to implement now.

TIP

Here are some forms of gamification that are more tactical and can be implemented with limited resources and effort on your part. It also helps when there are limited resources for rewards. These forms of gamification can address some tactical concerns as well, such as phishing reporting or security tool adoption. They essentially create a basic reward structure for exhibiting desired behaviors, which is gamification in its purest form.

Phishing reporting

If someone reports a phishing message, you provide some form of reward. It's that simple. It goes beyond the typical sentiment "Thank you for reporting the message" or "Congratulations! You detected our phishing simulation!" Though they sound great the first time, by the second time — and especially by the third time — a user reports a phishing message, the user not only believes that they receive no benefit but also may assume that the organization doesn't even care.

You need to do something more if you want to keep encouraging reporting of possible phishing messages. You need to either give an immediate reward for every report of a phishing message or track the number of reports and reward for a specific number of reports — and, ideally, better rewards for higher tiers of reporting. Most important, you need to let the user know that their reports are being tracked and they will be rewarded.

For example, the first tier might involve a generic "Thank you." However, it also includes a message that if they report two more potential phishing messages, they might receive a certificate for a free coffee or a similar item. You should also refer to a website that documents the tiers with the number of phishing messages reported and the respective rewards. Clearly, you need a reporting mechanism and the budget for the possible rewards, but it should have an impact in reported phishing messages. You should also mention that they will receive periodic phishing simulation messages so that they know they will have an opportunity to earn rewards.

WARNING

Some users might gratuitously report nonphishing messages, just to earn the rewards. You just have to be on the lookout for potentially abusive behaviors and adjust your program accordingly — or at least know how to deal with abusive users.

REMEMBER

You want people to report anything questionable because even generic spam messages indicate a weakness in your filters. The goal of reporting phishing messages is so that you can detect threats and remove them from the inboxes of users who aren't as aware as those reporting the messages.

Clean desk drops

Many organizations have a problem with people who don't physically secure their documents and computers. One of my clients wanted me to help them with this task, so we decided to engage in a late night exercise. Specifically, I printed up green and red cards and brought along bags of Hershey Kisses. The green cards said that the security team performed a physical security assessment and found that the desk was secure and then thanked them for that and offered a Hershey's Kiss. The red cards said that we performed a security assessment and found that the desk was insecure; we then asked the user to please secure their desk in the future, for which they might receive a reward during the next assessment. Both cards indicated that there would be future assessments and provided a link to a website explaining the assessment.

I then worked with a team of people to walk around the targeted facilities, and we examined desks to see whether computers were turned off (or at least whether a password-protected screen saver was active), laptops were secured in or to the desk, the physical desktop was clear of sensitive documents, and the desks and associated filing cabinets were locked. If they were properly secured, we dropped a green card and a Hershey's Kiss. If a desk wasn't properly secured, we dropped a red card.

We counted the cards before and after the exercise, which made metrics collection simple. Though you might consider the Hershey's Kiss a reward, the true reward was the acknowledgment as people felt that they passed a test. The fact that users were informed that there would be future assessments kept them on their toes. The future assessments allow for metrics tracking over time.

The one thing to be aware of when implementing this form of gamification, as well as similar efforts, is that even though the referenced website and the red card indicated that we were not tracking users individually, some people did reach out to ensure that they weren't in trouble. I provided language to respond to queries to assure people that we did not track individual desks, and no punishments were associated with this effort. We did, however, informally track which departments seemed especially insecure as a whole and decided to distribute extra posters or other nudges, related to physical security, to those departments.

Tailgating exercises

In performing an initial awareness assessment, I met with the CEO of an airline who, due to a rash of workplace violence incidents in the local area, was especially concerned about unauthorized people entering his headquarters facilities. To address this concern, I put together a tailgating exercise.

As I did for desk drops, which I describe in the preceding section, I printed green and red cards. The green cards thanked people for stopping the person from trying to follow them into the building and had $20 bills taped to them. The red cards informed the recipient that they should have stopped the tailgater, asked them for their badge, and referred the person to the main entrance, if they were a visitor. It also said that they would have been given a financial reward if they had responded appropriately.

One morning during the normal rush hour, I attempted to follow people into secured, employee-only entrances. If a person stopped me, I handed them a green card with the $20 bill. If they did not, I handed them a red card and walked away. I also had accomplices who themselves were performing the tests at different entrances.

Though you might believe this would be an expensive endeavor, the unfortunate reality is that few people stopped me or my accomplices. I expected this result. Likewise, the goal of the gamification effort was to get the people we tested to provide the awareness. We knew going in that we could do it only so many times without people being warned. As expected, people started telling their coworkers about the cards they received.

TIP

The number of cards we distributed at the beginning and the end of the exercise allowed for us to track metrics. We started each exercise with 20 red cards and 20 green cards and then counted the number of each color remaining at the end of the exercise. This allowed us to quickly calculate the percentage of people who stopped us compared to who didn't. If we gave out 7 green cards and 7 red cards, it meant that we were stopped 50 percent of the time. We performed the exercises several times over two months at varying times of day.

USB drop reporting

For USB drop reporting, I commissioned the creation of USB drives to use as part of an assessment. Lately, computers are rarely configured to autorun software, so I required special-purpose USB drives that will cause an executable to run on a computer upon loading. The program provided for tracking of the device and displayed a message that devices should have been reported to the Help desk, and requested people to send them to the Help desk. I then distributed the USB devices around the parking lots, cafeterias, and other common areas.

People who returned the devices per security procedures, without opening them, received a financial reward. The awareness program then promoted the fact that people who did return the devices received a financial reward. You can repeat this exercise on multiple occasions over time.

Reporting security incidents

This activity doesn't involve simulations, but I recommend that you establish a program to reward the reporting of potential security incidents. When you do so, be sure to identify rewards for the reporting of varying levels of potential security concerns.

TECHNICAL STUFF

This effort is primarily an outreach effort to inform people about what the security team should be alerted to, how to be sent an alert, and the potential rewards for doing so. From that point, you can either provide rewards as promised for individual incidents or track the number of reports over time.

This is simple and basic. The focus is getting people to report incidents.

Ad hoc gamification

After putting together awareness programs for years, I've had to deal on frequent occasions with tactical awareness concerns. These are due to incidents the organization suffered, strategic technology plans, or industry trends. For example, if an organization suffered from credential phishing attacks, there's an urgency to implement multifactor authentication. One organization I worked with implemented a Bring Your Own Device (BYOD) policy that led to the need for mobile device security. Sometimes you see industry trends with targeted phishing campaigns and you need to make an emergency awareness campaign of targeted attacks. Gamification is a great strategy for these efforts.

In one investment bank, there were incidents that led to the need to implement multifactor authentication (MFA). The bank could not force the highly paid traders to do anything, so we needed to find an incentive to get the traders to implement MFA on their systems. I created a contest where any trader who had MFA implemented would be entered into a drawing to play golf with the CEO, whom they all revered. The result was a 95 percent MFA adoption rate.

A high-tech organization likewise had a policy that they could not implement mandates. Unfortunately, this meant that the CISO could not force developers to implement security patches on their personal systems. Because it was a noted high-tech company, employees had free food already. They had unlimited time off. Their stock options were valuable enough that even monetary incentives were not impactful. I ended up playing to their pride. Though the CISO could not force the application of patches, the CISO could at least scan the systems. I ended up creating a gamification program that examined the proliferation of fully patched systems. We realized that technical people have a strong sense of pride.

I created a contest to reward the most secure department. We examined the percentage of fully patched systems for each department and created a leader board over the period of a month. We reported weekly on which department was the most secure. Department managers and teams in general did not want to be identified as the least secure, so they exerted peer pressure to encourage their teammates to implement autopatching (where the operating system installs security patches automatically). Almost all departments achieved 100 percent compliance and received a trophy for their efforts.

TECHNICAL STUFF

Business drivers tell you what behaviors should be rewarded, and then understanding the culture tells you how to best influence the users within that culture. You can hold a contest for people who follow your guidance, implement short-term rewards, or do whatever else you think will work. Remember, though, that the rewards must be meaningful for the users.

Putting Together a Gamification Program

If you're going to put together a full-scale gamification program, your goal is to reward a variety of security-related behavior over the course of a year or longer. Gamification efforts are independent of the other awareness program efforts, such as whether you implement your awareness program in quarterly or annual cycles. Gamification can be much more difficult to implement than the traditional programs I describe in previous chapters. The bad side is that it does require more planning and resources; on the good side, however, the continuous nature of the program allows for modifications and improvements as necessary.

Determining reward tiers

Reward *tiers* are the different levels a user can obtain within the scope of the gamification program. For example, frequent flier programs have levels like Basic, Silver, Gold, Platinum, and Diamond. It takes a certain threshold of miles flown and dollars spent with the airline to earn the different status levels. You need to define your own reward tiers.

I like to start by laying out the high-level structure of the program — how many tiers you want to have. The more tiers, the more effort is required by you in the planning and maintenance of the program. At the same time, the more tiers, the easier it is for you to maintain engagement.

TIP

In general, I prefer having five tiers. The reason is that you can make it easy for people to achieve the first tier, and reasonably easy to achieve the second tier, and then the third tier becomes more challenging, which activates people's competitive nature. Basically, you want to create it so that after people achieve a tier, they believe that the next tier, although more difficult to achieve, is within reasonable attainment.

The fourth and fifth tiers are then more challenging to achieve and are there to truly distinguish people who deserve recognition and the more desirable rewards. It isn't expected that everyone achieve, or even want to engage with, these tiers. The tiers are there, however, to encourage strong security behaviors and reward those who make the effort.

Assigning point levels

Now that you have your tiers, you should create a basic point structure to achieve the tiers. You have time to change it before you implement the program, but you need something to work with moving forward.

HOW POKEMON GO DEALS WITH POINTS

Niantic released Pokemon Go in July 2014 and within a year achieved 60 million regular players and more than $1 billion in annual revenue. Fundamentally, Pokemon Go is a simple game: You catch Pokémon. Despite this, the game developers have created engagement by implementing challenges, especially including completing the 40 different base levels. The first 10 levels were relatively easy to obtain. To advance from Level 1 to Level 2, you essentially had to achieve 1,000 points, which is catching 2 Pokémon. To achieve Level 3, you had to earn 2,000 additional points, which is again trivial. You can probably get to Level 12 with minimal effort. However, it grows more difficult as you go along. For example, to go from Level 19 to Level 20 involves earning more points than you needed to get from Level 1 to Level 10. Going from Level 39 to Level 40 involves earning more points than going from Level 1 to Level 34. Generally for the upper levels, you had to earn about 30 percent of the total points in order to reach the next level. You can assume that by that point, however, the players are invested. Over time, enough players earned Level 40 status that Niantic had to create 10 more levels to maintain engagement.

You clearly don't want to implement a point system like Pokemon Go (see the nearby sidebar "How Pokemon Go deals with points"), where you need to earn millions of points, because it would seem difficult, if not unachievable. I generally recommend considering a structure where you have to have a total of 100, 300, 600, 1500, or 3000 points to achieve the respective tiers.

Of course, you have to assign points to tasks that make the point system reasonable. I discuss this topic later in this chapter, in the section "Assigning points to behaviors."

Creating a theme

Salesforce, the major software company, created a security gamification program and used a *Star Wars* theme to name the different levels. The Salesforce CEO is widely known as an avid *Star Wars* fan, which was why this theme was chosen. It provided something for people to distinguish the tiers while recognizing the notoriety of achieving them. *Star Wars* was readily meaningful to the organization, so it was a natural fit.

TIP

Your organization might not have a natural fit, but you can find *something*. You can use a popular movie reference. If you're in the defense or intelligence industry, you can consider military ranks. In the corporate environment, you might consider security associate, security manager, security director, security vice president, or CISO. The security team might not approve, but at least you should see the theme of recognizing a title that represents the difficulty and significance of achieving a given tier.

Offering valid rewards

To have true gamification, you need to provide valid rewards. I've named a few different rewards in passing, but they generally involve certificates, tchotchkes, monetary rewards, executive recognition, or promotion consideration.

At the lower tiers, you generally give a certificate and an inexpensive giveaway. Mouse pads, squishy toys, stickers, and other items are inexpensive and easy to have. If you create a mascot for your awareness program, some version of the mascot can make a great giveaway. If you have a sufficient budget, you can look into more expensive items like T-shirts, other clothing items, and cellphone chargers, among others. Some organizations give away gift cards for Starbucks, Amazon, or other popular vendors.

You might also consider giving away security-related tools. For example, you can give a home license for antimalware, screen filters that prevent people from looking over someone's shoulder to read the screen, cable locks that prevent theft of laptops, and similar items. These things are just practical and reinforcing of security efforts.

TIP

Some organizations have other rewards programs where they let employees and departments give away points that can be used to trade in for different merchandise. If your organization makes use of such reward programs, get points specific for your rewards program. These programs not only provide rewards but also add legitimacy for your program.

At the higher tiers, you should endeavor to get the achievement something that can have a positive impact on promotions and salary increases. If your organization awards days off, cash, and other similar rewards, you want to attempt to allocate those types of rewards for your program. If your organization already has a rewards program, attempt to have a large number of points allocated for the higher tiers.

REMEMBER

What is most important is that the rewards are reasonably desirable to achieve the higher tiers of your program. At the lower tiers, you're generally allocating rewards that are appropriate to encourage someone to spend a minimal amount of effort. Once you get past the bottom two tiers, you should look for rewards that are truly desirable and worthy of those who are investing time in your program. This requires an understanding of your culture.

Assigning points to behaviors

After you have figured out what points people need to achieve different rewards, you need to identify how you will award users those points. If you will require 100 points to achieve the first tier, you need to determine how people can reasonably earn those 100 points.

REMEMBER

Your business drivers should ideally be how you determine those points. What behaviors do you want to reward? What are the simple and basic behaviors you want to reward?

Intuitively, you want people to take your training. You want people to report your phishing messages. You want people to lock their desks. You want people to attend events, read an article, and so on. These are the low-level points.

How long do you want it to take for people to achieve a basic tier? For example, if you want them to do it within two months, you might say that watching a mandatory video is worth 50 points. Reporting a phishing message or basic security violation might likewise be worth 50 points, and people can achieve the first the tier in less than a month. The second tier can be achieved in less than three months.

TIP

Then you consider what stretch activities you might want to reward. Report security incidents. Attend a focus group. Organize a local event. Attend a formal training class. Write a summary of an article to share. Contribute to a security newsletter. You may have other ideas about what is important to your organization.

These activities might be worth 100 or 200 points. It makes achieving the third tier reachable within a reasonable period, when combined with the lower-level activities. It is possible, and even likely, for everyone to achieve the third tier by doing only the basic activities, but it will take a longer period.

At the highest level, you want people to serve as your security ambassadors. You want people to find security vulnerabilities that are critical to your organization. You want people to make a contribution to your organization's security posture. These might be worth 300 to 500 points and make the higher levels achievable over time.

REMEMBER

All these generic recommendations have no specific knowledge of your culture and business drivers. Be creative as possible in how you create your point systems. This takes a thorough understanding of both your culture and its business drivers.

Tracking users and the points they earn

Clearly, you need a system that can track your users and the points they earn. This can be accomplished by using a spreadsheet. You can create a database to track the point structure and allow for retrieval. You may also create a web page that allows users to self-report their activities.

TIP

You can find commercially available gamification tracking software. Gamification is a well-accepted business function, and many companies created software tools to facilitate the implementation of a gamification program. These tools facilitate tracking. They're usually designed for large organizations implementing sales and customer retention programs, and might require a great deal of tailoring to meet your needs. It's also likely that security awareness vendors will begin to implement some form of gamification tracking in the future. A great resource I found for gamification tracking and implementation tools can be found at https://technologyadvice.com/gamification.

Your tracking system may be, ironically, the most complicated aspect of your program to implement. It's something to consider well before you implement your gamification program.

Promoting the Program

It may seem like a major irony, but to implement an awareness gamification program properly and effectively, you need to promote the gamification program. For gamification to work properly, people have to voluntarily engage with the program. They have to know *how* to engage with the program. They have to know the rewards and how to achieve them.

You need to promote the existence and basic structure of the program. You should look to Chapter 7 to look to find the best tools to promote the gamification program.

TIP

I found that the best way to promote a gamification program is to create a website that defines the program as simply as possible. You then promote the website and program via emails and other tools that are appropriate for the culture. I also recommend that, as people earn points in the program, the system sends them emails to inform them of their status and possibly includes tips on how to earn more points. Consider posters, events, and other communications tools, as appropriate, to further promote the program.

Announcing those people who have achieved different tiers, as well as some of those rewards, is possibly one of the most effective methods to promote the gamification efforts. Announcing awardees and their rewards provides social proof that your peers are engaged in the gamification program and that the awards are achievable.

IN THIS CHAPTER

» **Setting goals for your campaigns**

» **Planning the infrastructure**

» **Putting the infrastructure in place**

» **Configuring the simulations**

» **Performing the actual tests**

» **Dealing with those who can't stop clicking**

» **Reporting your results**

Chapter **12**

Running Phishing Simulation Campaigns

This chapter cover the basics of running a phishing simulation. A phishing *simulation* (frequently referred to as an *assessment,* a *test,* or a *campaign*) isn't a mandatory part of a security awareness program, but it is extremely common and is standard for just about all enterprise awareness programs. A phishing simulation is a legitimate component of any awareness program because a phishing attack is the most common type of cybersecurity attack used to target users.

Like all security countermeasures, the goal of phishing simulations is to improve security behaviors to reduce overall risk. The goal isn't perfection.

Knowing Why Phishing Simulations Matter

Safety science shows that if you remove threats completely, people become careless. Allowing incidents, including simulated incidents, keeps users on their toes. Given that spam and phishing filters have become incredibly effective, phishing simulations are the primary method for persuading users to maintain their vigilance.

Most phishing simulations improve security behaviors in limited ways, or at least as far as those that can be measured. These simulations are frequently Check the Box activities because auditors tend to ask for confirmation that phishing simulations are performed as part of an awareness program without discussing the quality of the program. You can go beyond Check the Box, however, and make measurable improvements.

Phishing simulations can help improve overall security awareness and general diligence. In addition to providing just-in-time training, which is the ideal use for these programs, the simulations overcome complacency.

TECHNICAL STUFF

Phishing messages used in simulations are referred to by many names. You might hear them called *lures, emails, messages,* or other terms with similar meanings. They're all valid. Likewise, the term *landing page* has various potential meanings. A *landing page* generally refers to a page where you end up after clicking on a link. The landing page you use for a phishing simulation can serve different purposes. It can lead a user directly to training. Or it might take a user to a fake site where you attempt to see whether they will enter information on a form (and if they do, they then encounter a second landing page).

Keep in mind that phishing simulations aren't real. The results you see in phishing simulations aren't the ones you would see in real-life phishing messages.

For one thing, phishing simulations occur with simulated messages. These messages are the type that are usually blocked by secure email gateways and other filtering software. To perform phishing simulations, you have to *whitelist* (mark as "safe") the sending domains and tune email filters to allow the messages to proceed. In real life, only more sophisticated messages get through the spam filters. The more sophisticated messages, of course, are the messages that are more likely to trick users.

Even so, phishing simulations are helpful (and often required). Your overall goal should be that more users detect and report real messages, which will allow your security team to mitigate the attacks in progress. The next section covers some specific goals you may consider for your phishing simulation.

Setting Goals for Your Phishing Program

If the goal for your program is to Check the Box, you just need to have your chosen vendor implement its default phishing service. Your job will then involve pulling reports from the system and tracking down people who don't complete their required training resulting from the video and phishing campaigns.

In this book, I assume that you want to implement a program that provides a real return on investment and reduces loss. Assuming that this is your mission, you need to set measurable goals for your program.

Checking the box

Even if your intent is to create a phishing program that drives better behaviors, you still likely need to Check the Box. Auditors and regulators frequently require phishing simulations. Even if you want to do more with your program than merely Check the Box, you may have to ensure that your company meets regulatory and compliance requirements.

TECHNICAL STUFF

No specific guidelines exist for checking the box. You can send out easy messages and ensure that anyone who succumbs to the phishing message receives some form of training. No need exists to demonstrate that you improve awareness. You just have to show phishing simulations are sent. If you hire a managed service, you can just show your auditors a report. You probably can get away with sending simulations once a year, but if you want to reduce susceptibility to real phishing attacks, I recommend that you engage in at least quarterly assessments.

If you want to truly reduce phishing susceptibility, you can run as many phishing simulations as you want. Minimal efforts will satisfy an audit requirement. So, if you're running a program designed for effectiveness, you will Check the Box in the process.

Producing easy metrics

One reason that phishing simulations are popular is that they produce easy-to-understand metrics. You send a simulation, and you can tell the results immediately. If you then send a later simulation, usually the number of clicks goes down. Improvement is easy to see and tout to management. Improvement is easy to track.

WARNING

Although the metrics you collect from a phishing simulation are easy to report, they can be misleading. The metrics reveal how people react to messages they don't usually see. If you send a highly sophisticated message, such as a spear-phishing email, which gets a lot of users falling for the message, and then send a basic phishing message on a later campaign, which gets a much lower click rate, it looks like your awareness program is effective, even though that isn't the case. This is manipulating the results, but it makes you look like you're running an effective program.

Benefiting from just-in-time training

Training is most effective when it's relevant. Just-in-time training involves providing training where and when the training is needed. When someone clicks on a phishing message, just-in-time training shows them that they can fall for a phishing message. This outcome increases the relevance of the information and shows people exactly what indicated the message was a phishing message so that they know what to look for in the future.

Differentiating between risky and secure users

It's difficult to know which users present the most and the least risk to the organization without measuring their susceptibility to attacks. By presenting users with an opportunity to demonstrate their level of awareness, you can determine which users are most susceptible to attacks. Though falling for a single phishing attack isn't necessarily an indication of a problem, someone who falls for multiple attacks will likely be a continuing problem.

At the same time, a user who repeatedly reports the phishing messages will likely practice better security in general. You can likely reduce the amount of phishing simulations that person receives. Similarly, the people who constantly click on messages should receive more frequent training.

WARNING

Identifying users who appear to present the most risk can be tricky. Some organizations consider terminating risky employees. For example, if a user who handles PII constantly fails phishing simulations, that user should perhaps be put in another position. Some organizations refuse to track this information because they err on the side of having no discipline for users. How an organization handles disciplining its users is up to the organization, but as an awareness professional, you need to run your program as you plan and cooperate with the appropriate stakeholders.

Planning a Phishing Program

Though phishing simulations can seem like a simple matter of sending mass email messages, it is far from that simple. Besides the technical issues, which are much more complex than just sending emails, you must consider logistical, cross-functional, political, legal, and countless other factors.

Before you implement a phishing campaign, you must define the technical infrastructure and address all nontechnical concerns. As with most efforts, how you address these concerns early on can determine the success or failure of your program.

Identifying the players

Many departments and individuals contribute to the success of a phishing simulation program. Some of these players provide information and other casual support. Others provide critical and ongoing support and can be either your best supporters or your biggest roadblocks in getting things done. If they provide the support, they simplify your efforts. If they don't provide the required support, such as if you don't receive the technical help or timely support you need from different departments, you will have an extremely difficult time being able to execute your campaigns.

Other critical players include, of course, executives and influencers. Executives provide funding and approvals. They can get anyone who is hesitant to work with you to prioritize your efforts. They can get you the access you need. The support of these people is critical.

In addition to the CEO and the chief information security officer (CISO), these departments are examples of stakeholders that may have a significant impact on your program:

» IT

» HR

» Corporate communications

» Physical security

» General counsel and legal

These important players likely influence all areas of your awareness program. Because phishing simulations are a more active form of communications, however, they require more support from teams within the organization.

Obtaining permission and buy-in

Generally, phishing simulations are accepted as a standard part of an awareness program, if not a security program as a whole. In many cases, however, you will encounter hesitance to use phishing simulations. Many of the reasons for reluctance are valid, and you need to consider them. If you anticipate the typical pushback, you can address it proactively.

Here are some common beliefs you have to address:

>> Phishing simulations are a waste of time.

>> Phishing simulations are an unfair gotcha game.

>> Users will feel targeted and betrayed.

>> Simulations create a distrust of the security team.

>> Everyone receives enough email already.

>> Phishing simulations are costly and time consuming.

>> Even if you do the simulations, people still click on phishing messages.

Prepare for these objections. Use the guidance from throughout this book, especially the metrics discussions in Chapter 8, and your own experiences to prepare to counter the objections. The objections are predictable, but be prepared for some questions unique to your environment.

WARNING

People will understandably be concerned about how users feel. You must acknowledge that some users will think phishing simulations are unfair no matter how fairly you design them. Assure your management and other stakeholders that you intend to create realistic simulations based on common attacks.

In an interview during an initial assessment, a manager once told me that they objected to the organization's phishing simulations because they had clicked on a simulation and felt that they were targeted and the test was unfair. I asked why they thought the test was unfair, because everyone received the same messages. The manager had no answer. In further discussions, they admitted that clicking on the phishing simulation made them more careful in the future. This may not seem logical to many, where a person would complain about something yet admit that it helped, but this isn't uncommon and you must be ready to address the situation.

TIP

From the list of stakeholders you identified in the earlier section "Identifying the players," you need to ensure that any one of those people or teams is supportive of, or at least not in a mindset to veto, your phishing campaigns. Typically, corporate communications is critical to your program, and may have to approve each campaign you send. Clearly, you likewise need management approval.

Allocating enough time for phishing simulations

Throughout all your efforts, you must ensure that you plan for how time-consuming phishing simulations can be. Maintaining these simulations involves much more than just sending emails.

TECHNICAL STUFF

You have to accommodate technical considerations of enabling and testing the simulations. There are issues in creating the email themselves and the landing pages, as well as the associated training. You need a tracking mechanism to ensure that users who require extra training receive it. If you implement gamification to reward people who report phishing messages, you need to take the time to implement a tracking and rewards program.

Even if you outsource the program, you must do remaining work to include the compliance aspects of the program. You need to proactively plan for the time required.

Choosing responsive tools

Consider the responsive of the tools you choose for your phishing simulations. *Responsiveness* relates to how Internet content displays across platforms. Websites that don't display well on a mobile phone are an example of poor responsiveness. Ask vendors whether landing pages are displayed properly on mobile devices. Ask whether the email interfaces allow for reporting phishing messages on mobile devices. Make sure you test the phishing tools on your mobile devices as well, before purchasing them.

WARNING

Many people are as likely to check their business email on their mobile devices as they are on their PCs, which means that they may react differently to a message depending on the platform or application they use to access it. For example, the phishing report button that is common on many organizational systems is not present on mobile devices, so users cannot report messages. In addition, mobile devices provide limited ability to review links. So the metrics you collect may be distorted, depending on the devices people use to access the message.

Minimally, you need to ensure that your message (the *phishing lure*) properly displays as well on a mobile device as it would on a PC. Likewise, you need to ensure that the landing pages and any training display properly on mobile devices.

Choosing a Phishing Tool

Phishing simulations can be quite useful, but they can be extremely resource intensive. It isn't just a matter of sending emails and seeing whether people click on links. You have to track the emails, provide training, create metrics, track individuals over multiple campaigns, space out the sending of messages so as not to overwhelm the email servers, create reports, potentially deal with multiple languages, and deal with varying landing pages and training formats.

I admit that I was personally shocked when I saw the price of PhishMe (now Cofense), one of the original phishing simulation tools available for purchase. Now that I have run hundreds of simulations and see how the requirements have become exponentially more complicated, I appreciate the simple brilliance in tools such as Cofense. Phishing simulation tools are a mainstay of awareness programs.

The first decision you have to make is whether you want to implement an in-house solution or use a vendor solution. It can be extremely tempting to save the costs of implementing a vendor solution, which can cost hundreds of thousands of dollars for reasonably large organizations. Implementing an in-house solution has its own costs, however, and will likely not be as comprehensive as most of the available vendor solutions. You need to consider the funds and other resources required to make the appropriate decision.

Creating custom phishing tools

An in-house, or custom, solution basically involves creating a system that creates emails, sends emails, tracks the emails, tracks the users, and facilitates the delivery of training to people who fall for phishing messages. After you create the system, you have to implement and maintain it. Custom solutions work best when you have a large team with substantial development experience as well as the ability to maintain the system.

WARNING

Implementation of a custom solution likely has no comprehensive toolset, so you have to perform a lot of functions manually. For example, you have to create the messages from scratch. You have to create the landing pages from scratch. You have to deal with the languages. You have to create the training from scratch. You have to create the reports from scratch. Again, you need to ensure that you have the skills and resources available to pull it all together.

On the plus side, custom solutions give you total control. For example, you control the branding of the messages sent out and the training you provide. On the downside, creating and implementing custom solutions involves more work than is obvious, and it's difficult to create a system that is as robust as what you can otherwise license.

If you decide to pursue a custom solution, you can use a couple of tools:

>> **The Social Engineering Toolkit (SET)** provides a phishing capability. SET, which is a freeware tool provided as a courtesy from TrustedSec, is available for download from `www.trustedsec.com/tools/the-social-engineer-toolkit-set`. SET is generally best for creating spear-phishing simulations versus phishing an entire company.

>> **Gophish** is a freeware tool designed for organizational phishing simulations. This tool is more user-friendly and provides more functionality than SET. You can download Gophish from `https://getgophish.com`.

If you want to work with SEC, Gophish, or a similar tool, be sure that you have technical knowhow. I once worked with someone who advised a company that it could use SET rather than acquire a commercial phishing solution. Company leaders purchased a PC to run SET. Then when the PC arrived, the advisor decided that they would implement it. When they downloaded SET, they realized it had to run on a Linux system. The person was unfamiliar with Linux and had to advise the organization that it was better to just get a commercial service. Be aware that these tools can be more effort to install and maintain than may be obvious.

Running your own phishing simulations with your own resources would seem to be the least expensive option. You also have full control over branding and just about all aspects of the phishing simulations. It is critical, however, to reiterate that it isn't as simple as it would appear. You likely won't have the tools and capabilities that a vendor would provide you. Additionally, the effort required to create a workable system is likely more costly than hiring a vendor. In general, you should consider something like this only if you have a large team with substantial development experience.

Choosing vendor options

Assuming that you are considering using a vendor or have made the decision and want to choose a vendor, there are a variety of considerations. Though many vendors are out there and you would think that they're all the same, there is a great variety in costs and capabilities offered. You should ideally look at what is available and choose the optimum balance between price and capability. The rest of this section provides considerations for choosing the vendors.

Knowing which options are available

Your organization may already have chosen a vendor that offers phishing simulation services. You may have acquired its computer-based training (CBT) service and the vendor provides phishing simulations as well. Some vendors that provide secure email gateways and data leak prevention also offer phishing simulation services, and they offer that as a benefit as well. So the capability is available for free for all practical purposes. If this is the case, it's significantly more convenient to continue to use that vendor as opposed to choosing another one specifically for phishing services.

Separating CBT and phishing vendors

WARNING

Most of the vendors in the awareness space offer both CBT and phishing. Frequently, these vendors started by offering either CBT or phishing and then added the other service later because they were losing business. This frequently means that one service is strong and the other is weak. Rarely is a vendor strong in both services.

Likewise, some vendors offer only one service or the other. Though it may be a difficult choice, consider whether the best solution is getting one vendor for phishing and another for CBT. Going with vendors who specialize can enable you to implement a best-of-breed approach. Doing so may be more expensive, but it can be worth the expense, especially if a vendor is strong in one service you need and weak in another that you also need.

Matching vendor features to your needs

Phishing simulation providers offer a wide range of features. You must determine which of these features best suit your needs. Some features sound great but have limited applicability.

If a vendor offers training and phishing capabilities in 50 languages, for example, and you need only a single language, there's no advantage to a vendor with 50 languages. If you do need those languages, however, you then must consider the quality of the lures and templates the vendor provides, because they may be extremely limited. Look into vendor claims to be sure that their features will benefit your program.

When choosing phishing vendors, you must assess how well the features they offer apply to your program. Be detailed in your assessments, and look into any grandiose claims made by vendors regarding effectiveness, quality, or other factors.

Here are some examples of the features you might consider:

>> Ease of sending messages

>> Importing Active Directory lists

>> Email lure templates

- » Languages offered, with depth of the languages that you need
- » Landing page templates
- » Training material offered
- » Integration of outside training
- » Variety of metrics collected
- » Reporting capabilities and templates
- » User tracking over time
- » Phishing reporting button integration
- » Integration with CBT and other training
- » Managed services offerings

You may have other requirements, such as interoperability with software and systems. Be sure to list your concerns when choosing a vendor.

Identifying features that can cause problems

Many features are useful, but some features you need to look for may cause concerns. Some phishing vendors, for example, include their own email addresses in the Sender fields. Even if a message is otherwise sophisticated and difficult to spot, if users realize that the sender has the phishing company's email domain in the sender field, they know right away that the message is part of a phishing simulation.

WARNING

Having a phishing reporting button is useful, but if clicking the button forwards the message to the phishing service provider for analysis, it could create a violation of a variety of data protection laws and be considered a reportable event. For example, if a user reports an email message that contains PII, the PII is sent to the service provider, who isn't an authorized recipient, likely creating a HIPAA or GDPR violation.

WARNING

Some vendors also like to tout how they think like hackers and sometimes de-weaponize actual phishing email messages. These sound like great features, but things can go wrong. One vendor became infamous for sending out messages that were unethical. For example, one message asked people to click on a link to register for COVID-19 shots. Another asked people to click on a link to confirm their Christmas bonus. You can argue that a real-life criminal would not hesitate to use these tactics, but these messages spurred a major backlash among employees and the buying public. A GoDaddy employee publicly complained about receiving such a phishing simulation, and people on the Internet started talking about boycotting the company. Remember that just because you *can* do something doesn't mean you *should*.

Hiring managed services

Even when you use a phishing simulation service, running phishing campaigns is extremely complicated and time consuming. Some companies provide phishing as a *managed service,* which means that they fully manage the service for you. They choose the lures, schedule and launch the campaigns, create the landing pages, and provide reports. They may provide the opportunity for you to have input into the process. They can also just provide you with the ability to look at reporting and you won't have to do anything else.

Integrating machine learning

Perhaps one of the more exciting developments in the phishing simulation market is the ability to integrate machine learning into services. Some vendors, such as HoxHunt, implemented machine learning to allow for phishing messages to be targeted to individuals via the organization as a whole. They essentially send out low sophistication to all users. People who don't fall for those messages then receive more sophisticated phishing messages. The process continues and everyone gets messages that are appropriate for their awareness level. Additionally, those people who have a higher level of awareness receive fewer messages.

This ability allows for learning to be tailored to the individual and is constantly challenging users at a level appropriate for themselves. The technology is relatively new, and it will be interesting to see how it is developed and proliferates over time.

Implementing a Phishing Simulation Program

Whether you chose a vendor or decide that you can use internal resources to facilitate phishing simulations, you then have to begin the implementation, and the steps are common. Even if your vendor will handle the implementation for you, you should at least be familiar with the steps required in the implementation. This way, you know what to expect and can more easily facilitate the effort.

Integrating Active Directory

To send out phishing messages, you need to have the email addresses of where they should be sent. Typically, most organizations have the email addresses stored in Active Directory (AD), which is essentially the enabler for all computers and users on most networks used in industry. Not only does AD have all of an organization's email addresses, it usually has the department, geography, preferred language, and other information associated with the user. All this information is intuitively obvious in assisting with not just the personalization of the phishing messages but also in the reporting.

TECHNICAL STUFF

Some phishing simulation systems require that you input a CSV (comma separated values) formatted file. For those, you can generally pull the information from AD and upload the CSV file into the phishing system. Ideally, the phishing system integrates directly with AD, and the system is constantly updated and better able to track user responses over time.

If the system isn't integrated with AD, you will have to pull the information from AD and regularly update the phishing simulation to account for users leaving, joining, or moving around within the organization.

Working with subcultures and geographies

As with other aspects of an awareness program, your phishing simulations program will be received across your organization's subcultures. (For information about how subcultures affect other aspects of an awareness program, see Chapter 5.) You need to ensure that you account for that. For example, phishing messages sent to users in the United States, such as tax form scam simulations, will be out of context in China. Messages relevant to the accounting department will rarely be relevant to factory workers.

TIP

Consider implementing different phishing campaigns for different subcultures. Each subculture should have relevant phishing messages, in the language appropriate for the subculture. Tailoring your program requires more work, but if you cannot put in the effort, you should reconsider the overall scope of your simulation efforts because your efforts will otherwise have limited effectiveness. For example, users won't even get to the point of considering whether a message is a phishing message if they don't understand the language used in the message.

Choosing languages

When you send out phishing messages, you need to consider how users would normally receive the messages in context, with special regard to the language. Clearly, if there is only the use of a non-English language and you send the message in English, which I have seen done, you're wasting your time.

I have worked with some companies where English is the business language used throughout the world. In that case, if you send messages that have a personal pretext, and send it in English, it won't be readily accepted. On the other hand, if you send a message to non-English language locations and the business language is English and you use a business pretext in the local language, it will be received skeptically. If you're going to make the effort to send out messages in a worldwide organization, you need to account for the languages used in context.

WARNING

Different dialects exist for a given language. Even American English differs from British English. For example, behavior is spelled *behaviour* in the UK. Differences exist between Spanish used in Latin American countries and Spanish used in Spain. Similarly, there are difference between Portuguese in Brazil and Portugal. I know of one phishing campaign that was created for Latin America but used a translator who used European Spanish, and it failed miserably.

Registering phishing domains

Some vendors send email messages from their corporate email systems, which can be a clear giveaway to users that a message is part of a simulation. The solution is to acquire domains that you can use specifically for your campaigns. Your organization may have already acquired spoofed domains as a proactive security countermeasure. For example, I acquired the domain SecureMentum.com to proactively address a likely misspelling for SecureMentem.com. The spoofed domains may be available for you to use in your simulations.

You can also acquire random domains that fit the context of an email message. If you're using a phishing provider, it likely has several domains it already uses.

Defining program goals

Frequently, when I ask awareness managers about the specific goals of their phishing program, they cannot articulate any. In essence, they're doing a phishing simulation either because they have to or it's just something they do because they think all awareness programs do it.

TECHNICAL STUFF

I highlight the importance of metrics throughout this book. Phishing simulations are no different. You should have specific metrics and goals for the metrics. For example, you may want to say that you want malware incidents to decrease by 50 percent, phishing reporting to increase by 100 percent, and so on. These are goals. You can also state simply that you want to meet compliance requirements. These are all legitimate goals to include. Avoid just saying you're doing phishing simulations "because everyone does it."

Collecting Day 0 metrics

As with all awareness efforts, remember to take Day 0 metrics so that you can prove the value of your efforts. Phishing simulations are one of the most reliable ways to generate positive, even if specious, metrics for awareness efforts.

REMEMBER

There are special considerations in collecting Day 0 metrics regarding phishing. To best do this, you don't want to provide training if people fall for the message pretext. For example, if the message intends to get people to click on a link, you should receive a report that the link was clicked. Clicking the link should return a generic error message that says something like this: "Site not found." The user should not know that they were part of a test; otherwise, they may be tempted to tell their coworkers about the phishing campaign in progress.

TIP

Collect metrics that indicate phishing awareness, regardless of whether the metrics have anything to do with the overall simulation. For example, you might want to collect statistics on the number of malware incidents the organization experiences, reports of phishing messages, reports of near misses such as DLP preventing the exfiltration of credentials, and any other possible metrics available to you.

Running a Phishing Simulation

Running a phishing simulation is much more complicated than simply sending email messages. The following sections describe the process for implementing a phishing campaign.

TIP

I recommend reading the entire chapter before launching your first campaigns, as some sections, such as "Tracking Metrics and Identifying Trends," toward the end of this chapter, provide information you must consider when you plan a phishing simulation.

Determining the targets

Though many people assume that all users are the target (the intended recipients of phishing simulations), that isn't always the case. As I describe in the earlier section "Working with subcultures and geographies," consider dividing your campaigns into different subcultures. You may want to avoid some geographies for a variety of reasons, such as not being able to create an appropriate context or language support use. You may determine that you want to avoid factory workers who lack access to work computers, because it's not worth the effort.

TIP

You can choose to target everyone, which is the default, even though the messages won't be relevant to many of the targets. You can choose to send different messages to different subcultures. You can choose just to target certain individuals with different spear-phishing simulations. It's up to you.

Before you proceed, you need to clearly identify the targets before planning the other aspects of the test.

Preparing the lures

Now that you know the targets, you can begin to figure out the pretexts you want to use to hook your targets. In a traditional campaign, you will generally want to construct one lure, or phishing email, for any culture you target. You want to construct the lures wisely.

You have a variety of issues to consider in the construction of the lures. Vendors typically provide more than 100 lures of differing types. They can provide a firm basis for starting. You still have some customization to perform, such as perhaps using your own logos.

Determining the sophistication of the test

Before you determine the actual lure to use, you want to determine the sophistication of the test you want to run. Though there is a continuum, I generally break it down to these three categories:

>> **Low sophistication:** Generic attacks that have no context or personalization. These tests are akin to telling people to click a message to see the status of a shipping package. They might just contain nonsense. Either way, they're generally easy to detect, and few people should fall for them.

>> **Medium sophistication:** Messages that have some context relevant to the user. For example, in the United States toward the end of the year, it's open season for choosing a health plan. A medium sophistication message would use that event to attempt to trick people into visiting a third-party site and entering their credentials. There could be a possible attack around a commonly known corporate event.

>> **High sophistication:** Generally spear-phishing messages targeted to individual users or small groups of people. This would be similar to sending a message to people within a specific division, such as human resources, and asking them to provide PII information related to the healthcare open season.

You need to choose the sophistication you want to use to target the users. Though low sophistication messages may attempt to bring everyone to a common baseline, if you only use them, there will be little improvement in overall awareness. Higher sophistication messages may result in higher counts; however, there is more likelihood that the overall security posture of the organization will increase. It also demonstrates that the users can become a victim to an attack.

CONSIDERING PHISHING SERVICE PROVIDERS

Some phishing service providers automatically send random messages from a library of messages to different people. These messages are usually pretty basic. After you provide email addresses, it randomly sends emails on some set schedule. If a person falls for a simulation, the system increases the frequency of messages. It seems like a reasonable strategy, but it provides only basic training. This basic training differs from that offered by companies that use machine learning capability to progressively increase the sophistication of the training.

REMEMBER

Most phishing simulations would never make it into an organization because of the filters most organizations have in place. Medium and high sophistication messages are more likely to be similar to real attacks that make it through the email filters. Even though click rates will be higher, you should definitely consider higher sophistication messages.

Constructing the lures

Once you have proactively determined the targeted sophistication(s), you can begin to construct the lures. In general, these are the elements you need to consciously determine for each lure:

>> Pretext

>> Sender

>> Email address

>> Intended action you're trying to solicit

>> Content including URL or attachments

>> Intentional errors injected into the message

You determine each of those elements with the intended sophistication in mind. If you want to have a low sophistication message, for example, you make it easy to determine that the sender is illegitimate. You hide the email address. You add typos and use bad grammar.

TECHNICAL STUFF

Phishing simulation messages solicit actions that reflect the primary tactics attackers use, as follows:

>> Get a user to download malware.

>> Send a user to a website to get them to disclose their credentials.

>> Solicit the user to send sensitive information.

You have to determine the attack you want to simulate and construct lures accordingly.

Finding lure ideas

TIP

If you want to create timely lures, there are a variety of potential sources. Criminals have their sources, and you can find inspiration from them. Current events are a big source. I already mentioned COVID-19 attacks. Whenever you see stories about compromised social media sites, criminals send phishing messages trying to trick people into visiting a fake site to attempt to change their passwords. If a big story hits the news, you can expect it may be used as a phishing pretext.

COOKING THE BOOKS

The term *cooking the books* is an intelligence term that refers to tailoring information presented to decision-makers in a way that leads them to make the decision you want them to make, or otherwise intentionally presenting information to lead people to making the conclusion you want them to make. With regard to phishing simulations, you can use sophistication to intentionally show that simulations change behaviors.

For example, if I perform a Day 0 simulation using a sophisticated phishing lure, I know that many people will fall for the attack. If my following simulations use low sophistication lures, the click rate will go down. This result is inevitable. So if I send a message that says people should go to a website to confirm their healthcare plans during healthcare open season, many people will fall for it. If I follow that message up a month later with a message filled with typos that asks people to click on a link to confirm their extended warranty on a Saturn automobile, few people would click on that. The click rate goes down drastically, and the phishing program appears to be a massive success. Some people do this intentionally. Other awareness managers have increased phishing sophistication without consideration of how it impacts their statistics, and then believe that they have a problem they don't have.

There may be industry-related issues to take advantage of. For example, when the SolarWinds Orion hack was announced, criminals would send phishing messages to technical employees trying to trick them into going to websites for information. This also happened with the Microsoft Exchange Server vulnerability and resulting hacks.

Seasonal attacks are also common. Sending fake messages spoofing shopping sites is common around the Christmas season. Similar attacks take place around tax season. Then there are scams related to summer travel. Again, you can anticipate these attacks and use them as potential fodder for your own simulations.

You can also potentially gather intelligence from organizations within your industry and use your internal threat intelligence team to find out which types of attacks similar organizations are having and what you should expect. You can then use those attacks in your simulation campaigns to proactively train people for the likely attacks.

Some phishing simulation vendors also provide secure email gateway servers and/ or phishing mitigation services. This allows them to see incoming attacks. They then de-weaponize the phishing messages and allow you to use them in your simulations. This allows you to see what might have happened if the messages made it through the filters. It also trains your users in case the attackers send the attacks to them via their personal accounts, which may not have filtering that is as effective as your organization's.

Adhering to ethical considerations

Criminals aren't bound to adhere to ethical standards. Many criminals know that emotionally triggering a person is the best way to trick them into taking an action, so they attempt attacks that target the emotions. So you may believe that anything a criminal would do is fair game for you.

Factors such as personnel issues, like raises or bonuses, trigger emotions. The pandemic triggers emotions. Potential threats to families trigger emotions. Criminals use this triggering to design their own attacks. Some people in the cybersecurity field argue that if criminals will do it, so should you.

I frequently perform penetration tests that simulate attacks. Criminals have kidnapped people to gain access to facilities. Does that mean I should kidnap people as well? Clearly not. I have to function within legal and ethical bounds that criminals will not themselves honor. It's the same thing for phishing simulations.

I was once brought in by an organization that was hired to infiltrate nuclear facilities. They asked me how I would get malware into the organization and on the targeted systems. I had the email addresses for the targeted individuals from a public user group. I said I would send a spear-phishing message that gets the targets to go to a website that would download and install malware on the targets' PCs. I was told that the organization mentioned that we would never be able to get in, so we could try anything. I asked, "Really? Anything?" The answer was, "Yes, anything." I then created a lure that looked like it was from the company HR department and said that benefits would be cut. I again verified that the company leaders were okay with this message. I warned them again. The message was sent to 20 people. However, 2,000 people clicked on the link. As I warned them, the message generated outrage, and the 20 people shared the message with coworkers, who themselves shared the message, and so on. I was against this strategy, but this is what they wanted and it had both the success and the negative pushback I expected.

WARNING

Though you may find some areas of ambiguity, getting people's hopes up to believe that they're receiving a large raise or bonus is unfair and messes with their emotions. It can even cause a rift within the organization. I have received complaints about organizations that do it. As I mention throughout this book, GoDaddy and other organizations suffered calls to boycott them because of such tactics.

TIP

If you're ever tempted to send an ethically ambiguous phishing simulation, just send out a "security alert" message instead. Send out a message that specifically warns your users that criminals are actively engaging in that type of phishing campaign. There is no reason to trick people, and also consider that if someone doesn't fall for your simulation, they will never receive the message. Not only do you not have to worry about being unethical, but warning users about a specific, active threat also gives them the impression that the awareness program is timely and relevant.

Creating landing pages

A *landing page* (the place where a link in a phishing message sends a user) can be used to inform an individual that they fell for a phishing simulation and tell them how they can perform more securely in the future. The landing page can also be used as an intermediate step to attempt to collect information and other credentials, or to provide a way to download malware.

If you're trying to collect information, such as by simulating a login page, you need to make the page look believable. That is, the page should look believable enough for the level of sophistication you're targeting. You may want it to look exactly like the login page, for example, or you may want typos.

Your landing page can also be a Google Drive or similar page because that's frequently how criminals attempt to bypass malware filters, by putting it on Drive and having the user download a file from there so that it isn't blocked by email filters. Again, you should make the sophistication of such pages match the level of sophistication you're targeting.

If the landing page is intended to inform users that they fell for an attack, you need to provide basic information. First, you need to inform them that they're on the page because they fell for a phishing message. That should be immediately followed by reassurance that they won't be punished for it.

The page should then describe in detail how the user should have been able to detect the phishing message they fell for. It should highlight what indicators were in the message. This page should be *responsive* — that is, able to properly display on different types of platforms and be relevant for the format of the message that "tricked" them. For more about the importance of responsiveness, refer to the earlier section "Choosing responsive tools."

Though you might just want to provide a CBT module on phishing in general, it does limited good without having specific references to the phishing message provided.

Addressing logistical concerns

Earlier in this chapter, in the section "Planning a Phishing Program," I discuss the high-level logistics of planning a phishing simulation program. The following sections cover specific technical concerns to consider before you run a phishing simulation.

Coordinating whitelisting and working around spam filters

Organizations expect phishing attacks, and they put filters in place to prevent the attacks from reaching their users. This a fundamental security practice. As I mention throughout this chapter, your phishing attacks would rarely make it through the filters. You therefore need to ensure that you work with the person who maintains the filters to ensure that your messages are whitelisted so that they get through the spam filters and function properly.

Adding gamification

If you're implementing a gamification program as part of your awareness program, you need to ensure that you have the appropriate tracking capability in place. Likewise, you need to make sure that if you give out rewards, you have the capability to readily distribute the rewards.

If you want to reward people for reporting the phishing messages, for example, you need to test that the reporting mechanisms are working and that you have the people in place to monitor the reporting and distribute the rewards.

For more details about implementing gamification, see Chapter 11.

Determining phishing frequency

When you plan your phishing assessments, you want to proactively determine how frequently you want to launch your campaigns. Theoretically, if there are compliance concerns, you can do it once a year. If you want to actually increase phishing awareness, however, you have to do it more frequently.

The expected periods for phishing simulations are monthly or quarterly. Any more than monthly and it's usually perceived as annoying or insulting to the users. Less frequently than quarterly won't have any possible consistent improvement in awareness.

You need to find the right balance. Part of that balance includes the resources you have available. If you don't have the people or time to perform the simulations monthly, you can't. If you can't monitor the reports, even if you have a vendor doing the actual phishing, you likely should limit the simulations. Whatever you determine, ensure that you do it properly.

Scheduling the tests

Assuming that you determined how frequently you want to run the tests, you need to then schedule the actual tests. I am specifically referring to the days and times that you intend to send the messages.

Most vendor tools allow you schedule sending windows. You can specify how many messages you want to send per hour so that you don't overload your servers. You can specify weekdays and time windows. This can have a significant impact on how many people will look at your messages to even consider acting on them.

One study found that people were more likely to open phishing messages if they were sent midweek, such as Tuesday through Thursday, during working hours. The researchers hypothesized that people had backlogged emails on Monday and were rushed on Friday, so they had less incentive to look at any questionable emails on those days. Likewise, if messages were sent during off-hours, the messages would appear in crowded email boxes the next morning and could be overlooked by users.

Considering this information, you need to make the best decision for your organization. This may even include different strategies for different subcultures. You may want to experiment with different times over different campaigns to see what works for you.

Anticipating user responses

Depending on the nature of the lures, you will draw differing emotional reactions. The greater the emotional trigger, the more likelihood of extreme responses. Even if there is a relatively benign message, you will find that some people will feel unfairly targeted if they fall for a phishing message. It's just human nature.

WARNING

To account for this, you should let your managers know what to expect and how to address the concerns. People who may be approached with user concerns should be informed that feedback is expected and that you have anticipated the likely concerns. The worst thing that can happen is that there are complaints and they are unexpected by influential managers.

Alerting the appropriate parties

Besides informing your management, you should alert anyone who may be contacted or asked to respond to potential incidents. Though you don't have to provide details, you should inform the appropriate stakeholders whom you've previously identified about the pending test.

WARNING

Be sure to alert any people responsible for responding to a potential incident that you're running a phishing simulation. You do not want to have your Help desk or incident response team treat the simulation as a real phishing attack.

Conducting a pilot test

Before you begin a full phishing campaign, you should test it out and send the messages to a test group. Be sure that the test group is aware that you're conducting a phishing test and that you have instructed them to fully test the messages. They should click on links, download files, enter data in forms, and so on. The purpose is to fully test the functionality. Ideally, the test team includes people from all geographies where the emails will be sent.

TECHNICAL STUFF

Using a test group that includes people from all geographies where the email will be sent addresses a variety of concerns. It ensures that the message will make it through email filters in all regions. It also ensures that all parts of the test appear properly and function as required. Different regions of the world have different technical controls, and you want to make sure that none of those controls impacts your simulation.

Ideally, you should be testing the messages on different types of end user systems to ensure that the responsiveness is implemented correctly. It's also important to run a pilot test for all campaigns. You never know if there were technological changes since the last test.

Tracking Metrics and Identifying Trends

When you run your phishing tests, I would contend that the most important aspect is the results, or *metrics*. I am not talking about the metrics of how many people fell for a given phishing message, but rather the overall state of awareness and improvement over time. Again, you have to show that you deserve more.

That being said, you have to collect metrics for each campaign individually. You can then track the trend in metrics over time. In addition, you should look to track metrics across the different geographies, business units, or other definable entities within your organization. This way, you can more accurately determine where you have potential weaknesses and strengths.

These are the basic metrics you can collect during an individual test:

>> No interaction

>> Message deletion

>> Opening of the message

>> Falling for the message's intent

>> Reporting of the message to the appropriate parties

Remember to consider that users may not be able to report messages from all platforms, such as mobile devices, so the "reporting of messages" is an unreliable metric. However, you should see trends.

TIP

An interesting metric to collect is the time users take to open the message after you send it. This gives you an idea of how long you will have to respond to an actual attack in progress. This metric should aid your phishing defense strategies.

In Chapter 8, I recommended that you collect metrics that can imply phishing awareness, such as the number of malware incidents. You need to track these types of metrics over time as well so that you can show an actual return on investment. Phishing simulations aren't an accurate representation of real phishing susceptibility. If you can show that actual incidents and their related losses are going down as well, you can imply the worth of your tests.

Dealing with Repeat Offenders

If a user falls for a simulation, you should add them to a list of people who need to be tested more frequently. For example, if someone failed a monthly test, you should retest them two weeks later to reinforce the learning. If they don't fall for the follow-up message, you can move them back to the regular testing schedule. If they continue to fail phishing simulations, you need to determine the appropriate actions to take.

One of the most controversial topics in cybersecurity is how to address people who fall for phishing simulations. They're a serious concern because, if they will fall for a low sophistication attack, they will fall for a real, targeted attack.

Consider what would happen if an employee was shown to make consistently bad work-related financial decisions, or otherwise could not execute normal business functions. They would inevitably be fired. Why is it different with cybersecurity?

REMEMBER

How these repeat offenders are dealt with depends largely on the culture of the organization. Earlier in this book, I tell how someone who works at a large investment bank explained that if you fall for one phishing message, you have to take training. If you fall for two phishing messages, you have to talk to the cybersecurity manager. If you fall for three phishing messages, you can be fired. The person understood why falling for phishing messages potentially represents fines or losses in excess of $100 million, so they now understand why that policy is in place and they accept it.

The reality is that few people consistently fail the phishing simulations, so the people who are at risk are relatively few.

WARNING

A repeat offender is both an outlier and a potentially significant risk to your organization. I recommend that you identify the repeat offenders if you're asked. If portrayed in the wrong context, these users imply that your phishing simulation program has limited benefit. You should, however, be able to demonstrate consistent reduction of phishing susceptibility among your organization as a whole. You need to be prepared to control the narrative and highlight your efforts as a security professional who delivers risk reduction.

Management Reporting

I want to highlight the importance of showing value in what is one of the most noticeable aspects of your awareness program. A phishing simulation is an active awareness tool and will not go unnoticed. A few people will complain about "being tricked." This is inevitable. You therefore need to be proactive in promoting the impact you're having.

Your goal is to deserve more. You therefore need to represent your metrics in the best possible light. Chapter 10 provides a detailed discussion of metrics and reporting, and you should work to incorporate your metrics into the management reports. You should present the metrics in a way that is clear and shows the appropriate benefit.

If you intend to present dashboards, as Chapter 10 discusses, you can summarize the results and trends of your phishing simulations. Ideally, they should be presented in a way that shows improvements. If you aren't summarizing phishing simulations in other reports, I recommend that you create a summary report to distribute to your management and others, as appropriate.

4

The Part of Tens

Chapter **13**

Ten Ways to Win Support for Your Awareness Program

I have seen dozens of ways that security awareness managers have attempted to win support for their programs; some of their ideas were more successful than others. Some security managers adopt guiding principles. Others take a more prescriptive approach. In this chapter, I describe the ten ways I find most effective for attracting the buy-in you need to launch an awareness program in an organization.

Finding Yourself a Champion

As I discuss in Chapter 7, security ambassadors, or *champions*, are users within your organization who serve as your outreach to other users local to them. You also ideally should find a management champion. This champion should have influence over executives and be willing to champion your efforts.

A management champion should have the influence needed to help garner extra resources, draw support from management as you establish when to roll out your efforts, and gain access to critical interviews (interviews with stakeholders, business owners, and other people whose buy-in and support are critical for the success of your program). Many people trivialize awareness efforts for a variety of reasons and personal biases; a management champion can help defuse these attitudes.

WARNING

You can run into a problem if a management champion has their own biases. I've worked with many people who said they supported awareness, and they actually did believe awareness could be a valuable tactic for an overall security program. Unfortunately, although they were willing to support the principles on which they thought an awareness program should be based, they hesitated to help beyond their biased understanding. In one case, I wanted to provide budgets for social engineering assessments, but the champion believed phishing was a form of social engineering, so there was no reason for other forms of social engineering tests. The person refused to approve funding for other forms of tests and metrics collection efforts. I tried to reason with them, but was in no position to either argue or alienate them, because the person was otherwise helpful.

Setting the Right Expectations

As I describe in Chapter 2, awareness programs often set themselves up for failure by proclaiming ludicrous expectations. The industry is filled with catchphrases like "the human firewall." Nobody believes a viable human firewall exists. Even if they do believe it, that human firewall will eventually fail. At that point, your efforts, and likely you, lose all credibility.

TIP

In my experience, most organizations have people within their management structure and security teams who believe security awareness is a wasted effort. This is why setting reasonable expectations is important — you can't afford to undercut your program's credibility by setting unrealistic expectations with people who already doubt its value. Though this is a common theme in this chapter, you must describe a reasonable return on your investment. You should have a few goals that seem reasonable and achievable, and provide value back to your organization. If you provide Pollyanna expectations, you won't be taken seriously, and if someone actually believes you, you lose the credibility at the inevitable incident.

Addressing Business Concerns

Setting the right expectations involves a combination of tasks you can achieve in a way that aligns to the business drivers of the organization. You therefore need to highlight how the objectives of your awareness program will improve the organization in a way that is meaningful to the organization. You then need to present your intended business benefits in a way that resonates with the organization and its leaders. Ideally, it also resonates with the average user.

TIP

Incorporate metrics into your efforts and into your reporting so that management can fully understand and support your efforts should questions arise about resources and requests of time on the part of management and other users.

Creating an Executive Program

Chapter 10 discusses awareness programs focused on executives. Putting special efforts toward a small group of people might seem like a waste of limited resources, but executives are among the most targeted people of an organization. More important for the purposes of this chapter, if you put together an effective and engaging program for executives, it will likely generate goodwill on the part of executives and increase their support for your efforts. You may even earn a budget increase for your efforts.

As many chapters discuss, you should have a special focus on topics of special interest to executives. This focus should include security issues related to their families. From a practical standpoint, the families of executives are potential targets because they have ready access to sensitive information. From an intangible standpoint, executives may appreciate the attention and value provided to their loved ones.

WARNING

If you choose to implement an executive-focused program, you must ensure the quality of the program. You cannot provide cartoons. You need to be engaging, but you can't be cheesy. If you're unable to create a quality program, you should probably avoid an executive program altogether rather than risk harming your efforts.

Starting Small and Simple

Before you launch an organization-wide program that implements what could be too many communications tools at a time, consider starting off with a smaller part of the organization. This way, you can reduce the number of variables you have to manage.

You may also want to restrict at first which communications tools you implement. For example, you may want to avoid rolling out your program in multiple languages around the world until you establish that you can handle a single language in a given geographical region. As another example, if you cannot roll out posters effectively, you will have greater difficulty rolling out table tents or desk drops (detailed in Chapter 7).

WARNING

You will encounter issues with distribution. You will experience delays in receiving responses from critical people. You may find that your translation services are unable to handle all the dialects you need. I once had to deal with a vendor who produced materials in Spanish. Unfortunately, the vendor produced translations for European Spanish and not South American Spanish, which of course was the one I needed.

REMEMBER

Start with a reasonable program and avoid being overly ambitious too soon.

Finding a Problem to Solve

If you want to garner early support, find a problem that is a priority for your organization and figure out how to address it. In one case, an organization I was working with was moving out of one headquarters building and into another. Moving security became a top concern. I put together a program that focused on securing a PC before a move, ensuring that employees left no sensitive information behind, and so on. It was relevant to corporate priorities, and it was one of the top priorities of the organization.

Another organization was going to begin implementing a bring-your-own-device (BYOD) program that institutionalized the use of personal cellphones for business use. Clearly, the security team wanted to ensure that users knew how to secure their devices and keep them safe. This naturally led to the creation of a mobile device/BYOD security awareness program.

You might not have opportunities that are as timely, but you should strive to find problems where awareness can help solve a business problem.

Establishing Credibility

Before many people will deem your efforts worthy of supporting, you may have to prove yourself. An inherent bias against security awareness is frequently in place because of the failure of past efforts, so you may face an uphill battle to win support.

TIP

The best way I have found to handle this issue is to find situations where you can prove that you have improved a situation. If you were able to help with a specific problem, promote how you helped. If you can find metrics that show your efforts helped to decrease losses or improve operational efficiency, promote that. Put out announcements and success stories. If possible, have management share or announce those successes.

Highlighting Actual Incidents

Though you usually want to avoid the FUD factor (*f*ear, *u*ncertainty, and *d*oubt), you can benefit by highlighting incidents where awareness failings led to significant losses. If you have had incidents within your own organization, you should ideally share those stories with the users. It allows people to understand the reason for your efforts.

TECHNICAL STUFF

If you have no incidents within your organization, you can find more than enough within your industry. If all else fails, you can point to stories of major breaches almost weekly. As I write this chapter, for example, the current major data breach is SITA, which is a company that is involved with airline reservations. You might be tempted to assume that this breach has limited impact, but many people reuse the password they use for airline reservations or their frequent flier program on their organizational and other accounts. This incident presents an opportunity to address password reuse.

Being Responsive

Though you may start out looking for a problem to solve, constantly finding business problems to solve should become engrained within your whole program. You should always be looking for timely issues and problems. You need to be looking to internal issues. You need to be watching news and pop culture to see what people are talking about in their outside lives.

By paying attention to external forces, you can keep the program timely and relevant, to not just work lives but also personal lives. This makes it more likely that people will embrace the behaviors you espouse as important, and improve their security behaviors.

TECHNICAL STUFF

Implementing your program in quarterly cycles allows for easier incorporation of timely topics. It allows for a natural transition of topics and doesn't disrupt long-term plans. If you aren't implementing your plans in quarterly cycles, you can potentially distribute, for example, a special newsletter via email. You can potentially have a special communications tool (or tools) devoted to timely topics.

Looking for Similar Programs

One way to jump-start your program is to look for other programs that are trying to change employee behaviors. Corporate wellness programs attempt to persuade employees to adopt healthier behaviors. Safety programs keep detailed metrics about what works and the success of those efforts. The people running these programs likely have experiences where they know what works and what doesn't. They know the best methods to create engagement. They also probably know what won't go over well among employees.

Before you design your awareness program, find out what other efforts have achieved success and failure in improving behaviors. Starting with proven processes and tools not only helps you avoid problems but also eliminates a lot of guesswork and allows you to incorporate accepted methodology into your program.

IN THIS CHAPTER

» **Winning over critical support**

» **Partnering with other departments and efforts**

» **Making requests personal**

» **Conveying realistic expectations**

» **Starting out strong**

Chapter 14

Ten Ways to Make Friends and Influence People

Whenever you launch an awareness program, you need the support of a lot of people, and you will likely have no authority over most of them. Those people over whom you have no authority will have no reason to support your efforts. You therefore have to rely on their perceived importance of your efforts and your ability to persuade people to help you. No single universal method exists for gaining support, but this chapter covers a few of the ways that I have found to gain support for awareness efforts.

Garnering Active Executive Support

Though executive support doesn't always mean that everyone in the organization will enthusiastically support your efforts, the reality is that it minimally doesn't hurt. I use the word *active* because support is meaningful only if it's useful — and there when you need it. People are used to seeing policy statements that broadly describe things as good or bad— and the description generally means little.

TIP

If you can persuade an executive to visibly participate in your activities, speak at your event, or record a video, this visibility provides evidence that there is true support for your efforts. Clearly, an executive's time is valuable, but you need more than lip service to show that the management team believes your efforts are valuable.

In one organization I supported, the CEO mandated the watching of the awareness videos. I was told that this was a major statement by the CEO in supporting the awareness program, because few other mandatory tasks were assigned to all employees.

Courting the Organization's Influencers

In all organizations, there are some people whom everyone seems to know. If the organization is large, there might be people in each defined demographic, such as a building or department. These people are frequently office managers, executive assistants, or executives. These *influencers* are typically early adopters of the promoted behaviors and actions, and if they are supportive of your efforts, they will actively encourage others to support you.

TIP

Identify an organization's influencers early in your interviews, and seek their input. Give them a sense of ownership, and then increase it by contacting them in advance, for example, and letting them know how you incorporated their input into your efforts. Whether or not you incorporate their input, you may want to periodically discus your plans with them so that they believe that they're an active contributor to the awareness program as a whole. All this effort combines to encourage them to use their influence to support and promote your efforts.

Supporting Another Project That Has Support

There are likely a variety of organizational efforts that provide a great deal of support, such as a pet project of executives or a critical upgrade to computer systems. In Chapter 13, I highlight a situation where the corporate headquarters of an organization was being moved and where supporting that effort allowed the awareness program staff to gain a great deal of support.

TIP

Find projects that attract significant support and see how you can become involved in the efforts. You don't want those efforts to consume all your resources for the sole purpose of supporting other projects, but if you can demonstrate how security awareness can benefit the effort already under way, you can obtain support for your current and future efforts. You will be considered a valuable contributor to the organization and will likely develop a great deal of contacts. With any luck, these contacts will feel a sense of reciprocity and return support for your awareness project. Either way, helping a program with perceived value increases the credibility for you and your awareness-related efforts.

Choosing Topics Important to Individuals

You clearly want to address business concerns, but try to incorporate awareness topics that also can be perceived to be completely personal to employees. For example, you can choose topics like how to protect your children on the Internet or how to protect your home network or a variety of similar topics. I spoke about the intangible benefits of addressing home and family concerns. Topics such as these create a perception that the security team cares about employees and can generate goodwill. Doing so might lead to better adherence to security policies.

WARNING

Surprisingly, I have seen pushback from executives regarding using limited resources to help people in their private lives. The executives thought awareness efforts should focus specifically on work-related activities. My response is that if people practice strong security behaviors at home, they will also practice strong behavior at work. They see the importance of protecting their family, and they're more likely to adopt strong behaviors for personal reasons — they won't suddenly stop those behaviors and become reckless at work. The goodwill will likely benefit the organization also.

TECHNICAL STUFF

Some companies have a policy of not telling people what to do outside of work. For example, they purposefully avoid any impression of an invasion of privacy and provide no comments or guidance on employees' social media profiles. This includes what information to post and security settings for social media sites. For companies with similar policies, you will likely have to ignore topics not directly work related.

Having Some Fun Events

Though I admit that I repeatedly say that you need an awareness program that's effective, not fun, you should try to incorporate some aspects that *are* engaging. You do need to go beyond traditional programs to gain some traction and inspire conversation among users. These events can involve bringing in speakers, holding contests, hosting a booth at different events, creating a true gamification program, creating a scavenger hunt, holding an escape room, and much more.

Depending on the size of your organization, you might have challenges in engaging many geographies. This is a case where your security champions or ambassadors can possibly help. They should be capable and trained to deliver any engaging content. Otherwise, though you may want to engage everyone, you have to limit the engagement to where it's logistically feasible.

Don't Promise Perfection

Making unrealistic promises is one of the fastest ways to lose support and ruin any credibility you have. The fact is that users will inevitably leak credentials, click a phishing link, or lose a USB drive. As an awareness professional, your job is reducing risk associated with user behavior. Do not repeat vendor marketing phrases making ridiculous claims. If you follow the advice in this book, you will create measureable risk reduction, which is typically evasive to cybersecurity programs. This is what you can state as your goal.

REMEMBER

Set realistic expectations. Focus on risk reduction and reduced incidents, and do *not* promise perfection. The more realistic the expectations, framed in clear business terminology, the more likely you are to gain and maintain support.

Don't Overdo the FUD Factor

At one level, you need to ensure that you let people know there are legitimate concerns about why you're advocating procedures that could in some way impede business functions. However, if you overuse *f*ear, *u*ncertainty, and *d*oubt (FUD), you may find yourself perceived as the proverbial boy who cried wolf.

WARNING

There is a fine line between showing that there are legitimate concerns that warrant modifying behaviors and overemphasizing threats that are unlikely to materialize. It also matters how you portray the threat. I have seen videos that feature the standard-issue "evil hacker" and people laugh cynically at it. You need to highlight legitimate concerns to a certain extent; however, you must not portray them in stereotypical ways or overhype them. If you do, nobody will take you seriously.

Scoring an Early Win

Little gives you more credibility or gains you more supporters than having a visible success in some form. Ideally, it can be helping a critical project. It can also be providing positive metrics involving large losses, such as reducing actual phishing incidents or a reduction of lost devices.

TIP

When you begin your awareness program, plan for some potential quick wins. Design your program with this strategy in mind. In the worst case, if you're using phishing simulations, you can highlight a reduction on simulation click rates. This metric might not be meaningful in the big picture, but it can seem impressive to people who don't know that you can design phishing simulations intentionally to show improvements by manipulating the phishing sophistication levels.

Using Real Gamification

As Chapter 11 defines, a real gamification program is a reward system. If a gamification program is designed reasonably well, many users score early rewards and are encouraged to participate. They then actively engage in security behaviors to collect the rewards.

REMEMBER

Gamification isn't just playing a game with people and giving them a participation prize. You need them to engage on an ongoing basis. When they do, they form a favorable impression of the awareness program and the security team in general.

TIP

When choosing rewards, think about what might motivate you. Chapter 11 offers more ideas, but it's great to give away money — well, obviously. If you have a budget, gift cards make useful rewards for people. In the absence of outright bribery, realize that certificates are nice but only go so far. Any free items (such as T-shirts, squishy toys, or pens, for example) are always welcome, and some people will take some extreme actions to obtain almost anything for free. That's just people being people.

Integrating the Organization's Mission Statement

Just about every organization has a mission statement that highlights the organization's social responsibility and ethical goals and sets expectations for behavior across the organization. In some organizations, the mission statement is as worthless as the paper it's printed on. In other organizations, every core decision is compared to the mission statement. If your organization values its mission statement, you must create a mission statement for your awareness program that incorporates the principles of the organization's mission statement.

If an organization's mission statement talks about the customer being the top priority of the organization, for example, your mission statement and your awareness program should likewise have a theme and should focus on protecting customers' interests and data. If the mission statement touts the value of employees, your mission statement should specifically talk about protecting the interests of employees.

If you can demonstrate that your awareness program is a critical part of your organization's overarching principles, you will make securing executive buy-in and support much easier. Connecting your program to an organization's mission may help attract enhanced funding for the program as well.

Chapter **15**

Ten Fundamental Awareness Topics

Awareness programs are not prefabricated, like a house — you must customize them to meet the unique needs of an organization. Helping organizations understand their unique needs and collaborating with their leadership and security teams are how you create an awareness program that works. That said, you also find certain building blocks that are common to many security awareness programs. This chapter covers these topics and explains why I often include them in the programs I create. Chapter 6 provides the details you need to consider on these topics.

Phishing

Phishing is the most common attack that leads to damage. Even if you're dealing with users who don't use computers regularly, you should likely cover phishing because people will be targeted on their personal systems and the attackers might try to spoof their organization.

Phishing is so important that it's worth covering as not only an individual topic but one that you should also enhance to cover different topics within the broader topic of phishing. These can include whaling, brand impersonations, fake charities, and more. When you implement the quarterly program methodology promoted throughout this book, it becomes easier to cover all these topics throughout a year. Either way, phishing can, and should, always be refreshed as a topic.

Business Email Compromise

In many cases, critical information is compromised when someone accidentally emails information to the wrong person. These topics are frequently related to verifying the recipients of an email, avoiding the choice of the blind Reply All option, and ensuring that the right information is sent to the right people.

In most cases, when such a compromise happens, no serious problem occurs. It does happen, though, and when it does, such a compromise can be devastating. There have been cases where someone emails personally identifiable information (PII) to the wrong party and it becomes a legally reportable event. Class action lawsuits arise from such cases. In other situations, business email compromise can lead to the loss of a large amount of money. In one case, a competitor clicked the Reply All option on an email message to a potential client and sent me and all other bidders a copy of their proposal. We all legally received it, and could consider that proposal in our own proposals.

Mobile Device Security

Just about everyone has a cellphone or another type of mobile device. Your users likely store information on their mobile devices that is relevant and potentially valuable to your organization. If your users have laptops they use for work, much larger quantities of your information are at risk on those devices.

Your users need to ensure that they properly physically and technically secure those devices, and you need to train the users to do so. This can include shoulder surfing, securely storing equipment, the use of tracking software, and the use of screen locks, among other topics. Just as phishing is presented as multiple topics, mobile device security should be covered from many angles. Again, Chapter 6 provides further options.

Home Network and Computer Security

The COVID-19 pandemic left every possible worker who could work remotely working from home. The security concerns became readily apparent. The reality, however, is that people were already doing work at some level from their home networks and computers. Even after people return to their offices when the pandemic is over, many will continue to work remotely and those who do go back to the office will still likely use their home computers and network to a certain extent. Working from home is here to stay because many employees now expect it, and many organizations appreciate the cost savings.

For this reason, no matter the state of work from home (WFH), your organization benefits if you cover a variety of topics related to people working from home. Your program might show users how to protect their home computers, configure their home routers, browse the web safely, and more. This is not only good practice from a business perspective — it also creates goodwill with the users, as they personally benefit from the information.

Password Security

Passwords remain the primary means of authenticating users. Even if your organization deploys multifactor authentication, you'll find that some applications don't provide the option. Also, most users rely only on passwords to protect their personal accounts and devices, and if work related information ends up on those devices, your information is at risk. Even worse, users often reuse their personal passwords on their business accounts.

Be sure to provide awareness materials on how to create, protect, and maintain passwords. Even if users have multifactor authentication, which should be incorporated into the training, users don't operate in a vacuum, and these points must be addressed. Your awareness program should help users understand that (or how) their personal habits affect the security of the organization. Chapter 10 provides details for how to accomplish this.

Social Media Security

Like it or not, most users access their personal social media at work. Even if they do so using personal devices, some users use social media communications to discuss work. People may also disclose sensitive work issues on professional social media sites like LinkedIn. Even assuming otherwise responsible use, social media can be a source of malware.

Responsible social media usage is a critical topic to provide to your users. Social media security benefits users' business and personal lives, also referred to as their *social media footprint,* and most should appreciate the information you provide.

REMEMBER

Some organizations mandate that the organization must not tell users what they can (or can't) do on their personal accounts. If your organization has such a mandate, you can discuss social media security without specifically mentioning personal accounts.

Physical Security

Physical security is a critical aspect for cybersecurity from a variety of perspectives. Devices and computers can be left vulnerable to theft or illicit access. Hard copy information can be left vulnerable to unauthorized people. Loud conversations can disclose a wide variety of critical information.

TIP

Physical security should be promoted to be as critical as any aspect of cybersecurity. Many aspects of physical security are embedded in the other topics discussed, which proves its importance. For example, locking mobile devices is discussed with mobile device security. Physical security lends itself to nudges (discussed in Chapter 7), which can be a valuable tactic to integrate into your program.

Malware and Ransomware

Malware, and especially ransomware, is devastating organizations and causing catastrophic damage. The city of Baltimore, Maryland, had a variety of civic functions crippled, causing long-term impacts to residents and businesses in the organization, because of ransomware. At the time of this writing, Acer, ironically a large computer manufacturer, was hit by ransomware. The criminals asked Acer for $50 million.

It is critical to provide information that helps users avoid ransomware and other forms of malware.

Social Engineering

Social engineering is a broad term and relates to any nontechnical attack. Phishing is a form of social engineering. Users should be made aware of the potential attack vectors, but, more importantly, instructed that the solution is to follow policies and not to be forced to act on emotions or a false sense of urgency. Users should also be made to feel comfortable telling someone "No," or, ""I'll get back to you," should they potentially face a circumstance beyond what is covered in your organization's policy.

REMEMBER

As I advocate throughout this book, you need to reinforce that users should focus on how to perform their job functions properly with security embedded into the process. Social engineering is a form of attack, and the best countermeasure is following well-crafted procedures. Again, you should focus on telling people how to perform their jobs properly, not on what to be afraid of.

It Can Happen to You

A portion of your awareness program should focus on the fact that incidents occur. Though you don't necessarily need to constantly focus on negative incidents, you do need to point out that they happen. If people form the opinion that you're crying wolf, they will discount your efforts, believing that it will never happen to them.

TECHNICAL STUFF

If you have none of your own incidents to discuss, you can readily find incidents from your industry or in the news. Attacks like Wannacry crippled major organizations, including a hospital system. Lives have been negatively affected. Though you don't want to create an environment of irrational fear, you want to justify the effort expended to take and follow your awareness program.

16.

Chapter **16**

Ten Helpful Security Awareness Resources

When I started to write this chapter, I thought it would be easy. You would think that there would be a plethora of free or low-cost resources available for security awareness.

ASSESSING RESOURCES BEYOND THIS BOOK

TIP

When you assess resources beyond this book, I recommend that you consider the answers to these questions:

- Is the material intended to guide you to buy a specific solution?
- Is the content grandiose, promoting platitudes and clichés?
- Is the content practical and implementable?
- Does the content help you have a broader view of the concept?
- Can you imagine the recommendations working in your environment?
- Does the advice sound good but is too broad to be actionable?

The reality is quite different. Most of the information available is from vendors promoting their specific product or solution. People provide their own materials to promote their personal services. The resources covered in this chapter provide consistent information that is generally free of hype and marketing content.

Security Awareness Special Interest Group

The Security Awareness Special Interest Group (www.thesasig.com) is a subscription-free, sales-free networking environment for more than 5,000 end-user cybersecurity practitioners. Professionals from other disciplines (such as risk, HR, legal, and supply) and representatives from government, law enforcement, and academia are also welcome. Membership is drawn from hundreds of organizations of all sizes from across the world and from all sectors — public and private.

Founded in 2004, many regard SASIG as a safe zone for users — suppliers, consultancies, vendors, and members of the press are routinely excluded. Before the pandemic lockdown began in early 2020, it was UK-centric, with some 35 physical meetings held mainly in London. But after the lockdown began, SASIG went online and has been transformed for the better. SASIG's reach now extends globally. Its daily online webinars covering the whole gamut of security topics have been attended by thousands of cybersecurity professionals, and its range of activities is growing.

CybSafe Research Library

As I continually tout the importance of applying good scientific principles to your awareness programs, it's important to have access to understandable sources to those principles. CybSafe, a company that focuses on improving cybersecurity behaviors, provides a database of different aspects of research related to security awareness.

This database provides a foundation of thought leadership as well as guidance on a variety of awareness subjects. The research library can be found at www.cybsafe.com/research-library.

Cybersecurity Culture Guidelines

Cybersecurity Culture Guidelines: Behavioural Aspects of Cybersecurity is a research paper from the European Union Agency for Cybersecurity (ENISA). It provides an overview of issues related to the human aspects of cybersecurity, with a great deal of information relevant to awareness practitioners.

The report offers a good discussion of aspects of awareness that are relevant to various user groups, and it provides guidance for running an awareness program. You can find the report at www.enisa.europa.eu/publications/cybersecurity-culture-guidelines-behavioural-aspects-of-cybersecurity/at_download/fullReport.

RSA Conference Library

RSA Conference is the largest event in the cybersecurity field. Over 30 years, the event grew from a small conference focusing on cryptography to having more than 500 speakers, each year, discuss all topics related to cybersecurity. RSA Conference recorded many of these sessions, and also evolved its web presence to include articles, webinars, blogs, and a variety of content formats.

The current content base on the website includes hundreds of videos and other content relevant to security awareness practitioners. You can find many of my presentations on the site describing the concepts presented in this book in detail. The RSA Conference site is at www.rsaconference.com.

You can also find more presentations on the RSA Conference YouTube page, at www.youtube.com/rsaconference.

You Can Stop Stupid

You Can Stop Stupid: Stopping Losses from Accidental and Malicious Actions (Wiley, 2021) is a book that I wrote with Dr. Tracy Celaya Brown. The book discusses how to address user-initiated loss in a comprehensive approach that involves technology, process, and awareness. In the book, we discuss how security awareness fits within a security program to address what the cybersecurity community frequently refers to as "the user problem," which, in my opinion, is more accurately "the security professional problem."

You Can Stop Stupid is available at Amazon.com and other bookstores.

The Work of Sydney Dekker

I discuss the parallels of safety science with security awareness throughout this book. Sydney Dekker, MA, MSc, PhD, is one of the leaders in the safety science field, and I strongly recommend that all awareness professionals look at his materials.

Dr. Dekker's website (https://sidneydekker.com) provides links to all of his books. If your time is limited, however, I recommend that you look at his brief YouTube video series, Understanding Human Error (www.youtube.com/watch?v=Fw3SwEXc3PU). It provides for a fundamental understanding of human error that is unparalleled. You should also make the time to watch his Just Culture video series (www.youtube.com/watch?v=PVWjgqDANWA).

Human Factors Knowledge Area

The Cyber Security Body of Knowledge project (CyBOK), run by the University of Bristol, tries to distill research in various cybersecurity fields into papers that are useful for academics and practitioners alike. The Human Factor Knowledge Area paper (www.cybok.org/media/downloads/Human_Factors_issue_1.0.pdf) is excellent.

The paper provides an easy-to-understand overview of a wide variety of topics related to security awareness. The paper is somewhat long, but reading and trying to understand the concepts it summarizes is well worth your time.

People-Centric Security

People-Centric Security: Transforming Your Enterprise Security Culture (McGraw Hill, 2015), by Lance Hayden, PhD, is possibly one of the most important books you can read and implement if you truly want to make measurable change in your organization's security culture.

Hayden is primarily a practicing security professional who had a long career as a consultant while also pursuing his PhD. He focuses his research to have practical implications. His book provides a model that allows for actual measurement of culture and its impact on your organization. The model he presents facilitates tracking of your security culture over time to allow you to show how your efforts improve the organization.

Human Security Engineering Consortium

The Human Security Engineering Consortium (www.hsec.org) was founded to address the fact that solving what the industry frequently refers to as "the user problem" requires a comprehensive approach that looks beyond security awareness. Stakeholder organizations are meeting to determine methodologies and infrastructures to mitigate user-initiated loss.

The Human Security Engineering Consortium is early in its founding, but the processes, guidelines, and recommendations will be supplemented with research and implementation guidance. A vendor infrastructure component will also provide for identifying the tools most appropriate to address the different aspects of user-initiated loss. A good portion of this information will provide detailed guidance on how to run a more effective awareness program.

How to Run a Security Awareness Program Course

How to Run a Security Awareness Program is a course I created that largely parallels the content of this book. The course is intended to further elaborate on the concepts of this book.

The course is modular to provide for experienced practitioners or others who want to learn about specific awareness concepts without taking the entire course. The course can be found at:

https://www.devopsinstitute.com/sme/ira-winkler

Appendix

Sample Questionnaire

Throughout this book, I highlight how important it is to know the culture of your organization, business drivers, stakeholders, and more. That is easy to say, but hard to accomplish. I have been developing and refining the questionnaire in this appendix for close to a decade. It provides a structured framework to collect information. Though a great deal of the information might appear to be basic and obvious, documenting it is still a critical task.

WARNING

In general, you can send the questionnaire to the relevant individuals, but I don't recommend doing so — the questionnaires are a way to start a conversation. I find that the content from the questionnaire takes up about one-third of the conversation. Ideally, the questionnaire serves as a conversation starter, and the resulting conversation is where the truly valuable information originates.

TIP

A good conversation develops rapport with stakeholders. Meeting with people can give them a sense of ownership in the effort, and they can become your biggest supporters.

As I mention in Chapter 9, start with a single awareness program to work out any kinks in the program. If this is your first time through, you should just collect for the entire organization any information intended for a single awareness program. If you're looking to implement separate awareness programs for multiple cultures, you should collect the relevant information for each of the cultures you intend to target.

Also consider that this questionnaire is just a starting point. I strongly recommend that you tailor these questions to your own needs. Also, a major aspect of this questionnaire is that it is designed to illicit conversation and free formed comments. I've learned more from the resulting conversations than the questionnaire itself. Determine from your personal experiences which questions are the most useful, potential questions to add, questions to delete, etc.

Questions for the CISO or Similar Position

1. **I work for the following sector:**

   a. Manufacturing

   b. Health

   c. Energy

   d. Retail

   e. Financial

   f. Technology

   g. Agriculture/natural resources

   h. Arts and entertainment

   i. Building trades and construction

   j. Education

   k. Hospitality/tourism/recreation

   l. Public services

   m. Transportation

   n. Government

   o. Other (please provide sector): _____

2. **My company has the following number of employees:**

   a. _____

3. **My company has offices in the following continents/regions:**

   a. North America

   b. South America

   c. Europe

   d. Africa

e. Middle East

f. Asia

g. Southeast Asia

h. Australia

i. Pacific Rim

j. Other (please explain): _____

4. **My company needs to translate materials into ___ languages:**

   a. 1

   b. 2–5

   c. 6–10

   d. 11+

   e. Other (please explain): _____

   f. List here:

5. **I have worked at my company for**

   a. 1 year or less

   b. 2–5 years

   c. 6–10 years

   d. 10–15 years

   e. 15 years or more

6. **My role in my organization is**

   a. CISO

   b. Security manager

   c. Security analyst

   d. Privacy officer

   e. Other (please specify): _____

7. **I have worked in the security sector for**

   a. 1 year or less

   b. 2–5 years

   c. 6–10 years

   d. 10–15 years

e. 15 years or more

f. Other (please explain): _____

8. **My security team consists of**

    a. 1–3 members

    b. 4–6 members

    c. 7–10 members

    d. 11–13 members

    e. 14 or more members

9. **My company has a security policy in place:**

    a. Yes

    b. No *(proceed to Question 11)*

    c. Other (please explain): _____

10. **The following topics are outlined in my security policy:**

Topic	Yes or No
Data classification	
General security	
Home networks/VPN	
Insider threats	
Mobile	
Passwords	
Patching	
Retention	
Social media	
Tailgating	
Travel security: Device use and Wi-Fi networks, for example	

11. **My company already has a security awareness program:**

    a. Yes

    b. No *(proceed to Question 14 and skip Questions 17–22)*

    c. Other (please explain): _____

12. My company has had a security awareness program for

    a. 1 year or less

    b. 2–5 years

    c. 6–10 years

    d. 10–15 years

    e. 15 years or more

    f. Other (please explain): _____

13. I collect metrics for my security awareness program:

    a. Yes

    b. No *(proceed to Question 15)*

    c. Other (please explain): _____

14. I collect metrics on the following aspects of security behavior:

Aspect of Security Behavior	Yes/No
General awareness (via survey, test, or module, for example)	
Clean and locked desk	
Data classification	
Encryption	
Malicious web browsing	
Mobile device (security controls in use)	
Password (strength)	
Patching	
Phishing (awareness)	
Phishing (detection)	
Reported incident	
Social engineering	
Social media (via social media monitoring)	
Tailgating	

15. My company has had a security awareness program falter but then improve at a later point:

   a. Yes

   b. No *(proceed to Question 17)*

   c. Other (please explain): _____

16. What did previous iterations of the program lack that caused the failure?

   a. Planning

   b. Cooperation from other departments (communications, legal, and HR, for example)

   c. Funding

   d. User engagement

   e. Support

   f. Other (please explain): _____

17. I use the following components:

Component	Yes/No
Article	
Blog	
Booth/event	
Cybersecurity Month event	
Internal social media account	
Knowledge Base	
Lunch and learn	
New employee orientation	
Newsletter	
Phishing exercise	
Poster	
Question inbox	
Quiz/survey	
Road show	

Component	Yes/No
Speaker	
Table tent	
Trinket	
Video-based training	

18. **I create a portion (from some to all) of my materials:**

    a. Yes

    b. No *(proceed to Question 22)*

    c. Other (please explain): _____

19. **I create all materials in-house:**

    a. Yes *(proceed to Question 22)*

    b. No

20. **What portion of your material do you create?**

Component	Portion You Create
Article	
Blog	
Booth/event	
Cybersecurity Month event	
Internal social media account	
Knowledge Base	
Lunch and learn	
New employee orientation	
Newsletter	
Phishing exercise	
Poster	
Trinket	
Video-based training	

21. I purchase materials for the following components:

Component	Portion You Create
Article	
Blog	
Booth/event	
Cybersecurity Month event	
Internal social media account	
Knowledge Base	
Lunch and learn	
New employee orientation	
Newsletter	
Phishing exercise	
Poster	
Question inbox	
Quiz/survey	
Road show	
Speaker	
Table tent	
Trinket	
Video-based training	

22. I update my materials

    a. Every week

    b. Every month

    c. Every 2–3 months

    d. Every 4–6 months

    e. Every year

    f. Never

    g. Annually

    h. Other (please explain): _____

23. Do you want to be able to use any components listed here but don't now use them?

Component	Yes/No
Article	
Booth/event	
Blog	
Cybersecurity Month event	
Internal social media account	
Knowledge Base	
Lunch and learn	
New employee orientation	
Newsletter	
Phishing exercise	
Question inbox	
Poster	
Quiz/survey	
Road show	
Speaker	
Table tent	
Trinket	
Video-based training	

24. Are you unable to use any components because of corporate culture?

Component	Yes/No
Article	
Blog	
Booth/event	
Cybersecurity Month event	
Internal social media account	
Knowledge Base	

Component	Yes/No
Lunch and learn	
New employee orientation	
Newsletter	
Phishing exercise	
Poster	
Question inbox	
Quiz/survey	
Road show	
Speaker	
Table tent	
Trinket	
Video-based training	

25. **What are the top three most successful components of your security awareness program (posters, newsletters, or interactive events, for example)?**

a. _____

b. _____

c. _____

26. **What are the top three least successful components of your security awareness program (posters, newsletters, or interactive events, for example)?**

a. _____

b. _____

c. _____

27. **Which standards and regulations do you need to be mindful of?**

Standard	Yes/No
FERPA	
FINRA	

Standard	Yes/No
GDPR	
GLBA/SOX	
HIPAA	
LGPD	
NERC/FERC	
PCI	
SCC	
Other	Please explain: _____ _____ _____

28. **What is the makeup of your employee base? (The answer should correspond to the industry/sector selected at the start; sample answers provided here):**

   a. Distribution centers

   b. Corporate headquarters

   c. Stores

   d. Manufacturing facilities

   e. Clinics

   f. Hospitals

   g. Banks

   h. Hotels

29. **How would you rank the following values within your corporate environment? (Rank the top 5 from 1 to 5.)**

Value	Rank the Top 5 from 1 to 5
Commitment	
Community	
Excellence	
Honesty	
Innovation	

Value	Rank the Top 5 from 1 to 5
Integrity	
Professionalism	
Respect	
Service	
Teamwork	

30. I can send out communications to my employees:

   a. Yes

   b. No *(proceed to Question 32)*

31. I can send out communications to my employees by myself:

   a. Yes *(proceed to Question 33)*

   b. No

32. I can send out communications only with the help of corporate communications:

   a. Yes

   b. No

33. I have a difficult time encouraging employees to take security seriously:

   a. Yes

   b. No

   c. Other (please explain): _____

34. I believe that the C-level takes security seriously:

   a. Yes

   b. No

   c. Other (please explain): _____

35. I believe that my management takes security seriously:

   a. Yes

   b. No

   c. Other (please explain): _____

36. **My security initiatives are greeted with enthusiasm from my department/company:**

   a. Yes

   b. No

   c. Other (please explain): _____

37. **I have a difficult time receiving funding for my projects:**

   a. Yes

   b. No

   c. Other (please explain): _____

38. **I have conflicts with my user base:**

   a. Often

   b. Occasionally

   c. Never

   d. Other (please explain): _____

39. **My team is contacted with security concerns:**

   a. Always

   b. Often

   c. Occasionally

   d. Never

   e. Other (please explain): _____

40. **Which three topics are of most concern to you?**

General security awareness	Phishing	Social engineering
Mobile security	Password security	Travel security
Physical security	Social networking	WIFI security
APT	USB drives	Patching
Encryption	Privacy	Insider threats
HIPAA	PCI	FERPA
NERC	Protect your home	Protect your kids
Security vocabulary	Security for executives	Security for developers

41. Do any departments present particular concerns to you?

    a. Yes

    b. No

    c. List: _____

42. How many distinct programs do you envision needing?

Number of programs: _____

List: _____

_____

43. Which products do you use that can be leveraged for metrics?

    a. AD

    b. AV

    c. MDM

    d. Web filtering

    e. Email provider

    f. SharePoint

    g. Google Sites

    h. DLP

    i. Social media monitoring

    j. Physical walk-throughs

    k. Others (please list): _____

44. How often can you test your employees for phishing?

    a. Once a week

    b. Once a month

    c. Once a quarter

    d. Twice per year

    e. Once per year

    f. Other (please specify): _____

45. How often can you test your employees for social engineering?

    a. Once a week

    b. Once a month

c. Once a quarter

d. Twice per year

e. Once per year

f. Other (please specify): _____

46. Have you considered gamification or incentivized awareness?

a. Yes

b. No

47. What kind of reward structure do you think would work among your employees?

_____

_____

_____

Questions for All Employees

1. I identify as:

a. Male

b. Female

c. Other

d. I prefer not to disclose.

2. Age group:

a. 18–22 years

b. 23–29 years

c. 30–40 years

d. 41–50 years

e. 50–60 years

f. 60 years or older

g. I prefer not to disclose.

3. **How long have you worked for the organization?**

    a. 1 year or less

    b. 2–5 years

    c. 6–10 years

    d. 10–15 years

    e. 15 years or more

4. **What department do you work in?**

    _____

5. **My company already has a security awareness program.**

    a. Yes

    b. No

    c. I do not know.

6. **Select the answer that best describes your impressions for each of the following statements:**

	Strongly Agree	Agree	Disagree	Strongly Disagree	N/A
1. I have learned something from my company's security awareness program.					
2. I have changed my behavior because of information I learned from security awareness.					
3. I consider myself to be a security-minded individual.					
4. I think my company's security awareness program is successful.					
5. I view my company's security team positively.					
6. I have had conflicts with my company's security team.					
7. I seek out the security team with security needs or concerns.					

7. Which components would most capture the attention of your team?

_____

Questions for the HR Department

1. What campaigns do you currently run to engage employees' awareness?
2. What have they had the most success with in their efforts?
3. What are the mediums of communication?
4. Do they have any specific guidelines or issues we should be aware of?
5. How do you want us to educate employees on how to report suspicious behaviors or internal threats?
6. Are there any issues you want addressed?
7. Are there any sensitivities across facilities?
8. Have they been involved with any security related incidents? How was it handled? What communications went out, if any?
9. Are people typically disciplined for security related violations? If so, what is the procedure?
10. What sort of awareness related training do people receive throughout their tenure?
11. Are there any compliance related concerns?
12. What is the off-boarding procedure? Are there established procedures for account deactivation?
13. Is there a procedure for attempting to recover IP or other sensitive information?

Questions for the Legal Department

1. What do you want users to know about security?
2. Any incidents (security related) with legal implications? Were any awareness related?
3. Do you believe that policies are properly documented?
4. Outside of incidents, have any awareness concerns ever come up — for example, any discussions with regulators?

5. Do you have concerns outside of HQ that are unique?

6. Do you run the data retention program? What do you do to communicate it?

7. Any data classification schemes? If so, what do you do to communicate it?

Questions for the Communications Department

1. How often do you send out communications?

2. Do you track metrics on your communications?

3. Will you be involved with the security awareness effort? Is your sign-off necessary in order to publish any materials?

4. What is the anticipated frequency you will allow?

5. Should we be aware of any guidelines we have to adhere to?

6. Can we receive a corporate template?

7. What is your preferred delivery method?

8. Do you have any concerns?

9. Have you had any problems in the past with other vendors providing communications to internal staff?

10. Are there communications we can be added to?

11. What is the frequency of our potential participation in those communications?

12. Have there been previous concerns for similar programs?

13. What has been the most successful method for attempting to improve employees' behaviors?

Questions Regarding the Appropriate Person for Physical Security

1. Do they catalog equipment and USB drives?

2. Do they perform rounds to check for locked computers inside office areas during off hours? If so, do they notify users who are not compliant?

3. Who controls physical security? Is it outsourced?

4. Can you leverage the staff to collect metrics? Put up posters? Distribute materials?

5. What sort of incidents have they encountered?

6. Do people generally wear badges?

7. Does it seem like people stop tailgaters (people who follow staff into facilities who do not display the appropriate access credentials)?

8. Are guests escorted?

9. Do people follow the guidelines?

10. Do they have any special concerns?

11. Do they have any suggestions to make awareness more effective?

12. Have they tried any awareness efforts of their own? If so, what was successful or not successful?

Index

About the Author

Ira Winkler, CISSP, is chief security architect for Walmart, where he focuses on behavioral cybersecurity. He is also a member of the faculty of the University of Maryland Baltimore County Center for Cybersecurity. He is considered one of the world's most influential security professionals, and has been named a "Modern Day James Bond" by the media. He did this by performing espionage simulations, where he used social engineering and espionage techniques to physically and technically "break into" some of the largest companies in the world and investigating crimes against them, and telling them how to cost effectively protect their information and computer infrastructure. Ira has been focusing on the human aspects of cybersecurity for more than three decades and has helped create and manage awareness programs for countless companies, from Fortune 1 to startups. He has lectured around the world on related topics and has been named a top speaker at countless events on six continents.

For his efforts, Ira received countless awards including the Hall of Fame award from the Information Systems Security Association. *CSO Magazine* named Ira a CSO COMPASS Award winner as The Awareness Crusader. Most recently, Ira was named 2021 Top Cybersecurity Leader by *Security Magazine.* He also has a patent pended for applying machine learning techniques to accurately identify user risks through clustering personality traits.

Ira is also author of six other award winning and bestselling books, including *You Can Stop Stupid* (Wiley), *Advanced Persistent Security* (Syngress), *Spies Among Us* (Wiley), *Through the Eyes of the Enemy* (Regnery), *Corporate Espionage* (Prima), and *Zen and the Art of Information Security* (Syngress). He has contributed chapters to many books mostly on subjects related to social engineering and security awareness. He has written more than 1,000 professional, academic, and trade articles.

Mr. Winkler began his career at the National Security Agency, where he served as an Intelligence and Computer Systems Analyst. He moved onto support other US and overseas government military and intelligence agencies. After leaving government service, he went on to serve as president of the Internet Security Advisors Group, chief security strategist at HP Consulting, and director of technology of the National Computer Security Association. He was also on the graduate and undergraduate faculties of the Johns Hopkins University, University of Maryland, and several other colleges considered Academic Centers of Excellence for Cybersecurity.

Dedication

This book is dedicated to Howell McConnell and Pete Sutton, the two best security awareness practitioners you could ever meet. They trained generations of NSA and other intelligence community professionals and were incredibly effective at it. I only wish I could have a fraction of the impact that they had with their awareness efforts.

Author's Acknowledgments

With any book, there are countless people to thank. I have to thank literally hundreds of leaders at companies around the world who brought me in to assess and improve their awareness programs. Unfortunately, I can't mention them by name, but I couldn't write this book without all the real-world lessons learned as to what worked and what didn't without serving these organizations.

From a publishing perspective, I owe immense thanks to Katie Mohr, my original acquisitions editor. She shared my vision for this book, and for anyone unfamiliar with the publishing process, the acquisitions editor is in many ways the driving force to get a book from concept to bestseller. Steve Hayes took over in the middle of the process, and his efforts were appreciated. I owe an incredible debt as well to Colleen Diamond, my editor. It takes an immense talent to take someone else's content and make sure what is intended to be written is translated to the page. Not only is this a difficult task under normal circumstances, it is especially difficult for the *For Dummies* series, as it requires an extra level of accessibility, and therefore an extra level of talent on her part.

There are also many experts who deserve thanks. Among the most influential to me have been Dr. Lance Hayden, who was among the first to define culture as distinct from awareness in cybersecurity; Martin Smith and Jo Wise of the Security Awareness Special Interest Group, who have provided incredible service to me and the awareness community as a whole; Andrew Rose from Proofpoint, who knows as much about the awareness space as anyone and is a great person as well; and Masha Sedova of Elevate Security, for being the first in the cybersecurity field to really define what gamification is and can be.

Publisher's Acknowledgments

Executive Editors: Steve Hayes, Katie Mohr

Project Editor: Colleen Diamond

Copy Editors: Colleen Diamond, Becky Whitney

Production Editor: Tamilmani Varadharaj

Cover Image: © panida wijitpanya/Getty Images

Leverage the power

Dummies is the global leader in the reference category and one of the most trusted and highly regarded brands in the world. No longer just focused on books, customers now have access to the dummies content they need in the format they want. Together we'll craft a solution that engages your customers, stands out from the competition, and helps you meet your goals.

Advertising & Sponsorships

Connect with an engaged audience on a powerful multimedia site, and position your message alongside expert how-to content. Dummies.com is a one-stop shop for free, online information and know-how curated by a team of experts.

- Targeted ads
- Video
- Email Marketing

- Microsites
- Sweepstakes sponsorship

20 **MILLION** PAGE VIEWS EVERY SINGLE MONTH

15 MILLION **UNIQUE** VISITORS PER MONTH

43% OF ALL VISITORS ACCESS THE SITE VIA THEIR MOBILE DEVICES

700,000 NEWSLETTER SUBSCRIPTIONS TO THE INBOXES OF *300,000* UNIQUE INDIVIDUALS EVERY WEEK

# of dummies

Custom Publishing

Reach a global audience in any language by creating a solution that will differentiate you from competitors, amplify your message, and encourage customers to make a buying decision.

- Apps
- Books
- eBooks
- Video
- Audio
- Webinars

Brand Licensing & Content

Leverage the strength of the world's most popular reference brand to reach new audiences and channels of distribution.

For more information, visit **dummies.com/biz**

PERSONAL ENRICHMENT

Staying Sharp

9781119187790
USA $26.00
CAN $31.99
UK £19.99

Facebook

9781119179030
USA $21.99
CAN $25.99
UK £16.99

Guitar

9781119293354
USA $24.99
CAN $29.99
UK £17.99

Investing

9781119293347
USA $22.99
CAN $27.99
UK £16.99

Beekeeping

9781119310068
USA $22.99
CAN $27.99
UK £16.99

Digital Photography

9781119235606
USA $24.99
CAN $29.99
UK £17.99

Meditation

9781119251163
USA $24.99
CAN $29.99
UK £17.99

Pregnancy

9781119235491
USA $26.99
CAN $31.99
UK £19.99

Samsung Galaxy S7

9781119279952
USA $24.99
CAN $29.99
UK £17.99

iPhone

9781119283133
USA $24.99
CAN $29.99
UK £17.99

Crocheting

9781119287117
USA $24.99
CAN $29.99
UK £16.99

Nutrition

9781119130246
USA $22.99
CAN $27.99
UK £16.99

PROFESSIONAL DEVELOPMENT

Windows 10

9781119311041
USA $24.99
CAN $29.99
UK £17.99

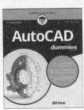

AutoCAD

9781119255796
USA $39.99
CAN $47.99
UK £27.99

Excel 2016

9781119293439
USA $26.99
CAN $31.99
UK £19.99

QuickBooks 2017

9781119281467
USA $26.99
CAN $31.99
UK £19.99

macOS Sierra

9781119280651
USA $29.99
CAN $35.99
UK £21.99

LinkedIn

9781119251132
USA $24.99
CAN $29.99
UK £17.99

Windows 10 All-in-One

9781119310563
USA $34.00
CAN $41.99
UK £24.99

SharePoint 2016

9781119181705
USA $29.99
CAN $35.99
UK £21.99

Fundamental Analysis

9781119263593
USA $26.99
CAN $31.99
UK £19.99

Networking

9781119257769
USA $29.99
CAN $35.99
UK £21.99

Office 2016

9781119293477
USA $26.99
CAN $31.99
UK £19.99

Office 365

9781119265313
USA $24.99
CAN $29.99
UK £17.99

Salesforce.com

9781119239314
USA $29.99
CAN $35.99
UK £21.99

Coding

9781119293323
USA $29.99
CAN $35.99
UK £21.99